DATE DUE	

SOUL IN EXILE

SOUL IN EXILE

LIVES OF A PALESTINIAN REVOLUTIONARY

FAWAZ TURKI

MONTHLY REVIEW PRESS
NEW YORK

To Camilla Spain,
with gratitude for all the rebel songs
from the liberated zones of Ireland

Copyright © 1988 by Fawaz Turki

Library of Congress Cataloging-in-Publication Data

Turki, Fawaz, 1940–
   Soul in exile.

    1. Turki, Fawaz, 1940–   . 2. Refugees, Arab—
Biography. 3. Palestinian Arabs—Biography.
4. Jewish-Arab relations—1949–   . I. Title.
HV640.5.A6T87   1988   956'.04   88-1455
ISBN 0-85345-746-8
ISBN 0-85345-747-6 (pbk.)

Monthly Review Press
122 West 27th Street
New York, N.Y. 10001

Manufactured in the United States of America

10 9 8 7 6 5 4 3 2 1

PROLOGUE

Most people, not least of all Arabs, consider the capital cities of the Maghreb countries of North Africa to be steeped in French culture. That may be true of Tunis and Rabat. Not so Algiers. Here people have thoroughly scrubbed all the grime of the colonial past off their national body. Streets, squares, parks, marketplaces, and other city landmarks are named after heroes of the war of independence. People read *El Mojahed,* not *Le Monde.* Road signs are in Arabic. Cafés have *terraces,* as in Paris, but they are filled with a generation of young Algerians who have grown up with little recollection of the *Pieds Noirs* nightmare. This is a blue-collar city, not without its share of drabness. But its inhabitants, unlike those of other cities in North Africa and the rest of the Arab world, are not so helpless economically that they have to import their matches, their soap, and their pencils.

Algerians forever remind you, and each other, how costly it was for them to gain their independence. True, this independence has not produced economic miracles. Life here is still lived close to the bone. It does not allow, as in Western society, or monied society in some Arab countries, for afternoons of brie and beaujolais nouveau, for annual vacations by the seashore and shopping sprees at department stores. Thousands of Algerians still emigrate each year to Western Europe in search of a place as "guest workers."

In the Middle East, however, Algerians are seen as the Germans of the Arab world, hard working and persistent, though at times stolid and humorless, respected for their accomplishments in national reconstruction. Respected, but not, unfortunately, emulated.

At the Algiers airport, the clean and spacious VIP lounge is located in a separate building. Its officials speak in soft, polite tones. Attendants attired in national dress serve coffee.

The main terminal, however, resembles all main terminals in the Arab world, crowded with passengers and their relatives and veiled women and children and peddlers and lottery-ticket sellers and taxi drivers and pickpockets and porters and policemen. And soldiers everywhere with submachine guns. You choke in the heat. You are overpowered by the pungent smells and the dust. And you wonder if you are going to be arrested or questioned or delayed. You worry about that even if you are a citizen of Algeria. But if you are a Palestinian, you worry more. You know that you have no recourse to justice. You have no state, no embassy, no institution of any kind to protect you in a moment of crisis. That's how it has always been for Palestinians; but you don't mind or care.

You have worn your sense of otherness all these years as a consciousness more intimately enfolding than your own skin. Statelessness is your only state, and you have long since developed an aboriginal sense of how to live there. You have grown up thinking that only in hell is there likely to be a halcyon statehood without the implosive stresses of national struggle. Perhaps a state is only a fantasy in the crazed dreams of your people, devised to contain the terrors of their history.

No matter though. The five thousand Palestinians who have been arriving in Algiers around the first week of February 1983 know they need not worry. They are received at the VIP lounge. As celebrities. As revolutionaries. They are, after all, arbiters of the destiny of the Palestinian people and are in the Algerian capital to attend the sixteenth session of the Palestine National Council (PNC), their parliament-in-exile. Among them are the 355 council members, all manner of council officials and functionaries, observers, journalists, and activists, as well as foreign dignitaries and solidarity group representatives.

I too stand there clutching my passport. There is something formidably, unendurably pitiful about the way a person, stateless all his life, clutches a passport once he gets one. I look at all the other Palestinians around me, coming from a bewildering multiplicity of countries, and experience a kind of emotional vertigo. We have all grown up and lived not only in diverse locales in the Arab world, but also in Western and Eastern Europe, in North and South America, in Africa and the Far East. Yet we have managed to keep our communal sense of national reference bounding and rebounding among us, like jugglers' weights, from year to year, from place to place, from generation to generation, so that we now understand each other, as if through a common trick of feeling.

As I sit in the lounge, memories of more flamboyant times cross my mind. A mere eight months before, what had taken a whole generation to build had been at its magical height. There was not a Palestinian alive then on whose life the Movement, the Revolution, the Resistance (as it was alternately called) had not etched a deeper national sensibility and inner excitement. There was not a Palestinian alive between the battle of Karameh in 1968 and the siege of Beirut in 1982 who was not radically transformed at the core. Our society had experienced a dynamic awakening at its vital centers of query and apprehension. Our national folk troop had found in music and dance a liberating function of culture and was recreating *dabki* dances and the use of our musical instruments, the *yarghoul* and the *oud*. The Palestine Film Institute was projecting lucid imagery on the screen and showing how a society, once held inert by its sense of refugeeism, could, through national struggle, impose coherence on the botched landscape of its everyday reality. The Palestine Research Center had amassed the world's largest library on Palestinian history, along with a large number of artifacts, artworks, and old manuscripts dealing with our culture. A whole institute employing hundreds was established to

7

resurrect the ancient art of embroidery. Our poetry, fiction, belles lettres, science, and system of education were enriched at their core of meaning.

A new tense, a tense of reality brought to a higher pitch of subtlety, was being added to the grammar of our cultural life, flourishing even under the occupation. To elude the censorship and restrictions while remaining responsive to the native sensibility, our writers were compelled to sharpen and restructure their metaphors and allusions, their use of image and style.

For two decades our Movement continued to release intense energies of spirit, and exploit possibilities of perception that would otherwise have remained fallow. We were growing up to see our-selves as inseparable from the national struggle, or separable from it only by abstraction. Our struggle for statehood, for freedom, for self-definition was, in effect, our window on life. We knew that if the Palestinian Revolution lost any of this energy, every Palestinian would, in a vital and central way, become less Palestinian.

This process of renewal seemed active wherever we chose to pitch our metaphorical tents, not only in Lebanon, but elsewhere.

Then, a walk through the Arab University district, where the Movement's offices and institutions were located, quickly proved—to a native son who had grown up in the streets of Beirut—that beyond the outward circumstance of anarchy lay a greater reality of revolutionary dreams. And the streets teemed with Iranian revolu-tionaries out to topple the Shah, Turkish leftists training to form a native underground, Egyptian Communists organizing to overthrow Sadat, Sudanese poets hiding from Numeiri's repressive regime, Nicaraguan Sandinistas out to liberate their society from Somoza, Arab Marxists who believed that armed struggle was the only instru-ment of liberation in the Arab world, Tunisian intellectuals coming to grips with their inability to write a coherent theory of the "Arab nation," plus European Trotskyists, U.S. pacifists, English ideologues, East German labor unionists—they were all there, not to mention all manner of Arab-American hucksters who had a readymade formula to "turn American public opinion" in our favor in return for this amount of money, or to put out a publication or open a "lobbying office"for that amount.

Though at times shrill and naive, our political values and the subversive energy of our outsidedness as a nation-in-exile had thrown their shadow across the entire Arab world, the third world, the Islamic world, and the socialist world.

Here in Algiers today, however, no one knows that our objective reality, along with these same political values, has already turned on its hinges.

To these Palestinians, and others like them around the world who follow the ten-day proceedings from afar, this is just another Palestine National Council session. A very important one to be sure, since it has been called to reassemble our political ethos and redefine our tactical direction in the wake of war, but nevertheless just another gathering of our parliament-in-exile. With a long catalog of ruin stretching behind us, all the way from the dismemberment of our homeland in 1948 to the siege of Beirut just eight months before, and with death sweeping over our history with such cruel frequency, we have thought that the 1982 war was just another firestorm, from which we will emerge intact, even purified. None suspect that each one of us (for in national struggle history is Everyman's affair) is destined to suffer, however uniquely, some part of the tragedy and dislocation that followed the siege of Beirut. None suspect that the fall of movements, or causes, from grace could be accompanied by a festive mood such as the one characterizing this sixteenth session of the PNC. None suspect that the arrow of revolt we had shot twenty years before has started its downward flight. And none understand that, whether we like it or not, whether under duress or in agreement, we will have to hand over the leadership of this national struggle—a struggle that has become so ingrained in our daily lives—to another generation of Palestinians.

No. Made haughty by our grief over Sabra/Shatila and arrogant by our ritual of resistance in Beirut, we remain unchanged, unyielding, unmoved in our repose of illusion. A generation of Palestinians that, in its impudence, expected, as we have become accustomed to expecting, that the Arab world, and maybe the world beyond, owes us a living. And support. And respect. And here we are, five thousand of us, to reenact our private anguish on a public stage, unaware that the last authority of reason in everything we had built and struggled for is shattered. We strut about as if we still occupy center stage in the international arena as heroes of a national struggle supported by a consensus of humanity at all its international forums.

At the airport, I sit in the VIP lounge—for where else would men

9

and women who had conducted daily transactions with history sit?—and clutch my Australian passport as other Palestinians arriving on the plane with me clutch their equally hollow travel documents. The man sitting next to me is Mahmoud Darwish, one of our national poets and a friend of many years. He confides that *surely* there will be trouble soon with the Algerians, a confrontation of sorts with some Palestinian or other. This is an *airport,* for God's sake, isn't it? Where have Palestinians been more wounded at the core than at airports, refused entry, detained, expelled, questioned, humiliated, and so on, because of their travel documents, their national identity, and their revolutionary reputation? I respond that this has happened more often at airports in the Arab world than in the Western world. For this and other reasons, I add, we have become elitists, looking down our noses on Arabs in general, not just on their governments.

Indeed, Palestinians have traditionally considered themselves the most outstanding theoreticians, ideologues, novelists, belle lettrists, bankers, and engineers in the Arab world. They have believed that they were chosen, if not by God, certainly by history, to be the vanguard of the Arab renaissance and to fall into the garb and glove left to them by the Vietnamese after *their* victory in 1975. Somehow Palestinians have believed all these myths and tried to lay them on people everywhere. And though they have not, after two decades of struggle, liberated any part of the homeland, they have carried within them no germ of preordained failure. It is the world that has failed, not them.

For ten days and nights, we wander around attending General Assembly sessions and various closed-door meetings in the spacious halls of the Palais de Nations by the shore of the Mediterranean. All the well-known heavies of the Revolution are here, striding around the hallways, talking animatedly, gesticulating, and giving speeches, trying to find an idiom of struggle, a political paradigm, to correspond to the new realities of our times. None of them betrays a hint of unease, uncertainty, about our condition. Perhaps it is a statement about us as a people and a nation in struggle that they do not.

Instead there is an incredible flow of energy, even pride. It is, after all, a major accomplishment for the Palestinians not only to be holding a parliamentary session so soon after the devastating events of the 1982 war, but to be holding a parliamentary session at all. For a nation severed from its native ground, with its people fragmented around the world or living under occupation, with its movement, cadres, and leaders constantly hunted down by enemies from within and without the Arab world, to have its own parliament and convene it yearly is no mean accomplishment.

Moreover, to establish the Palestine National Council, a forum for democratic discourse that adopts resolutions then acted upon by the Movement's executive branch, in a part of the world where institutions of this kind are seen as a threat, is no less than heroic.

And the people who have made it all happen are right here, having converged on Algiers from diverse locales around the Middle East.

In my nihilistic mood today, I see intimations of doom everywhere. Are these men capable, *still* capable, of comprehending, indeed mastering, the workings of our historical destiny? Whom does one blame—our leaders, ourselves, history, God—for allowing the enemy to chase our *fedayeen* to the four corners of the Arab world and for allowing the women and children they left behind to be chased to their mass graves in Sabra and Shatila? Whom does one blame for allowing the numbing image to enter our consciousness of the evening sun casting vacant shadows on the fly-covered bodies of our men, women, and children as they lay slaughtered like sheep in the muddy lanes of our refugee camps?

I observe that I am not completely alone in my gloom. The calamitous nature of our condition today, and the swift descent of our movement from center stage, is written on the faces of a great many of our leaders.

But not on Yasser Arafat's. What is it about this man? Why is it that he does not at least appear to grow old in years, slow in gait, pessimistic in mood? What makes him able to emerge from each upheaval in our national life with renewed vigor, to rebuild, to start all over again? Why have Palestinians rallied around him all these years, these long arduous years, although he has not brought them anything for their labor and sacrifice?

Unlike other Palestinian leaders, whose pronouncements on our condition have always somehow retained a feel of conscious acquisition, Arafat has an intuitive, aboriginal grasp of the Palestinian psyche. His métier as a revolutionary derives from a sense of tenancy, an ability to work from within, the national heart. He operates from a popular, historically based center in Palestinian life. He is in organic accord with the Palestinian people's idiom, culture, and aspirations, as well as their elitism, prejudices, and chauvinism, at any moment of immediacy in their struggle. His political logic is not charged with Mao's stylistic genius or Lenin's interpretive audacity or Castro's universal currents of meaning; it is, however, a folksy, literal, political logic nearer the source of Palestinian life than that of any other Palestinian leader. When Arafat speaks, Palestinians hear words close to their own. He strikes a chord in their collective soul, not only with his words, but with his style. He is the essential Palestinian Everyman, living a more authentically Palestinian life-style than any of them—no family, no home, no passport, no country, no property, consumed by Palestine and nothing else. That is why Palestinians, or at least most, engagingly call him *Abu Ammar* (the Building Father), *el Khityar* (the Old Man), *el Kaed el A'am* (Commander-in-Chief), and, at times, *el Waled* (Dad). And that is why the overwhelming majority of Palestinians have chosen Fatah, the movement that Arafat and half a dozen of his fellow revolutionaries created, as the expression of their mass sentiment. Fatah is an ensemble of their sensibility, no less than that. Unfortunately, it is also no more than that. For Fatah is impermeable to another flow of meaning. It is, at this point, an essentially nationalist movement—a reflection of the people it leads.

I spot Dina Ta'amari standing with a group of men. Dina was King Hussein's first wife. She is a woman with an outstanding history as an Arab patriot. In the late 1950s, for example, she had used her yacht to transport arms to the Algerian revolutionaries, who were then in struggle against the French to gain independence. Her involvement in civic and nationalist causes has not ebbed since. Now she is married to Salah Ta'amari, the military commander of the Palestinian forces in southern Lebanon. A dashing, intellectual, and handsome guerrilla from a poor, refugee-camp background, Salah became the model of the Palestinian protagonist in John Le Carré's novel *The Little Drummer Girl.* Le Carré had been a friend of the Palestinian leader for years and had stayed at his house in Sidon on a number of occasions.

During the invasion of Lebanon in June 1982, Salah was injured and later captured by the Israeli army and placed in Ansar, a sort of concentration camp that then held about fifteen thousand Palestinian and Lebanese prisoners. Dina's preoccupation these last eight months has been to publicize the atrocious conditions the prisoners lived under and to petition international organizations to demand their release.

I go over to shake hands.

"What's the news from Salah?"

"No news," she responds, sighing to indicate her sense of hopelessness. "What makes it worse is that the prisoners think we don't care about them. They think we've forgotten them."

"I don't believe that."

"Well, they have no access to news from the outside world. Every now and again they see a Red Cross official or two and that's about it," she says wearily.

I tell her that sooner or later we'll find a way to get them out of that hellhole.

"I hope so. Have you seen the exhibition of posters about Ansar that we put up?"

I tell her that I have, and was impressed by it.

Hundreds of people mill around the corridors and the lounge. It is early evening. In three hours, the PNC, the ultimate legislative authority of the Palestinian Movement, will meet again to elect a new executive committee for its executive branch, the Palestine Liberation Organization (PLO).

There are old people and young people, people in traditional dress and others in jeans. People who have been in the struggle since 1965, or were in it during the 1936–39 revolt inside Palestine, and some who have grown up not knowing anything else. And the foreign guests. Slavic faces, Germanic faces, Anglo-Saxon faces, African faces, Oriental faces, Indian faces, Latin faces. Outside the Palais de Nations, three Algerian destroyers patrol the coast.

I join some friends in the lounge. Among them are May Sayegh, president of the General Union of Palestinian Women (GUPW), and her husband, Abu Hatem, a PLO official.

May is reminiscing about an incident in the old days, in the early 1970s, when she and two other women from the union went to the Tel Zaatar Palestinian refugee camp to "educate Palestinian women politically, about their role in society."

"I mean," May laughs self-deprecatingly, "here we were, a bunch

13

of bourgeois Palestinian women, graduates of the American University of Beirut, and we meet this middle-aged woman, with that typically haughty look on her face that most women of the camps have, hanging her laundry on a line outside her ramshackle hut, with its tin roof held down by rocks and pieces of wood and branches and what have you. We tell her we've come from the GUPW to teach her—we actually said teach—about the politics of the Revolution. Well this lady says, 'Listen *khaltes*, my loved ones, I want to tell you this. If these sheets of tin,' she says and hits the wall of the hut with her fist, 'did not teach me, all these years, what the politics of my life and revolution is all about, then *you're* not going to.' "

"Yes," says Abu Hatem, "You can't underestimate our people's intuitive view of the world. This man I knew in Bourj el Barajneh kept telling me, every time I saw him after an Israeli bombing raid, 'Don't worry, it's all vitamins for our nation.' "

We continue talking. We reminisce about Majed Abu Sharar, a mutual friend who had been killed three years before, about the *Takhikhas*, the fighters and civilians who were shooting in the air when the *fedayeen* evacuated Beirut; about Black September in 1970, our first major confrontation with an Arab army; about the battle for Sidon in 1976 against the Syrian army, when a rocket-propelled grenade (RPG) hit a Syrian tank and sent it flying up to the roof of a two-story building, where it stayed right through the summer of 1982. We talk about who is living where now, since the evacuation. And in the end we talk, as if sensing that we needed relief from the excruciating subject we had been addressing ourselves to for over an hour, about May's hometown, Gaza.

"Brothers," says May mock-seriously, "in Gaza we eat hot peppers for breakfast."

We all laugh.

"And don't tell me you fellows from Haifa," she continues, pointing to her husband, "eat anything resembling hot peppers, even for dinner."

"You are the crown of my head," Abu Hatem responds.

At this point another friend joins us, a man in his late twenties whom I know only be his *nom de guerre*, Ben Bella. My acquaintance with him was superficial, but the others know him very well. Ben Bella, an expert in karate, had spent many years in Japan, where he acquired a reputation as a champion who would not "retreat" in combat. When he returned to Lebanon, he worked in the South under Salah Ta'amari as an instructor for the Palestinian youth movement, the *ashbal*. The *ashbal*—literally, the cubs—aged anything from nine to fifteen saw themselves, and were seen by Palestinian society, as an elite group who excelled not only in sports, but in combat. Karate was their major sport, according to Ben Bella. Though "violent," he tells us, it teaches practitioners to be "calm." The *ashbal* weapon was the RPG, known in the Soviet Union, where it is manufactured, as "the weapon of the brave." The *ashbal* were expected to fight "like ten *fedayeen*." "Every grenade in an RPG costs 34 *liras*, and you only have six, so don't waste them," they were told. "Don't hit your target"—usually a tank—"until it gets close to you, and then immediately move away."

Indeed, the Israelis dubbed them "the RPG kids" in the 1982 war for the devastating number of hits they scored with their grenades and the agility with which they moved. In every battle the Palestinians waged, all the way from the battle of Karameh in 1968 to the Syrian invasion of Lebanon in 1976, from the Israeli invasion of 1978 to the one that came four years later, the *ashbal* played a major role.

At Karameh, by literally throwing themselves at Israeli tanks with their explosives strapped to their waists, the *ashbal* may have turned the tide of battle. In June 1982, at the Rashidiyyeh refugee camp in the South of Lebanon, Ben Bella tells us, a group of thirteen *ashbal* kept firing at the attackers, "meanwhile running around like frogs," till they ran out of ammunition. Then they marched out with military salutes, to surrender to the enemy.

Ben Bella also tells us about the last days in Sidon, around the end of June; how Salah Ta'amari decided to stay rather than leave the *ashbal* behind and join the battle in Beirut.

"They all fought until they had no more ammunition," he says with finality.

Not more than twenty feet away, Salah's wife, Dina, is busy hanging drawings done by Ansar prisoners, smuggled out recently, on the walls of a room set aside for their exhibition.

The conversation turns to internal politics. Abu Hatem, bitter because he was prevented from giving Fatah's presentation on the Lebanon Zone because of his "radical" views, complains that the PNC's major contribution in this session was to coin a new word for the Arabic lexicon—*la'am*, a contraction of the words *la* (no) and

15

na'am (yes). All the resolutions that mattered, including the one on the Reagan Proposals, were couched in innocuous, ambiguous terms. In effect, this exposed the helpless, eviscerated spirit of our Movement.

Ben Bella takes exception, and submits that this is all part of the "tactics" of our postwar policy.

"Isn't it interesting," I say, "that most of the declarations dealing with our history have emanated from foreign capitals and were proposed by foreigners? Look at the Peel Commission, the Rogers Peace Plan, the Geneva Conference, the Camp David Accords, the Fez Plan, the Reagan Proposals, and so on."

"The first session of the PNC, which gave birth to the PLO, was held in Jerusalem," Ben Bella reminds me. "*That* is significant, isn't it?"

I admit that it is; but I don't add that it is equally significant that we are here in Algiers and not in Jerusalem. What is the point of getting into these arguments now? Isn't it enough that I've discussed that issue a million times in the past, in the early hours of the morning, with diverse Palestinian friends, all the way from Sydney to Paris, from Washington to San Francisco?

1

In the panic, some children suddenly found no hands to hold. They ran up and down the coast road looking for their parents. Clusters of men and women, tired from the long trek, sat by the bushes to rest, staring into the horizon as if crazed by sorrow and incomprehension. A few miles before we reached the Lebanese border, a crowd of people gathered around a woman who lay by the wayside screaming with labor pains. No one knew that this was our last day in Palestine, that this chaos would leave a gap in our soul. And we, the children, did not know that the memory of it was later to haunt the inner history of our whole generation.

In our refugee camp in Beirut, my father complains that the Lord's way has become wanton and absurd, but adds that every event in His creation has reason, meaning. If it had not meaning, then what has happened to us would not have happened. He could not explain the meaning of the events that led to our last day in Palestine. He just trusted that it was there, somewhere. The beginning of every act in His creation was simply the beginning of another.

Maybe he was right. No one can say. I just know that for my own generation of Palestinians our last day in Palestine was the first day that we began to define our Palestinian identity. Like the olive trees and the land and the stone houses and the sea and the *dabki* dances and the ululation at weddings. Everything was where it belonged. Everything coalesced into a coherent whole. It had never occurred to anyone to define it, or to endow it with any special attributes. Until we were severed from it.

I was just another eight-year-old child growing up in the refugee camps. All around me people talked about Palestine as if it were the center where all the impulses of their human identity intersected. And everybody was angry. Their anger tangled in the hair of the tents and the muddy lanes of the refugee camps. The men and women were angry because they had to count their years without the harvest. The children were angry because, as they began to acquire a past, moment by moment, touch by touch, encounter by encounter, they discovered that a sense of otherness governed their lives.

In exile, Palestinians lived in their little world and waited for a kind of deliverance. And soon our lives would intertwine with the lives of other people in the world. Then, in the overlapping of strange sorrows, it would be difficult to say whose mouth should turn angry.

In the early 1950s it was still unclear who was in exile, we or our homeland. The refugee camps we lived in were beginning to resemble the people who inhabited them.

In the winter it rained heavily. The dirt tracks of the Bourj el Barajneh camp turned to impassable mud. Families stayed in their tents or, the lucky ones, in their mud huts. After the torrents came the bitter frosts. The cold ate into our flesh. The whole camp was transformed into a swamp, with steam coming out of the belly of the earth and our mouths, and the walls of the mud houses.

The people were wrapped in rags given to them by the United Nations Relief and Works Agency, UNRWA. Rags originally "donated by the American people." The girls walked around wearing baseball hats. Out of the sacks our UNRWA flour rations came in mothers cut underpants for their sons. I often walked around with my behind covered with a handshake and the proclamation that the contents were a "gift from the American people."

Everybody shivered. All over the camp, the emaciated dogs died. Every day had a thousand and one wrinkles and a thousand and one knots. The men looked for employment, for food. They avoided the police, who were then implicating Palestinians in everything from inflation and communist plots to cold spells. And once every month they lined up, as if in a funeral procession, to receive their UNRWA rations of flour, powdered milk, and dates. The rations lasted a week. Then people ate words. The words led to orange groves in Jaffa, to olive trees in Tershiha, to cloudless summers in Haifa. And back again to Bourj el Barajneh.

In the summer it was fiercely hot. Big bowflies buzzed in the air. A sense of ennui, of resignation, ruled the camp, our lives. It was going to take a new generation to bring down the camp's flag of surrender and raise a flag of rebellion in its place.

In the 1950s I lived in the streets of Beirut. There was nowhere else to go. I worked in the streets, played in the streets, grew up in the streets, virtually all the streets of the city. In those days, Beirut was owned by street people. They poured over them, day and night, in an intricate communion with a city crazed by its colonial past and class dichotomies. Street peddlers, lottery-ticket sellers, shoeshine boys, hustlers, pimps, black marketeers, as well as Palestinian children in oversized business jackets down to their knees, donated by UNRWA, selling chewing gum and trinkets. At the age of ten I sold chewing gum, trying to hide my Palestinian accent for fear of getting beaten up by Lebanese kids who called me "a two-bit Palestinian" and a coward who "sold his land to the Jews." That is, till I learned to band with other Palestinian kids in the streets for protection, for union, for commonality.

We wandered the streets of Beirut together, peddling, shining shoes, hustling, stealing. And talking. We were all Palestinians and we all came from the camps. We spoke the same language, lived the same tensions. The geography of our souls intersected. We called ourselves Awlad Falasteen. A name that you choose for yourself, that you endow with your own symbolic constructs, has an indefinable exquisiteness. It unifies you, brings you close to yourself.

The streets of Beirut, as we worked and lived and played there, held a pain that gave us meaning. The image of children wandering around selling Chiclets chewing gum outside sidestreet cafes and restaurants and schools and office buildings has meaning. The

19

aimlessness of street life has meaning. The sun was so hot it made the streets sing. The sounds came from everywhere, as they always do in the streets of third world cities. These ancient streets were so narrow and the houses were so close to each other on either side that people were constantly on their balconies, talking, shouting, shrieking at each other. The peddlers, with their carts, shouted the virtues of their goods to heaven. All of this overpowered us, demolished us, till we learned to assimilate it and make it a part of our consciousness. And when the streets breathed, the smell blew at us as if it had come past centuries, after circling the oceans and the deserts and the stars. And always the faces. The faces of people earnest with impatience or quiet resignation. In some streets it seemed as if there was not an inch of space to spare. Human beings were walking, living, working, riding their buses and trams, tending their shops, sitting in their cafés, as if shoulder to shoulder. Nobody knew for sure why they cried or mourned. They just did. And waited for a Messiah, a prophet, a revolutionary, a rebel, an ideologue to explain their subjective pain, and give it objective coherence.

In the midst of all of this, we Palestinian children tried to make a living. Going to school was still a dream, a precious thought, like first love.

Ibrahim Adel became my friend almost the first day we arrived in Beirut. His family's tent was next to ours. We took to working the streets together. He shined shoes. Some of his customers called him Baldy. In fact, most Palestinian children were called Baldy in the streets. When our parents sent us to a barber (usually to one from Palestine who now made a living with a chair and a small table with the tools of his trade on it, propped up against a mud wall somewhere down the end of a dirt track in our refugee camp), we had all our hair shaved off. That way, because we needed a haircut only every three months or so, our fathers could save a lot of money. We often held that against our fathers. Ibrahim did not. He worshiped his father.

Abu Ibrahim* was revered by everyone at the camp because he had been a guerrilla in the 1936–39 revolt in Palestine and two of his brothers had fallen in battle. He was also a "people's poet," an activist who composed poetry orally and recited it to the masses, often political poetry about the land and struggle and freedom and life and

*"Abu" is a title conferred on a man who has one or more sons and means "father of." Usually a father is called "Abu" followed by the name of his eldest son.

20

death in the cause of Palestine. When people in the camp, sitting in the evening around the kerosene lamps in sidestreet cafés sipping their tea and smoking their waterpipes, came across a metaphysical question to which they were hard put for an answer, they murmured the common Palestinian phrase: "Surely the answer, brothers, lies only in the heart of the poet." And if Abu Ibrahim happened to be there, they all turned silently to him. He would pull gently on his thick moustache, sheepishly looking down the bridge of his nose, and begin: "Brothers, as the Prophet Mohammed revealed . . . and the poet confirmed . . . "

Ibrahim would always be there, looking up at his father, hanging on his every word.

In the streets, Ibrahim never learned to hustle, to fend for himself. We called him Maktabi (the library) because he was always reading books and because we were awed by his ability to write the English alphabet. He did not know any English yet, but he could transliterate any word in Arabic into English letters. All of which was never an asset in the streets.

One day Ibrahim and I are downtown working a street together. He with his shoeshine gear slung over his shoulder and I with my supply of chewing gum. On formidably hot days like this one the heat takes your breath away. If you walk for more than a block, you feel you are about to choke, your lungs struggling for air. On such days we worked the cafés, where it was cool inside, and even cool outside because the waiters would splash buckets of water every now and again on the pavement in front of the tables. Ibrahim and I have not eaten. We are both anxious to make some money, enough money to buy a *falafel*—a vegetable patty—or better still a *shawarmeh*, a chopped meat sandwich.

Usually when there was no food around the house because the UNRWA rations were gone and we had to leave without breakfast, the kids from Awlad Falasteen could be seen around the Beirut port, picking up oranges, apples, tomatoes, and the like that had fallen from the vegetable and fruit crates being shipped to the Arabian Peninsula and beyond. Sometimes Ibrahim and I would go to the American University of Beirut campus, sneak into the architecture department, where students would have their lunch bags ready for them before they went on their regular outings to study city buildings, and simply walk off with four of five of the bags. We were never caught.

21

Today it is too hot to go anywhere. Ibrahim walks around the Mashrek Café, near the Corniche, desperately soliciting business. He looks even to me, so little, so trusting, so vulnerable, as he maneuvers his way around the tables offering to shine shoes.

When he stops by Abu Majid's table, I know there is going to be trouble. Abu Majid is a neighborhood *zaim*—in the Lebanese tradition of the 1950s a huckster who lived, and earned his living, by the code of the bully. Like other neighborhood *zaims*, Abu Majid is known to have extensive holdings in business and politics—established politics being, in those days, as authentic a source of income as any other. His friends, like him, are thugs who prey on the poor and the helpless in the neighborhood.

In addition to this, Abu Majid hates Palestinians. Sitting at his table at the Mashrek Café surrounded by his friends, he is often heard mimicking our accent and talking, between giggles, about how he had just picked up his food rations at the UNRWA depot.

I stand in a corner of the café watching Ibrahim. The damp penetrating heat I feel is the heat of hatred. I hate this man and his friends. And his world. And ours. When a child hates, it is the voice of reason traveling home over lost roads, with the sound of blood rushing to the ears. One does not "learn" to hate. A child hates because it has been robbed of conditions of love. Standing in a corner of the Mashrek Café that day, I hate this man and his universe.

"Do you want your shoes shined, *zaim*?" Ibrahim asks Abu Majid.

"Well, son of the camps, son of Palestine! We love Palestinians here," he says, turning to his friends with a knowing smile. "Right brothers?"

They all mumble their agreement. I know immediately that this repulsive creature, made inhuman by his calling as a *zaim*, is about to play a practical joke on Ibrahim, to humiliate him, because that is how people like Abu Majid and his friends derive their enjoyment.

"I will shine your shoes for a quarter of a *lira*," Ibrahim says.

"I will give you half a *lira*," the *zaim* replies, again looking knowingly at his cronies.

Ibrahim's face lights up and he proceeds to put down his shoeshine pack.

"Before I give you the money, you have to do one thing."

My friend looks up as if nothing unusual is about to happen. "Sure, what would you like done?"

22

"First, you have to kiss my foot."

Ibrahim remains squatting behind his gear, staring at the man. The request has taken the will out of his muscles, his ability to respond.

Around the café, no one seems to notice. Busboys are running around with burning coals for the customers' waterpipes. Waiters are shouting to other waiters to bring a new deck of cards to a table whose occupants, in turn, are shouting greetings to people sitting at other tables. Outside there are beggars and lottery-ticket sellers and vendors and veiled women. And children in rags, with no hands to hold theirs. And people haggling over prices of food and soap and rosewater and a respite from pain.

"You want me to kiss your foot?" asks Ibrahim incredulously.

"For that you get half a *lira*."

I can see Ibrahim is getting flustered at the strange proposition. I cringe with mortification as I see my friend prepare to kiss the *zaim*'s foot, looking abjectly at the gathering. I am consumed by hate. I am hating Ibrahim with all my might because I know he is going to do it. I am furious at him. I am furious at everything around me.

"Kiss my foot, boy, kiss my foot, son of the camps," the man is saying, almost shouting with delight. His companions are roaring with laughter and anticipation of the result of their practical joke.

Ibrahim squats there in front of the man and waits for the excitement and laughter to die down. And I am thinking of that day, about a year before we left Palestine, when my uncle had brought home a hand grenade and I was allowed to hold it for a moment. I remember feeling the cool of the metal on my skin, contemplating the web of lines on its surface and being fascinated by the magic it transmuted to me. The terror of knowing how such a small object could wreak devastation on an enemy. Now, as I stand in the café, I am holding the same grenade, shouting "die, die, die, you mob of two-bit Lebanese sons of whores. *Die.*" I am throwing the hand grenade into the crowd of people as they contentedly drink their glasses of tea and torment us. Because we have less than they do. Because we are hungry. Because we are Palestinians. But when it explodes, it explodes only in my head and my soul. It is only my sense of worth that explodes. My rage. At the whole world. At the whole community of civilized nations and peoples that send us blankets and figs and powdered milk. That give us a tent to live in. And a foot to kiss. No one dies in this explosion, no one is mutilated, except us, the hewers of wood and drawers of water, as we silently go about our business of growing up.

We Palestinians often picture ourselves as a proud people, a people hardened by adversity to the point where we would not compromise our meaning. Well in the 1950s we were, as children, hungry. And hunger has a meaning, a logic, all its own. Just as our metaphysical need to be free declares its own form of meaning, so does our physical need to eat. A human being, triggered uncontrollably to gratify either need, will do anything—and a child will more readily than an adult.

The man puts his foot forward and Ibrahim bends down to kiss it. Just as my friend is about an inch away, the man withdraws it. There is a sudden explosion of laughter. The *zaim*'s friends are slapping their knees and doubling up with joy. Ibrahim demands his half *lira*, and the *zaim*, in between roars of laughter, repeats: "But you did not kiss my foot, you did not kiss it."

"I want my money," Ibrahim is demanding, virtually in tears.

"You will get your half *lira* only after you have kissed my foot."

The man puts his foot forward again. "Kiss it now. You'll get your money."

Again Ibrahim tries. And again the man pulls his foot away and his friends break up.

I go over to Ibrahim and drag him away. We walk out of the Mashrek Café and head to the Corniche, where we sit by the water.

Ibrahim, my friend. Ibrahim, whom we called "the library." Ibrahim, whose full name translates to Abraham the Just. Ibrahim, who is like me, and other Palestinian children growing up in the streets, learning what living in exile means.

We sit by the water for a long while, not saying much.

"Sons of whores," he suddenly shouts. "May the Lord destroy their homes."

"And pour acid on their souls," I add. "May they all die away from their homeland, in the *ghourba*, in the countries of others."

"Hey, tell me," Ibrahim asks with passion, "when do you think we shall return to Haifa?"

"I don't know for sure. A year or two. Maybe three."

"You think it's going to be that long?"

So you are abused by time. And wizened by it. For every moment in your existence, as a Palestinian child, thrusts you beyond your fixed meaning, a meaning that is difficult to explain to others. Meaning, after all, is hardly neutral or reducible to a static definition divorced from its existential setting. The range of significance that we endow ourselves and our history with is irreducibly Palestinian, the product of infinite adaptations in our social system. And it is, in the common sense of the word, private.

How the fuck do I explain why I am angry at the West, at the rich and powerful in the Arab world? How do I explain why I am now a revolutionary, why the vision of the return to Palestine has been, all my life, indispensable to my feelings, as it was to the feelings of my parents' generation and later became to the feelings of the generation of Palestinians that grew up after mine? How do I explain any of that without explaining the overlap of every event in my life and my history and my social system? And how do we go about repudiating the sense of otherness thrust upon us, without repeated spasms of despair, without muttering cruel prayers and drinking rain?

In the end you just return to the streets, which you have come to know so well and with which you have developed a subtle relationship of hate and love. In Beirut, as in other third world cities, the streets have a way about them, a magic to them, an intensity evocative of ancient energy and ancient memories that only the eye of hunger and love can see. There is a kind of order to everything, to the fusion of the odor of urine from the open latrines with the smell of uncollected garbage in alleys and on the pavements, with the political (always political) graffiti on the walls, with the sounds of pain from every direction, with the smell of spices, the intimacy of bodies, the notion of a humanity suckled on the same misery. And with the subtle absence of anonymity in the midst of it all. The streets do not tolerate anything anonymous. If you live there, everybody knows your name and your family and your nationality and your class background and your place in the hierarchy of power that the streets, in the wisdom of diversity-within-unity that they create about them, will give you. The peddler's status is known vis-à-vis that of the shopkeeper. The lottery-ticket seller, the cardsharp, the black-marketeer, the pimp, the policeman, the local *zaim,* they all know where they stand in relation to one another. Who oppresses whom, who reveres whom, who robs whom, who lives off the labor of whom—all of this has been determined by historical forces in the streets, forces whose origins are buried by time or beyond individual

25

recall. And if the streets do not decay it is because every available space is occupied, because everything has an intricate structure and an intricate function.

Westerners who live in their suburban outback will not mistake these streets for a happy place to live in. But those who have lived there, graduates of the higher education that city streets can confer on its denizens, often emerge as inspired men, as poets, as revolutionaries, as angels in armor. Few emerge as dead souls wounded by the crush.

And we, the children of the Palestinian diaspora, coming as we did in 1948, had to fight for our way there, acquiring an aboriginal sense of where we fit in the general scheme of the city—pending our return to Palestine, our homes and homeland. In the meantime, ours would remain a reality scorched by alienation. We were destined to wander the face of the earth, creating a ceremony of shadows that was to become our homeland in exile. And living in it, in the dark fullness of ourselves, we would end up affecting the world as forcefully as it had affected us. The only difference between us and others growing up in the world at the time is that we, unlike them, never had a childhood. In the end, people like us are a necessary component of change in history. Progress has never been made by contented people. In the midst of oppression, only the oppressed will abolish injustice. Only those who are defined as the footprint of a shadow emerge from the night with a dream. The dream soon sours, as all dreams do, and other outsiders, armed with the complex energy of their outsidedness, come forth to be agents in history, propelling it forward.

In Beirut, a year or two after we left Palestine, my father's hair began to take the color of snow. I would not leave him alone. I repeatedly badgered him about my bicycle. He had bought it for me a short time before we left our country. I want to know what is going to happen to it. Will the Jewish kids, who had been coming to Palestine from Europe, take it? Is it safe? Is it? Will it still be there when we return? And he assured me, earnestly, faithfully, that since our house is locked and we have the key, everything, including the bicycle, will be there just as we had left it. But I was not satisfied. I leaned against him, in tears, pleading to be taken back to Haifa, just for the day, just for the short trip across the border, to pick up the bike. Why can't we go? Why not? Why? Why?

Suddenly my father bursts into tears and begins to mumble: "I wish I were dead. I wish I were dead."

Soon after his wish was granted.

How do I mourn my own father's death? Had my father died of natural causes, of a recognized disease, of old age, or had he even died a violent death, I would have known how to mourn. But my father died of something else. He died from not being able to answer the question that he must have repeatedly asked all those years: Why had all of this happened to us?

In 1948, my father lived in Haifa. He was poor, like most Palestinians, and like most Palestinians he was also proud—that he lived in his city, had his own petty business, played backgammon with his friends in the sidestreet cafés of the city, and supported his family. After 1948, he found himself transplanted to a world of nonbeing in a refugee camp where his humanity and identity were reduced to a fragment. The move was so sudden, so inexplicable, that it took his breath away. The more he thought about it, the more the thought splintered his soul into pieces of raw wounds, of dizzy incomprehension. At the beginning of each month, he would line up at the food depot to pick up our food rations. His family lived on charity. Away from home. In the homeland of others. And they were alone. And destitute and hungry. He did not know why everything had crumbled around him. He could not deal with his sudden transformation from a proud, self-sufficient Palestinian Arab to a helpless nonentity belonging to a people being pushed off the pages of history books. Armed only with his traditional images, with his traditional system of logic, which had served him well to define the peasant society he had been a product of, he was unable to explain why he had been robbed of the right to live in his country. That is why my father's hair, which had been jet black in Palestine, was turning the color of snow. He was shriveling up and his hope, like his voice, was losing its edge. He had no answers, and he just wanted to die.

Yet I know I should not be concerned. My father lived his history and responded to it, in life and in death, the best way he knew how. And I had mine. When I reflect on it, I find that I have grown up with death like I have grown up with my skin. Violence and death flourished within close proximity of every moment, every encounter

27

in my life. Even as a child I was learning of the violence that history is capable of inflicting on the soul.

Violence in both its psychological and physical forms had always dominated my life. Yet in this period along with my memory of pain and devastation, I had an equally strong feeling of compassion, an affirmation of the possibility of human justice and freedom—denying violence a monopoly of the soul. Even as an eight-year-old boy, I had memories of what I had left *behind*. Of walking, resting, and walking along the coast road to the Lebanese border to seek refuge. A peasant woman giving birth on the wayside, emitting ghastly sounds. My mother fingering her prayer beads, pleading with the deities to let us through safely. Stragglers from Haifa, and Acre, and other coastal cities joining us along the way, all heading in the same direction. My mother tying her shawl in knots around her back and shoulders and putting my two-year-old sister there. When we pass the Zionist settlements, everybody walks straight on, looking straight ahead, as if this will protect us from being seen or shot at. *What are these settlements? Who are the people who live in them? Why did they choose our country to come to? Who are these people? Who are they? Who are they?*

The year before, in the village we lived in, I keep remembering . . . the house was blown up and the family in it ran out, the woman, her body burning, clutching a pillow as she ran. I hear a scream. In the room that night everybody is getting up. My eldest brother carries a gun and leaves in a hurry. The sound of gunfire is getting louder, closer, and the animals in the village are running loose, down the dirt tracks, behind the houses. The Committee for the Defense of Balad el Sheikh is giving instructions while the sky rains fire on our village. Maybe God in His heaven has gone mad. *They are here again.* It is still night in the room and my mother is reciting verses from the Koran. *The Stern Gang is here again.* There is a kind of frenzy in the Koranic words my mother recites. Her voice is drowned out by the sound of shooting and then I hear it again, so loud, so frantic, when there is a gap, a short silence, as the firing stops. *They are here . . . who are these people? . . . They are taking our homeland.*

We left the village and went down to Haifa to live with my grandparents and uncle. My grandfather worked at the Haifa port with the British Port Authority . . . and the underground. Every night he came home with guns that he would smuggle through the gates at the port and bring to my uncle. Guns he would steal from the offices where he worked. Guns he would buy from drunk British soldiers. Guns brought on friendly ships arriving from Beirut, Latakia, and Alexandria.

My uncle and brother would go off for days together. They were called *mojahedeen* in those days. In my own generation, two decades later, their counterparts were known as *fedayeen*. But everything was dying. There were only remnants—disorganized and alone—of the 1936–39 revolt.

Outside my grandfather's house, along the main road, a group of *mojahedeen* are standing beside cement blocks. They are armed with machine guns and hand grenades. They take up their positions on the road to Mount Carmel only minutes before the ambush begins. My uncle is running back and forth issuing instructions. The convoy of trucks arrives. Six brown trucks covered with canvas and thick rope. One driver and a passenger in each. I am crouching by the window with my father's arm around my waist. Everybody in the room is watching. All at once, machine-gun fire rakes the trucks. Hand grenades explode. The shooting is incessant for over a minute. Two of the trucks are on fire. I do not know where to look. Something is happening in all directions. To all the men. To all the trucks. I keep watching the truck nearest to the cement blocks. I see the driver with one hand on the steering wheel, the other clutching a pistol that he places on the outside, against the windshield. His co-driver, next to him, is dead, his body half out of the open door. The man now jumps out of his vehicle and takes cover behind some of the cement blocks. He crouches there with the pistol still in his hand.

When the British soldiers arrive in their tanks and army trucks, my uncle and his men hurry back to their homes with their weapons. There are bodies in the street. The trucks are burning. The smell of gun smoke fills the air. The man behind the cement blocks waves to the soldiers. I see him as he walks away with them. I wave to him, tentatively, innocently. I begin to endow him with a private history that I create for him. A private life that is embellished with time. His memory has lived with me ever since I left Palestine in 1948. Ever since our land was flattened by bombs, and political edicts denuded our history of its metaphor and its idiom.

After the man is rescued the tanks and soldiers stay in the

neighborhood. Soon more soldiers arrive. Hundreds of them. With their blond hair, freckled noses, and tattoos.

We hear them climbing up the stairs. My grandfather's part of the house is on the second floor of a two-story building. We hear foreign voices. It is always foreign voices. Foreign people telling us what to do. They order us to open the door. They shout something about the authority invested in them by the King of England. That is how it was in those days—the King of England invested his people with authority to issue orders in Palestine. And in India. And Africa. And Kenya. And Hong Kong. Of course, no Englishman would ever have allowed us to send people over to England and invest in them the authority to push around English men, women, and children.

The soldiers rush into our house, six or seven of them. We are herded into one room. They ask my grandparents if they have guns around the house. We are standing, all of us, with our arms up. Only my mother looks funny, with her prayer beads over her head, muttering incantations to scare away the evil spirits. The soldiers open wardrobes, smash the dressing table, throw my grandmother's sewing machine against the wall. They wreck the place. The two soldiers who are doing most of the ransacking are shouting abuse at the top of their voices. "Filthy wogs," they keep repeating, "filthy wogs." All this time I feel nonchalant. For I had seen that, and much more, done in the village. I had seen them grab people by the hair and drag them to the center of the square and kick them till they became unconscious. Often they took suspects with them who never returned. In the 1936–39 revolt, before I was born, the British hanged three men from our village. Three *mojahedeen*.

Though my father was never a *mojahed*, he transmitted their ethos to me. The mythology of the *mojahedeen* is an integral part of our oral history. Every Palestinian child who sits on his parents' knees listens, entranced, to the tales of men who defied the hated British and later the Zionists. How bands of *mojahedeen* came to the village during the 1936–39 revolt, with guns and checkered headdress, and the women came out to the square and gave them flowers and bags of food and the children pointed at them. Suddenly a woman would stand close to them, put her hand over her mouth, clasping her lips with two fingers, and start ululating. The other women joined in and the square, the whole village, reverberated with the resonant sounds. The men in the village became reverential, their voices hushed, as

30

they greeted the *mojahedeen*. *"Ahlan Wa Sahlan, Ahlan Wa Sahlan fi el Abtal"* (Welcome, Welcome to the brother heroes). And before leaving, the fighters were joined by some of the young men, who would leave the village fields to live in the hills with them.

My father never went away. He was a small shopkeeper. One day three British soldiers get off their jeep outside his shop and talk to him. They are drunk. One abuses my father because there are flies on the goods displayed in the open. How do you expect anyone to eat this shit with flies on it, he wants to know. Another takes his rifle and knocks over the bags of olives, cheese, oranges, whatever is nearest him, right on the ground and jumps on them, roaring with laughter. The third soldier grabs my father by the neck, throws his *hatta* off his head and slaps him across the chest. And my brother became a *mojahed* at the age of seventeen.

When we left Palestine the dawn was blowing around us like the rage of God. Our city had fallen and burnt on supine bodies. And the world applauded. But I did not hate. I could not hate at the age of eight. April is always a good time of the year where I was born. The sun shines and the smell of olives and oranges permeates the air. That April, in 1948, was my father's last in Palestine.

The day before we left the city, we sat in the house off the highway and heard foreign voices shouting into loudspeakers, "Get your women and children out." I hated those foreign voices. "Get everybody out. Get everything out." This is going to be somebody else's country now. "Get them out." Around the streets, in the distance, there was intermittent gunfire. "Get your women and children out." Flares and smoke and fireworks exploding in the heavens, above the houses, beyond the port, near Mount Carmel, around the center of town. Something was dying. Something was coming to an end for this generation of Palestinians. *Get out.*

The men and women who were defending Haifa were gone. They were alone. They were dead. They were dying. They were wounded. Then the people went. The radio was dead. Before it died someone issued Declaration 15 on the air. And what was Declaration 14? And 8? And 4? And infinity? There was no Declaration 16. The ether was choked with fire. And despair. And death. And ever since that time, people have wondered why I use double negatives around my house, unhindered by my walls lined with books; and why I use terms like nation and homeland and inalienable rights, unconcerned that I

31

have become over the years the citizen of a community of beings much larger than Palestine.

In Beirut, however, at age thirteen, I could not explain my father's death without looking for Declaration 16, and for a liberated zone I could go to, live free in. At that age I could not explain the tradition of refugeeism my father was transmitting to me as I listened to his mumblings about how soon—for surely it had to be soon—we would all return. All our agonies would be over. The cosmos would be restored to its preordained course.

In the first three years of our *ghourba* a frightening sense of my father's refugeeism ruled Palestinian life in our refugee camp. Everything was slow-moving, quiet, dormant. The dogs, like the children, had bones showing under their skin and lay in the shade of the tents. In the hours after noon people were nowhere to be seen, except occasionally a woman walking up the dirt track to the water pump with her bucket. No one acknowledged our presence. Whether we were being ignored or forgotten no one could say. After a while, it ceased to matter. In the evening, the old men sat in the sidestreet café with its kerosene lamps talking furtively. Their words were at times impassioned. At times angry. They talked about Palestine. About the Return. Trustingly, hopefully, about UN debates. None of them doubted that their stay in Lebanon was temporary. Instead, they discussed the difficulties that the majority of Palestinians encountered making a living, getting a work permit, a residence permit, a permit to cross borders; they discussed which Arab leader stabbed us in the back more than the others. Which Arab state was good to the Palestinians and which was bad to them. Palestine would always be there as they left it. And it was also right there that night, around the kerosene lamps, transmuted to us in their images and recollections and passionate idiom, in the encapsulated world of the refugee camp that had already been home to me for three years.

I sit in the café next to my father and watch him and his friends drink their tea and suck on their waterpipes. I am eleven years old.

My father is talking to Abu Saleem, a newcomer to the camp. My father asks him where he comes from in Palestine.

"I come from Hawassa," Abu Saleem replies.

My father recognizes the village near Haifa. "Hawassa, hey?" he asks quietly, elongating the name and dwelling on it as if it has some mystical, healing effect. "Hawassa is a pretty village."

Such an exquisite verb that my father has just used, bristling with the stuff that makes people defy history and the heavens and the powers that be. For to both my father and Abu Saleem, Hawassa, along with all the intangible realities of the village, is something that will remain eternal and real in the essential repertoire of their consciousness. To them, Hawassa *is* and not *was* a pretty place. And Palestine *is* and not *was* their country.

To my parents' generation the present was insanity. Not a natural continuum of what was. The only way they could relate to it was to transform it into an arrested past, governed by Palestinian images, rites, rituals, and dreams. That was the only way to impose harmony on their daily life, which terrorized them. They looked at themselves in the mirror of their past, for had they looked at the present the mirror would have been cracked. The image of their reality blurred.

A whole mosaic of folklore began to emerge that captured, and froze in the mind, the portrait of Palestine as our parents' generation had left it. The vernacular exploded spontaneously with the mass sentiments of those who came from Haifa, from Jaffa, from Acre, and other towns or isolated villages in Palestine. *Haifa,O beloved city, we left thee with the fish that our fishermen had caught still thrashing about on the sands.*

Jaffa, its denizens would counter, *we fled thee O sad city of the north, with our Dabki song not yet finished.* And those who came from Acre would say, *Acre, we built thee unafraid of the roar of the sea.*

I am eleven years old and my father and I are walking down the dirt tracks of our makeshift world in the refugee camp. The walls are covered with political slogans. One of these says, "May a million calamities befall the British, enemies of the Palestinian people." I read that aloud to my father, deliberating over the words.

"May the Lord hear your prayer," he responds earnestly.

"The Zionists are also the enemies of the Palestinian people."

"That they are. May a million calamities befall them too."

With such vehemence was I acquiring a past and a consciousness.

My father is in his traditional *shirwal* and headdress, clutching three *liras* and some change for the tram fare. We are heading to the marketplace downtown to buy food. The money, though so little, is

33

precious. My brother had worked all day the day before at a construction site to earn it. Today maybe we can eat something other than the powdered milk, bread, and dates that the UNRWA rationed out.

I am carrying an empty wicker basket in one hand. I ask my father eagerly if we will be buying cake today.

"Why cake? Who do you think we are? We are not of the landed gentry, you know," he reprimands me. Everything he utters nowadays, every phrase he formulates, seems to be infused with land. We are not of the *landed*. We are not of anything except Palestine. Palestine, which housed within it the passions of two hundred generations.

"When we return to our homeland, you shall have all the cake you want. Believe me, it won't be long now. Just be patient."

In the marketplace we mingle with the shoppers. It is hot and humid. My father haggles over prices, spending the whole morning, to make the three *liras* last. The flies buzz in the air. Peddlers shriek. The porters walking around with huge wicker baskets over their backs frantically solicit work. We have to walk all the way back to the refugee camp because we don't have enough money left for the tram fare. In the heat, it is a long trip for my father. He and I alternate carrying the basket, now full of vegetables. Every five minutes or so, my father sits down, panting. I sit down with him along the Basta road. My father's face pours with sweat, which glues some of his hair to his forehead.

"Soon we shall go back to our homeland, son," he says to me suddenly. "We are not from this country. We are not even of it. God in his wisdom will know when to help the heroes of the Return regroup and help us fight for our rights."

I ask him if his store in Haifa will still be there when we return. He smiles happily at the image, and says of course it will, like everything else.

"And our home will still be there. And the Makha el Sham Café near it, where Abu Murad used to play the *oud* and make it cry," he adds.

I glance at him intently, studying his face, as if I am seeing my future in his past. To him everything is in either the mind of God or the heart of the poet.

Soon after that I took to the streets. This was no time, no place, to have a childhood. At home my father hung a picture of Nasser up on

34

the wall, hammering a bent nail in with an ashtray. What else was there for him to do? At the dinner table everybody watched someone who reached for the sugar or the bread or the beans, ready to shout "Hey, leave some for the others." I say that to my younger sister. There is so little of everything. More than one spoonful of sugar and everybody cried, "Hey, leave some for the others; we are not of the landed, you know."

I was growing up very cynical in my early teens, cursing the world and its angels and gods, and the mumbling incoherencies of my father. And the whole world outside the camp, which was venting its hostilities and aggression on us.

The Egyptian president smiled benignly on our misery in the mudhouses of our refugee camps, promising my father salvation he never intended to deliver. My father trusted Nasser because he had nowhere else to turn. I tried to be understanding but found it difficult.

If I was later to become a revolutionary, it was simply because a revolutionary idiom and the tensions of revolutionary life raged around me in the streets as if they were part of the elements. The struggle between rich and poor? This was a concrete everyday reality we literally bumped into it as we walked the city streets and saw Arabs from Lebanon and elsewhere driving imported sports cars to the nightclubs of Beirut, where they could drink and gamble themselves silly while the masses of the city starved. Their preoccupation with Western gadgets had long since turned them into caricature Arabs. I only had to go to Hamra Street, as I did in my first year selling chewing gum, to see them sitting around in places called Uncle Sam, Queen's, and The Horseshoe, speaking French or English to each other. To them, we were *tres sauvages, complétement sauvage!*

And the ruling elite in the Arab world? I could not reconcile their pious claims with what we Palestinians endured in their states. Before I reached an age to have acquired any recognizable political history, I could already tick off a whole catalog of fears, terrors, and mendacities that they had made a part of our lives.

"Why the hell do we need a picture of Nasser around here?" I ask my father flippantly.

"Watch your language," my mother intones.

"Can we still trust Arab leaders?"

"Not Nasser? *Nasser?*" someone in the room asks incredulously.

"If God were an Arab leader, I would not trust him."

"Atheist! Communist!" This one from my mother.

I start swearing vehemently and my mother starts her Koranic incantations. "I ask forgiveness from God Almighty, the Great. No power and no solution except from Him the Exalted, the Omniscient."

My father, as if on cue, stands up and tells me to leave the room. As I do, my sister picks up where I left off.

"He is right, don't you see, dad?" she is saying. "Can we trust anyone, except ourselves, to liberate our country?"

Jasmine. My kid sister. With her glasses and teenage pimples and jet-black hair. With her pamphlets and booklets on the "solidarity of the working classes" hidden in her school bag so our parents won't see them. Her fear of the dark. Jasmine, who, like every other Palestinian kid, never had a childhood. As much a product of the violence in our history as I. Working as a servant in the Ajloun Mountains of Jordan at age 12.

We were learning rich metaphors from those who came before us with full memories of Palestine. And adding our own metaphors from exile. Our struggle for self-definition took on the freshness of a new beginning, resonant and self-assured, as theirs did when it started in the 1920s. And like everything that is newly born, our struggle carried elements within it from the past, all Palestine's past.

As we grew up, we lived Palestine every day. We talked Palestine every day. For we had not, in fact, left it in 1948. We had simply taken it with us. Palestine was an indivisible part of my generation's experience. Just as there was nothing in the Garden that Adam did not know, nothing that he could not isolate, identify, and interpret. It could not have been any other way. Our involvement was as much forced upon us as it was a genuine and spontaneous inward preoccupation of our soul. This became evident soon after we all began to go to school again.

The first school I went to in Beirut was not far from the camp. It was run as a business by a Lebanese from the neighborhood. The classrooms were crowded. And always cold and damp. The teachers were semi-literate. But for me even this school was an exciting place to go to every day. For Ibrahim, with his craving for education, it was heaven on earth.

Every school day, for me, was an exotic experience. After years in the streets I was truly enchanted by the idea of a formal education, by

36

school activities, by sports, by the concept of boy scouts. I joined the boy scouts. And I was totally consumed by the idea of a camping trip to Cyprus that the group was organizing. For three months I made preparations. I saved money. I peddled chewing gum again in the evenings. The anticipation of the trip gripped my senses. I told the people at the camp. I told the whole world. I was a fourteen-year-old boy, a boy scout, going on a camping trip to Cyprus. I was, at last, no different from the other children. The tension of this transformed me, ruled my life for three months.

Three days before we were to go on this trip, the Palestinian kids in the boy scout group were called into the principal's office. Because we were Palestinians, he said, we were stateless. And because we were stateless, we had no travel documents. And because we had no travel documents, the principal adds with the gestures of a man who had just discovered the solution to a major problem in his life, we could not go to Cyprus. We should have informed him of our status before, he continued reprovingly, talking to us, as the rest of the world did, as if it were our fault that we were stateless.

The other kids went on their trip. And we returned to Palestine. I am from Haifa. *Haifa, O beloved city, we left thee with the fish that our fisherman had caught still thrashing about on the sands.* Haifa now means more to me than it did to my father. It is more graphic in my mind than in his. Its image more enriching, more engulfing as I grow up.

Still, there was nothing wrong with *being* a Palestinian. Or *living* at the camps. We went to school. We fought the boys outside the Bourj el Barajneh. We fought each other. Samira sat next to me in class and my arm brushed hers. During the *Eid* following the holy month of Ramadan, the UNRWA distributed clothes and shoes and baseball hats to the refugees. I am a refugee. I get an old pair of moccasins from America. That's right, from America. I have painted slogans on the walls: Down with America.

For Palestinians, passion for politics and political activism began at a very early age. By the time we were halfway through high school, we were already veterans of a number of demonstrations, strikes, protest marches, and ideologies, as well as arrests, beatings, and worse.

For Ibrahim, politics was now more than a passion. It ruled his life. Every waking moment. Long before he graduated, he virtually

37

controlled political activity at school. He became the one to decide when to go on strike, what demonstration to join, what petition to sign. He was becoming incredibly self-assured, haughty, aggressive, and extremist. It was he who organized Awlad Falasteen to uproot the UNRWA trees. The United Nations organization had been doing a lot of building, renovating, and construction around our camp. The trees, planted along the dirt tracks, were presumably put there to beautify the area. But around the sidestreet cafés, people were wondering about them, about the better shacks they were building.

A woman shouted to a gathering of Palestinians around the water pump, "O sisters, I swear to you by the blood of our fallen patriots that I will not hammer one nail in a wall while we are outside Palestine. We shall build only when we return to our land. There we shall build!"

The woman was Um Ali, who became famous in the movement in the 1970s because she lost all her six sons, her two daughters, and her husband in battles the Palestinians waged after 1967.

Are they going to deny us our right to return to our land, everybody was complaining, by making our stay here comfortable, acceptable, and hence permanent? "They" were the UNRWA officials, the American government, the Zionists, the British, the Arab states, and everybody else who lived outside the camps with their backs to us.

The trees looked so incongruous in the midst of our misery and destitution. So Awlad Falasteen attacked the trees, uprooted them, and burned them. We danced around the fire, singing lines of doggerel then common among Palestinians: Who am I/Who are ye?/ I am the returnee/I am the returnee.

And always the police came to the camps. And always Captain Constantine was in a jeep, accompanied by three or four of his gendarmes. Nobody was afraid of us in those days.

He climbed up on a box, in the manner of a man about to pontificate, and waited for the people of the camp to come and listen to his abuse. If they did not, he sent his men to drag them out of their homes. He talked as if we were children.

"I don't want to see any more Palestinians peddling in the streets without a permit," he hollered with a hint of contempt in his voice. "I don't want to see any more Palestinian sons of whores going across the border to Syria without a travel permit, or working 'whether paid or unpaid' without a permit." If someone asked him a question he raised his voice contemptuously as he replied. He even slapped men across the face in front of their sons. "Uppity Palestinians," he screamed, and went on to do the same thing at other camps.

At the café, a man complained, "The son of a whore doesn't even wear a moustache."

One day someone killed Constantine, with a dagger, as he was coming out of his house in the Mazra'a district. Immediately everybody began to speculate whether it was the Nasserites, or the Arab Nationalists, or the Communists, or the Baathists who did it. Shopkeepers gave out free candy to the children.

Then Squad 10, police who were the terror of both Palestinians and poor Lebanese, came to the camps. They arrested an eighteen-year-old boy called Hatem Arabi. He was never seen again.

Three middle-aged, very American-looking evangelical ladies come to our school to distribute toys. They are patting kids on the head and speaking deliberate, enunciated English to them when a boy of eleven or twelve walks up to one of the ladies, and ever so gently, pats her behind. "Your buttocks are so beautiful," he says innocently.

The three evangelists want to know why the older pupils outside the school gate are making such a din. We are going to join yet another demonstration organized by the Arab Nationalist Movement in support of the Algerian struggle against French colonialism. Everybody is already shouting slogans. The girls are in the front, standing three abreast, holding Palestinian, Lebanese, and Algerian flags. The boys are arguing among themselves about which route to take to reach the Makassed school, where we will join its detachment of demonstrators.

"*Tahya el thawra el Jazairia,*"someone shouts. And we all shout back, Victory to the Algerian Revolution. "*Fi el thawra tahreer Falasteen,*" another shouts. And the slogan is repeated *en masse.* In struggle shall Palestine be liberated.

As we move on, dirty versions of political doggerel, old ones from previous demonstrations or new ones coined for the occasion, echo across the streets. The slogans condemn American imperialism, the British government, the French colonists in Algeria, Arab reactionaries, the "lackeys" of the West and Zionism in the Arab world, and virtually all established Arab leaders, with the Hashemites in Jordan and Iraq heading the list. When we get to the Makassed school, Ibrahim runs back and forth to confer with the leaders of its detachment of demonstrators. He is sweating profusely, with his shirt clinging to his small body.

"The sons of whores say we can't go for a while," he says loudly, contemptuously, "because the stupid Baathists are at it again with their rigid instructions to their followers. For God's sake, these people are so dumb and irritating!"

He talks as if his whole life depends on the success of the event, gesticulating wildly, pleading with everybody to stay in place and not disperse.

We ultimately get moving and pick up more people on the way, heading to the American University of Beirut (AUB) to combine with its own students demonstrating there. From the AUB we are all going to march down to the Borj, the main square in the center of downtown Beirut, to the Lebanese Foreign Ministry.

On the way, the shopkeepers throw flowers and rosewater at us. Some shout slogans such as "Down with colonialism" and "God is with those who seek to be free." Others, more religiously oriented, shout Koranic phrases. By the time we reach the Borj, our numbers have swelled immensely. We stand all bunched up together, surrounded by a large number of gendarmes. The demonstration today, unlike many others before and after it, is legal. The Algerian Revolution in the late 1950s, like the Palestinian Revolution in the late 1960s, was too popular for the government to ban.

Outside the Foreign Ministry building the various groups from different schools or different parties or different ages mingle together. Ibrahim and I hold the wooden poles supporting a banner that says "Western imperialists, colonists, and occupiers in our homeland—the Arab world shall become your graveyard." Salim Solh, the prime minister of Lebanon, steps onto his third floor balcony to address the crowd. Ibrahim and I are directly below, standing near the steps leading into the lobby of the building. For about ten minutes Solh dwells on the sympathy that the Lebanese and other Arab peoples have for the Algerian struggle for independence. But then he says the Lebanese people have always sought friendship and cooperation with the French and the Lebanese government does not want to endanger this special relationship. Ibrahim begins muttering loudly under his breath. Then suddenly, as if he has gone mad, he screams *"La, la, ya Solh, la solh ma'a el istimar?"*—No, no, O Solh, no peace with colonialism. Ibrahim is punning on the name "Solh," which in our language means "peace." He keeps screaming the line over and over again, at the top of his voice. Full of uncontrolled fury, he lets go of his side of the banner to wave his fists at Solh. Then he climbs up on the steps and proceeds to give a counter-speech.

For God's sake. Ibrahim Adel. The sixteen-year-old boy with whom I grew up at the camps. Who has a lyrical name like Abraham the Just and a nickname like "the library." Who shined shoes around the Corniche with me. Ibrahim, the boy with the shaved head who had tried to kiss a *zaim*'s foot not so long ago, is now giving a counter-speech to the one that the foreign minister of Lebanon is giving to a crowd of ten thousand demonstrators.

What is happening to us, the first generation of Palestinians growing up in exile? It is as if we are growing up challenged to talk about and deal with more than we knew. Each question we ask to which we find no answer becomes a blow, merciless and brutal.

Ibrahim is, of course, picked up by the police and taken into custody. In those days, when you were arrested the police did not bother to file charges, release you on bail, or enable you to inform your next of kin. Very simply, you were beaten senseless, made to sit in a cell for a day or two, a week or two, a month or two, or when necessary, a year or two. Till the emergence of the Palestinian Revolution in 1967, it was illegal for Palestinians to engage in any kind of political activity. In Lebanon, Palestinians were considered aliens.

When we went to visit Ibrahim at the police station the day after his arrest, laden with bread, black olives, and yogurt, he seemed in incredibly good humor, despite his swollen face and bruises. He even joked with us about what the police had threatened.

"To deport me," he said mock-seriously, "if they caught me in a demonstration again."

"Deport you," we all asked in unison. "Where? Where could they deport you?"

"That's the joke, don't you see?"

Ibrahim was soon released because Abu Ibrahim (like everybody else) knew someone, who knew someone, who knew someone in the

Lebanese Parliament who, for a bribe, did favors for the families of prisoners. Under the then existing system, someone who could come up with the appropriate amount of money could literally get away with murder.

In Palestinian society, when someone is released from jail for a political offense, everybody in the neighborhood, and even outlying neighborhoods, visits to offer "congratulations." The visitors may be total strangers, but they come, sit down, drink tea, talk Palestine, and offer their congratulations. If male, the ex-prisoner wears his headgear in a special way, tilting his *hatta* at an angle to indicate rakish defiance of the authorities and to declare to his friends that he had not been crushed. He is, in other words, proclaiming publicly his willingness to go back to jail if need be. If the victim died under torture, or has been killed in battle, then his family buries him attired as a bridegroom, *arisse el watan,* married to the nation. Again, congratulations, not condolences, are offered by the visitors.

These are old, traditional arrangements that Palestinians (in struggle for well over a century) had established sometime beyond anybody's recall; arrangements that, for various reasons, still appeal to their internal psychic economy.

So Ibrahim basks in the "congratulations" that people from Bourj el Barajneh camp come to his home to offer.

Abu Ibrahim, however, is enraged at his son, not because of his political activism but because he is "endangering his education." "How are you going *to live* without an education?" Abu Ibrahim is shouting at his son. "You keep forgetting that you're a Palestinian. *A Palestinian.* You're worth nothing without an education. No one will give you a job without an education. Do you want to grow up to be a shoeshiner? And tell me. How will you support us when your mother and I are old? You're a *Palestinian.* Can't you wait till we go back to our homeland? Do you want to struggle in the lands of others? May the Lord damn them and damn the lands of others? May the Lord damn them and damn their lands and their corrupt governments and police. May the rainbow never appear in their skies. May the Lord pour acid on their songs and fire on the tongues of their poets. Wait till we return to Palestine. Your education is more important than politics."

In Palestinian society, you do not talk back to your father. Ibrahim listened, and said nothing. In exile, however, our fathers have become too debilitated, too drained, by the effort they have made, all these years, to transmute the ethos of Palestine to us. In their old age, they have become conservative, cautious, terrorized by the exigencies of life and the imminence of death in exile.

2

The objective conditions in our situation—which are themselves an externalization of our subjective condition—were changing us, transforming our picture of the world and ourselves at a dramatically accelerated pace.

At school, I am consumed by a paper I am writing about the Russian Revolution for my history class, trying to deal with why men and women struggle at such danger to themselves; why certain individuals readily offer their lives for a cause although this means they will not be around to enjoy the rewards of the ultimate victory. At home I am consumed trying to pacify my mother, who berates me and my sister for "endangering" our education. Our mission in life, she insists, is to become educated and liberate Palestine, not to change the Arab world. "Leave politics alone," she shouts. "We are just Palestinians, for God's sake." She does not respond to our argument that Palestine and the Arab world cannot be seen in

44

isolation from each other, and that our destiny as a people cannot be divorced from its relation to politics, and to political events in the rest of the world.

The argument that everything in politics is interconnected in an intricate web of relationships spanning the whole world had come to me from my friend Samir Salfiti, who worked as a peddler at the Corniche. I knew Salfiti from the camps and from Awlad Falasteen. We often called him Abu Saksuki, Father of the Beard. More often we called him Brazil-Japan, an engaging name we gave him because he was always wont to begin an argument, in that systemic logic of his, by saying: "Hey listen brothers, if you want to know what's happening in Brazil you have to know what's happening in Japan"—what happens in one place is related to what happens everywhere else.

Unlike many of us, Brazil-Japan, or Bee-Jay, never made it through high school. He had to drop out when he was fifteen because his father died and there was no one to support the family. So he bought himself a cart and sold peanuts, *kaak*—a crispy bread—and roasted corn around the Corniche. We often went there, his old friends from the streets, to chat with him, talk politics, and, above all, recite poetry. Poetry is not the exclusive idiom of the educated elite among Palestinians. Rather, the opposite is true. Poetry to us is a currency of everyday exchange, a vital starting point to meaning. A child recites poetry. A politician quotes a line of poetry, to prove a point. A personal letter contains, always, at least one line of poetry. Moments of despair in everyday life, moments of joy, are celebrated or defined in poetry. There is so much poetry in the air, poetry from pre-Islamic times, poetry composed by countless poets at the height of Arab civilization, poetry during that civilization's decline, modern poetry, obscure poetry. People define themselves and their environment in verse. Palestinians take all of this for granted—until they live elsewhere in the world.

The poet's craft has so shaped, organized, reordered, and revitalized the tenor of our society's life and mythology that it has become ingrained in our existential habits of spirit, our manners of ceremonial life. That is why Palestinians forget, outside their own milieu, how affected they seem, how rhetorical; and how hard it is for outsiders to understand that a people's national anguish, or personal grief, can be best articulated in poetry—that poetry, in fact, is every Palestinian's idiom.

45

At the Corniche, we would sit by Bee-Jay's cart and recite poetry incessantly. We had memorized so much of it, even before we had gone to school, that we played a well-known game with it. One of us would recite a line, and the fellow next to him would be challenged to recite another beginning with the letter with which the previous one ended. We went on for a long while before someone got stuck.

Palestinian poetry, whether oral or written, is so rich, and poets so ubiquitous, that no aspect of Palestinian culture and no introspection of the Palestinian national psyche is irrelevant to it.

All the poetry that was then being composed, or at least that we were then committing to memory, would have been considered subversive by the Arab governments and their police. Our poets were forever exhorting the masses to struggle for freedom, for Palestine, for the Return. The struggle for freedom, whether against indigenous oppressors or foreign ones, the theme went, is a unified statement that needs no explanation. It is encompassed in forces that transcend us. Ordinary people should plunge into the tumultuous stream of history, so that articulate self-determination and political experience are not the prerogatives of princes and presidents and statesmen alone.

Despite its somber theme, the poetry we grew up with also had a kind of innocence to it, a roundedness, a celebration of the impulse to be free, a moral optimism, and an aboriginal reduction of history so that it became everybody's concern.

The ideal of a poem whose meaning "remains hidden" is alien to us; not only because our language leans more, in its drift and form, to verse than to prose, but because it is in the craft of the poet, rather than of the theoretician or polemicist or analyst, that people seek a reflection of their mass sentiment. For centuries, in a development originating in the overlap of infinite social adaptations whose exact origins are beyond recall, our poets have appropriated the role of speaking the language of the people, of drawing on the universality of their struggle rather than on the particularity of a personal malaise.

The poet in Palestinian society, hence, has been a hero. The hero of the poet, however, has always been the fighter, the man or woman who dies in the struggle of the masses. The myth of the fighter, "the blood of our fallen patriots," has always pressed to the core of our historical meaning.

God will free us, Palestinians used to say in the old days, at moments of crisis before our struggle began. Then soon after the turn of the century, the fighter became a sort of God himself, supplanting the real God here on earth, as His agent in the now, while He sat back to deal with issues of the hereafter.

Three successive generations of Palestinians, inside and outside Palestine, have immersed themselves in struggle, conducting their own dialogue with history. Our children have never had occasion, a respite, to adulate or emulate Davy Crocketts and Robin Hoods and football stars. Their heroes are the same as their elders'—individuals whose sacrifice for the cause of Palestine had already entered into legend, the kind of legend necessary to any society created, shaped, and organized to be responsive to situational and psychological needs such as ours.

The spell of martyred Palestinian fighters does not lie wholly in their willingness to give their lives for the people. To us, to those Palestinians who knew these fighters, lived alongside them in the villages in Palestine or with them as sons or brothers, and to those of us growing up in the refugee camps on their exploits, these fighters have signified an uninterrupted continuity in a tradition of struggle, a tradition of life, that stretched back to the turn of the century.

To us, the tradition of the *mojahedeen* of the 1920s (literally, those in holy struggle for the people), like the *fedayeen* of the 1960s (literally, those who sacrifice their lives for the people), means that every moment in our present establishes intimate links with our past, thus making our future not only tolerable to contemplate but a vital center in our historical experience. In this context, Palestinians do not have to throw furtive glances behind them; they are, rather, forced to proceed afresh every morning, leaving failed history behind.

The poet, then, simply appropriates the enormity of this collective sentiment, internalizes it, endows it with poetic form, and gives it back to the people, from whom it came. And of course the people respond.

So we, the children from Awlad Falasteen, strolled around the Corniche, or more often congregated around Bee-Jay's cart, and recited poetry—poetry whose subtlety and richness were actually structured by, as much as it was now structuring, our own self-definitions.

Bee-Jay never felt insecure because he was possibly the only kid among us who was not going to school. He just took it for granted that since his father had died he would, as the eldest son, support the family. Luckily, his family was rather small by Palestinian standards, with only six of them around.

Still, the death of Bee-Jay's father had come as a surprise to everybody, since he had seemed so healthy. So massive and strong. He had a thick mop of hair and keen, piercing eyes, in addition to an incredibly resonant voice, which he often used effectively to recite *mawal* and *awf* peasant songs.

Back in Palestine, Bee-Jay's father, Abu Samir, had spent his life almost entirely on the land, with the land. He knew what was and what was not coherent with his world—which for him was the only world around—without knowing the history and the politics of Palestine. When people around him, at the refugee camp, discussed the Balfour Declaration or the White Paper or the role of Arab reaction in the *nakbi* of 1948 he was lost. But he had a cogently aboriginal sense of our historical life. Once, the men were arguing at one of the sidestreet cafés at the camp about how strong the Palestinians would have to be in order to defeat Zionism and return to their land. Abu Samir interjected: "Brothers, the answer is simple. Ask yourselves how many enemies we have and that is how strong we have to be. We have to have as much strength as the Zionists, the Arab governments, and America combined."

Abu Samir would have no truck with the political banter and heated discussions around the camp's cafés. Peasants have no business discussing intellectual issues. Is not everything they need clearly defined, with every question being its own answer, in the condition of the land, of the seasons, and in the way men and women, animals and trees, wind and sky, express themselves every day, how they were born and how they died, having lived out their life spans and then returned to the land whence they came?

Abu Samir, like the true Palestinian peasant he was, *loved* the land and his family and his village and his goats and even the cheese that his goats gave him. But while he had them all he never once, Bee-Jay told me, used the word *love*. He never once said to his wife that he "loved" her.

"I don't believe that my father had ever kissed my mother," Bee-Jay once explained to me, in talking about the concept of affection in the peasant milieu. "Only when we came to Lebanon did my father begin talking about how he loved, and missed, the land and our village and our way of life in Palestine. Only then did he begin to seem affectionate, loving, intimate, with my mother."

Abu Samir's own father, around the turn of the century, had worked in a camel caravan, transporting goods back and forth among Amman in Jordan, Sidon in Lebanon, and Acre in Palestine. He was bitten by his own camel and died a few months later.

He had carried all his family's savings on him in a money belt, all in gold coins. With that, Abu Samir, then in his late teens, bought the land. Working the land in third world countries is not, as is often pictured, a bitter struggle for peasants who own their land. It is in fact a labor of love. When the harvest was in and sold, peasants like Abu Samir would buy their wives printed fabric to make dresses, slaughter a cow, and invite other families from the village for a feast so they could meet children of marriageable age and see which of them was gifted playing the *yarghoul* and dancing the *dabki*, who was strong and healthy to work the land and who, among the girls, had accumulated a good trousseau.

In 1955, a journalist from England, one of those wretched "area specialists," complete with cameras and images of the Palestinians as the noble savage, came to the camp to conduct a series of interviews with the men around the cafés. She talks to them, through an UNRWA interpreter, as if they are children—in a slow, deliberate, patronizing manner.

"But why, why must you go back to Palestine?" she asks Abu Samir, thrusting her microphone close to his face. "Why Palestine specifically? There are many Arab countries you can be resettled in."

She was too ignorant of our culture to know how profoundly insulting she was being. No one can make sport of a Palestinian peasant's gods without eliciting a fierce response, yet Abu Samir simply straightens up stiffly in his chair and waits a while before he answers. He has learned over many years how to handle a goat or a mule possessed by a fit of obstinacy. You are gentle with it, suspending your fury a while, till it comes to its senses.

"Sister, let me tell you this," he intones, his eyes almost closed as he puffs on his waterpipe. "The land is where our ancestors were born, died, and are now buried. We are from that land. The stuff of our bones and our soul comes from there. We and the soil are one. Every grain of my land carries the memories of all our ancestors within it. And every part of me carries the history of that land within

49

it. The land of others does not know me. I am a stranger to it and it is a stranger to me. *Ardi-aardi,*" he concludes. My land is my nobility.

What an English journalist, coming from a culture that wants to "conquer space" and "tame nature," did with that bit of peasant self-definition, no one can say.

When it rained and no people strolled up and down the Corniche, Bee-Jay left his cart at home and engaged in politics. Politics ruled his life, as it did, in one degree or another, the life of every Palestinian of my generation. He had been in and out of virtually every political party and movement found in Beirut at the time, and was as comfortable, in that man-child confidence we possessed in those days, dissecting secular Arab ideologies—Baathism, Nasserism, and Pan-Arabism—as he was holding forth on Marxism or John Lockean liberalism. In addition, he was a hardened street tough, the stereotypical "son of the camps" who was living a quintessentially political life.

Sometime in the early 1950s, he and his family left Beirut to live and work in Cairo, only to return in disillusionment after less than two years and reintegrate themselves into the camp. While in Cairo, Bee-Jay became involved in student politics and was detained a number of times. His most memorable arrest, ironically, was the result of a seemingly nonpolitical offense. He was working as a janitor at one of the hospitals in Cairo. One day he noticed two women in labor and recognized one of them as a Palestinian from the neighborhood where his family lived. She was in extreme pain and screaming furiously. So Bee-Jay went over to console her, presumably because her husband was not around. The doctor told him to get out.

"She is a Palestinian," Bee-Jay responded shouting, "I'm responsible for her."

The doctor scolded the woman for screaming, saying she should be quiet "like the Egyptian lady next to you, who is also in labor."

Bee-Jay turned around and screamed at the doctor: "What the fuck do you know? Do you expect a woman giving birth to a guerrilla fighter to act the same as a woman giving birth to a bellydancer?"

He was dragged out and taken to a local police station, where he continued to play his defiant act—which kept him there for a few days instead of a few hours. While in jail he met a Palestinian boy in his early twenties whose story he never ceased narrating to us when he returned to Beirut. This boy, presumably from Gaza (which was then under Egyptian administration), had been picked up by the police for some unknown, undocumented offense having to do with being "associated with communists," and tortured so brutally that he lost all his memory. He could not recall his own name, or anything about his background except that he was a Palestinian. When it was time for his release, the authorities discovered that he did not possess the thirty dollars to pay his fine. So they dumped him back in jail. He tried to commit suicide once by throwing himself onto the yard from the second floor. He just broke his legs and his collar bone.

When Bee-Jay got to jail, the boy was a mess. He had lost his glasses and could barely see, and was no longer in control of his motor responses or bowel movements. Bee-Jay took care of him the short while he was there and after his own release he immediately collected the thirty dollars for the boy's freedom. When Bee-Jay and his parents left Cairo the boy was still under treatment, looked after by various Palestinian families in the neighborhood.

Back in Beirut, when Bee-Jay spoke of that boy, he always referred to him as *el batal*, the hero. But more than that, he always ended the story by saying: "We shall burn down their religions and their gods, destroy the house their ancestors built, and suck the blood of those who rule the Arab world."

Around that time, Bee-Jay became a Baathist and often smuggled party literature into various West Bank towns, where it was, of course, banned. He usually took the last bus from Amman and arrived late at night in Nablus, where bookstores distributed the material surreptitiously. The Communists and Arab Nationalists did the same thing. In those days in the Arab world, literature that mattered had to be distributed through an underground.

One night Bee-Jay's bus was stopped at one of the check-points where Bedouin soldiers routinely searched passengers and examined their identity cards. He was arrested, not because the soldiers discovered his contraband publications, but because he had given the soldiers a lot of back talk, as was his wont with authority.

He was held overnight but the soldiers never discovered that he was carrying "subversive literature," he told us derisively, because they were "all illiterates." And he would repeat rhetorically, over and over again, "Imagine the Hashemite Kingdom of Jordan. The *Hashemite* Kingdom. A country named after the name of the ruling family. Imagine! A country where labor unions and political parties are banned, where voting in elections—when elections are held—is confined to male property owners. Son of a whore king. Feudal pig."

Bee-Jay was growing up violent. In demonstrations he would taunt the police. When arrested, he would be the one to throw the first blow. When called a two-bit-Palestinian, he would spit at the cops and holler obscenities at them.

I was witness to a fragment of this violence one day when Ibrahim Adel and I met him at the Corniche just as he was ready to close up shop.

Except for him, we were all now going to school, but we had learned by this time how to swing our proud Palestinian egos around. Ibrahim and I were in our late teens (Bee-Jay was already twenty-one) and had become too street-smart to be terrorized by local *zaims* and their thugs. Certainly not when we were with Bee-Jay.

We stop at a nearby café and take a table to ourselves. As we drink our tea, Bee-Jay suddenly stands up and points to the wall inside with a look of horror on his face. From where we are sitting on the terrace, we have to squint against the glare of the setting sun to see what he is pointing at. Before we realize that the object of his change of mood is a framed picture of King Hussein, he had grabbed his glass of tea, run in, and thrown the glass with all his might at the picture, uttering obscenities in a ferociously loud voice.

"Son of a whore king," he says to the proprietor. "We shall drag his body in the streets of Amman and let the people spit on his soul—as they did to his cousin Faisal and the Butcher of Baghdad, Nuri el Said. That's what we shall do to this king, this son of a whore, dirty offspring of illegitimate birth whose mother screwed a foreign occupier, this oppressor of the people, son of oppressors, lackey of the British, agent of the Americans, this puppet, this savage. . . ." He spits on the picture and swears loudly—at Hussein, at the British, at the Americans, at God. He spits and spits. And he swears and swears.

Rarely did I see hatred of Hussein manifested so savagely by other Palestinians—at least before the events of Black September in 1970.

Today, when I meet Bee-Jay at the Corniche, he seems quiet. Subdued. Almost too relaxed for a man usually possessed by an incessant flow of energy.

"Brother, I'm so happy to see you," he says, kissing me on both cheeks. After we talk for a while, he asks me if I want to join a new organization currently operating underground. It has cells in Gaza and the West Bank and Beirut and Kuwait and other places where there are Palestinian communities, he says.

He is always talking about some political organization.

"Brother," he continues, "this organization is prepared to fight, not just talk. This is a movement based on the belief that Palestinians, and only Palestinians, can liberate Palestine and help our people return home. Brother, this is it. It embraces no half-baked ideology kicking around the Arab world. This organization believes that the only appropriate ideology for a people is one that grows organically from their struggle. From our struggle, from our everyday struggle, we will get the formulas and theories and strategies to found our ideology on."

I tell him wearily, almost absentmindedly, that this is what I have been thinking for a while, that we have been banging out heads against the wall looking for salvation in Baathism and communism and Nasserism and Arab nationalism and the rest of it.

"Arab nationalism!" he sniffs contemptuously. "To think that we were tortured for Arab nationalism, with its vision of reaction and fundamentalism. Tortured for reading or distributing their stupid underground newspapers."

Bee-Jay looks around him conspiratorially and draws a four-page, smudgy newspaper out of a lower compartment of the cart.

"Brother, this is it. This is our newspaper. *Falastinuna*," he says proudly. The paper is the original organ of Fatah. He asks me to keep it, read it, and think about what it is saying. And if I wanted to join, he would be happy "to introduce" me to the comrades in his cell.

I tell him that I am too tired, too spent, too abused, by political activism. The Arab world can go fuck itself. I'm getting out of it. As far away as I can go. I need a respite from it and from my own pain.

From the time I was eight years old, to be at the Corniche with my friends beneath the bright skies, with the Mediterranean waves breaking a few feet away from us against the rocks, had always seemed natural, to talk about who we were and, in recent years, about the dangerous issues and concerns that arose from who we were. It seemed our lives were ordered, organized, and defined around the Corniche.

"Brother, I'm finishing high school in a couple of months. And I'm leaving this place, for good, till Palestine is liberated."

"And who will liberate Palestine?"

"I want to liberate myself first, from the Arab world. I'm choking here. I'm going to wither away and die if I stay here. I want to be somewhere else, where I can be free."

"Then, brother, permit me to tell you that you are naive. How can you separate your destiny from the destiny of Palestine, how can you separate yourself from the self of Palestine? Palestine and the Palestinians are two components of the same system. Brother, we need to return to our homeland, not go away from it."

I blurt out that maybe I need to get away from a place in order to understand it.

"Where will you go?" he wants to know.

I tell him I have no idea. Anywhere in the world where my stateless travel document will be accepted. I say I am going to Syria to see my aunt in Aleppo within a couple of weeks. Then I will return to Beirut for high school graduation and make preparations to leave.

"But where will you go?" he persists.

"Maybe Australia. They're taking immigrants there," I say, adding flippantly, "They're not wise to us yet."

"Australia? What kind of a son of a whore place is that for a Palestinian to be in?"

There is silence between us for a minute or two. Then he says, with finality, "Brother, have you noticed how most of our friends have left Beirut? Those who haven't left are thinking about leaving. And I swear to you by the blood of our fallen patriots it is wrong. What if they don't come back? All of us, the sons of *el balad,* the country, are leaving *el balad* behind."

Bee-Jay turns away and begins to roast corn on the cob and rearrange his goods around on the cart. Suddenly he starts shouting the virtues of his merchandise, his voice reaching to heaven.

Two months before I graduated from high school, on a typically hot, oppressive, Beirut summer day, I packed a few necessities and headed for Syria, first by service cab to Damascus and then by bus to Aleppo.

It was a mystery to me why someone like by aunt would want to live in a place like Aleppo, where she had lived since the early fifties. Now with my uncle gone, she was all alone, away from her traditions of activism spanning a quarter century of struggle inside Palestine, in everything from women's unions to the Great Revolt of 1936–39. Was she drained of life like others of her generation severed both physically and psychically from Palestine, ready to die?

For a Palestinian, Aleppo is nowhere. It is a city that has virtually no Palestinians living in it. It has no Palestinian refugee camps, no Palestinian ghettos, no Palestinian emigré centers, no Palestinian coffee shops, no Palestinian activist groups, and no UNRWA, that ubiquitous symbol of shame in our lives. To live in Aleppo is to have no feedback from other Palestinians, a process that Palestinians have often found necessary for the retention of their sanity. But my aunt has always been an eccentric—or was so seen by others— motivated by a dialectic in her life that always baffled those who knew her.

During the three years she and my uncle lived in Beirut before they left for Aleppo she had developed a reputation as a humorless, abrupt, almost rude woman. Of course she was not. She was simply forward and uncompromising, with one particular weakness—she could not tolerate mediocrity. I loved her in those days for the way she refused to be obsequious in the presence of officials, as other Palestinians were to get a work permit or travel permit or police permit or peddler's permit or any of those other wretched documents that reminded us of the helpless side of being Palestinian. She always had a cynical look on her face, or a distant look or a look of aloof contempt—but never the look of defeat or resignation many older Palestinians were acquiring.

On day when I was ten, I wanted her to run with me after a tram that had just pulled up. She grabbed my arm firmly and said coolly, "Don't run. Don't run. It's not worth running after a tram in this country, in the land of others."

I loved her. I loved her observations on our existential condition, cryptic though they may have appeared to me at the time, and I loved her haughty posture, which I intuitively understood as a challenge to the decline of pride among her generation.

I arrive in Aleppo and call. My aunt says she will come to pick me up right away. Walking up the street, she looks so frail and emaciated, so old and weak. Her hair, tied neatly in the back, has gone totally gray. She still, however, looks as dignified as she did years ago in Beirut. But then she looked middle-aged, full of vigor and defiance. And the woman I see now . . . well, she is old and helpless.

She recognizes me immediately. "You are here," she says, hugging me slowly, gently. "Let me look at you, let me *look* at you. You have grown, Oh, how you have grown, with all these muscles on you. And your face, you have grown in your face. Come, come, let us go. I'm so happy to see you. To have you here with me."

When we get home she cooks for me. What else would she do? She is still the daughter of her culture, where food is sacred, the most precious gift one can offer a guest. She wanted to share *ni'mi* with me, the blessing of food that has given its life to sustain ours.* So my aunt fusses in the kitchen and I help her cut and peel. Her movements are so slow, so cautious. Her voice has lost much of the resonance and edge that it had in the past.

Suddenly I feel sad. This is a tragic moment for me, dense in emotional concentration, and I know it will retain a vivid immediacy in my mind for the rest of my life. I realize its pathos even then: a generation of Palestinians is passing, fitfully, from the stage of our history into limbo and death and obscurity and defeat. Leaving us a kind of void, a dull void. A psychic severance in the soul. Except for what we have made of the images they have transmitted to us. They left Palestine with cogent memories, tangible metaphors derived from the very roots of the land. And in absorbing this self of our history, we—our generation, the first born or growing up in exile—are transforming it, and endowing it with new attributes acquired from the sensibility of the *ghourba*.

Will this stored material, as we work from and within it, be sufficient to inspire us to leave their failed history behind and

*In Palestinian culture, when partaking of food, you even have to sit properly because you are in the "presence of *ni'mi*." Leftovers are never thrown out—if they are thrown out at all in a poor society like ours—with the rest of the garbage, but separately. If you find a piece of bread on the floor, for example, you must pick it up, reverently bring it to your lips and forehead and put it aside where it may later be disposed of with other leftovers of *ni'mi*.

proceed afresh? What if we fail too? What will be the response and responsibility of the generation that will come after us? What will we be doing then? Falling into the garb and glove of my aunt's generation, assuming the gait of the fallen and whispering to each other across the bewildering rubble of our history?

My aunt walks around, the rawness and disorder of her generation evident in every gesture. She fusses over me. She feeds me. She asks after various members of the family. We sit on her balcony, smoke waterpipes, and drink tea in small glasses. Am I active? she wants to know. I tell her that I am. But I do not tell her about my plans to go away. Just away. I do not tell her I am convinced that to know my native ground, to revitalize the pivot of my self-consciousness, I have to inhabit a remote, entirely alien world of expression.

Every morning, my aunt gets up and sits by her desk to write. She works till lunch time. When I ask her what she is writing, she says she is writing about myth, or *ostoura*. *Ostoura* is the force in culture that binds the past-present axis in society along which we conduct our lives. The closest approximation to *ostoura* in English is "active myth," a living habit of spirit that recognizes no apartness or extra-territoriality for itself in the time continuum of past-present.

"You are writing about myth?" I ask.

She nods.

"What kind of myth?"

"Palestinian myth."

Since I do not respond, she continues, "But do you know why I am writing about myth?"

I sit down on the couch close to her desk.

"I'm writing about myth because that's all I have left. People like me have been robbed of everything in their lives except myth."

"I am beginning to think, at my age, that in myth there is more subtle a bridge to wisdom than in verifiable truth. The truth of what has become of us, the truth of our history. I am writing about the past. About the 1920s and the 1930s in Palestine. Like us in our day, you are today in yours living a time of *ostoura*, of active mythology. You don't know it, of course. And like you, we did not know it at the time. That's what we did then. That's what you're doing now. People create myths around them to house their visions in. You are all part of a living myth yourselves, part of a generation created in the image of the land that gave you birth."

57

I look at her intently, fascinated by the mystical dialectic she is developing.

"Son, I am an old woman. I cannot deal with the pain of Palestinian nationalism anymore. With my past and your present. I have no present left. It is only my past now that I must, in the few years I have left, try to impose harmony on. Do you see that?"

Wherever I go nowadays, there are explosions in my brain. In my soul.

My aunt prepares waterpipes for us and I make tea. We can hear the street sounds from where we are sitting on the third floor. The peculiar sounds of the streets of Arab cities, originating from the central knot of our social history.

"Honor me," I say to my aunt, offering her a cup of tea.

"*You* honor me, son."

"Blessings," I say and sit down.

"Blessings."

I'm overwhelmed by a desire to ask her what it was like in Palestine in the thirties. What she did. I crave to hear her talk about it. It is as if I have a desperate need to convince myself that the link between my Palestine and hers is real, that the continuum has not been severed, that our history is not arrested. It is as if I am to derive strength, great strength, from this frail woman sitting across from me puffing on her waterpipe.

"Do you hear from your uncle Akram?" she asks. My uncle Akram is her brother who had been involved along with other *mojahedeen* in the ambush of the trucks outside our house in Haifa in our last days in Palestine.

I tell her that I have not seen him for a number of years but that we all knew that he now lived and worked in Kuwait and, in fact, he wrote to us from time to time.

"He was an active one, Akram was. Right to the end. He kept right on while all his mates were falling. All our fallen patriots, God bless their souls. None would give up."

She sits in silence for a moment. Even her memory is now fading, she says, but the recollections she has chosen to keep are clear in her mind. She asks if I remembered the *shahid* [fallen patriot] Salim el Bard. I say that I do indeed, and that his son now goes to grade school in Beirut and lives with his grandparents, since his mother had gotten married again and her husband did not want the boy living with them. Salim el Bard was the eldest son in his family, which lived on the floor below in my grandfather's building in Haifa. Less than a week after Salim got married, at age twenty, he fell in an engagement with a British patrol outside the village of Hawassa, north of Haifa.

"God bless the souls of all our *shahids*," she says. "Salim and Akram were in the same unit and close friends, although Akram was a lot older and a mentor to Salim. Their greatest hero was Izz el Deen el Kassam. They had plans to organize an underground modeled on his tactics and appeal to the poor.

"I was much older than Akram, of course," my aunt continues. "And I remember Izz el Deen distinctly. I remember when he first suggested that in our struggle against the British—and mind you that was before the White Paper came from the London Foreign Office tentatively agreeing to the idea of our national independence and to the imposition of limitations on Jewish immigration—our fighters, the *mojahedeen,* as they were called in those days, and all of our people should wear the *hatta* so the *mojahedeen* could go around undetected by the authorities."

She pauses for a moment, a smile on her face.

"You know there were a lot of freelance fighters operating all over Palestine in ignorance of each other's existence. They were mostly simple folk—their land had been expropriated, or their sons imprisoned, or their freedoms taken away by the British—so they just picked up their guns to avenge their grievances.

"It was so incredible in those days. The struggle was every man's, every woman's, every child's preoccupation. You've read about the general strike of 1936. Son, this wasn't one group of workers, such as letter carriers or bus drivers, or even one social class, such as peasants or workers, going on strike. This was the case of the *whole* nation going on strike to protest their political condition and demand independence. Everything was closed. The whole nation came to a standstill for eight months. For eight long months. There was never anything like it, to my knowledge, in history."

My aunt is becoming increasingly animated, narrating a story that has been the mainspring of her existence since she was a child.

"But we failed in the end. We failed not because the people did not fight or did not want to fight, but because we were not, from the outset, in control of our Movement. We were not the determining force behind the revolt. The leadership of our revolution, after the death of Izz, was embodied in the "families"—the Husseinis and the Nashashibis and their clique—the landowners, the indigenous overlords, the reactionaries, who wanted to protect their own interests. They were in league with the Hashemites of Jordan and Iraq. And as you know, when indigenous overlords inflict pain it is no less acute if they happen to be an Emir Abdulla and a King Faisal rather than a Commissioner Gordon or a Zionist. By the time we took over and ousted the reactionaries it was too late. We had missed the turning point in our history. That turning point was in the late 1930s and we didn't turn with it."

My aunt and I talk on, discussing "the problem" in an abstract sense, for over two hours. The effort is getting her progressively more tired, but she is still animated. I ask her how she happened to join the Movement.

"I knew I was going to join it when I was fourteen years old, in the late 1920s. In the street. I killed a British soldier, you know. In downtown Haifa. Right where we lived in the Niknass quarter, where I went to school with Akram. Some months before the incident took place, the British had hanged two men for possession of weapons. One of them was Abu Marwan, a relative of ours. I had loved him. I saw him hanged and later I saw his body put in a canvas bag by the soldiers and dumped in the street where his family was supposed to pick it up, as was the custom in those days. That's when I began to hate the British. I hated them desperately.

"You know how important, how sacrosanct, *el thaer*—committing yourself to avenging an injustice by verbalizing your promise in front of a witness—is in our culture. Well I made that promise then to Akram. He and I fought because he wanted to pledge *his* commitment instead.

"As you know, your grandfather's house in Haifa was an active *mojahedeen* center and there were always guns there. Well, one day I took one of them, a handgun, and put it in my school bag. I kept it there. For weeks on end I would take it to school and during the recess take it out and play with it. Keep in mind that in those days we knew about guns the way children know about toys. I would take the bullets out and put them back in again. I would hold the gun in my hand, close my eyes, and imagine a situation where I would confront a British soldier or policeman in the street and fulfill my promise of *el thaer*.

"One day on my way to school I saw a British soldier harassing a peddler. All those weeks—all that time, you know, during which I had thought about avenging the horrible death of Abu Marwan and getting used to my gun—I had never thought it would be real. It had become a fantasy, a game, a glimpse of power over a hated occupier. But that morning when I noticed the figure of a uniformed British soldier, I froze. There I was at age fourteen possessed by a demonic, uncontrollable urge, an urge to commit an act that in those days was universally considered by every Palestinian, all over Palestine, to be *hallal*—a blessed duty ordained by God and his angels, like giving alms to the poor and making the pilgrimage to Mecca. In the late 1920s, remember, no one had money to give to the poor or the time to go to Mecca, because we were preoccupied with the British and their Balfour Declaration. Zionist settlers had not yet started coming in great numbers. Our concern was getting the hated British out.

"It was a hot day. God it was so hot, and I was wearing that ridiculous uniform that the British commissioner insisted all urban school children wear—black stockings and a black skirt with a blue blazer. Just like in Britain. They wanted to make nice English girls out of us. And the street was full of people already. Everybody peddling or buying something, right there in the street—chickens, soap, fruit, clothes. The soldier had his back to me. I never saw his face. And he never saw mine. And believe me, son, that's how it always was in Palestine. For even if we saw their faces, and they ours, we looked through them. How could we have said anything to them? How could they have communicated anything to us? Between us was a gulf, an oppressive kinship of colonizer and colonized. It was the confrontation of two opposites never destined to converge, never destined for anything other than a fierce duel in our land. They came to us from two thousand miles away as slave masters, and it was inevitable that we would reject them even if we were subdued by them. But we were not subdued by them. We were just beginning to regroup our political resources, to manifest our mass sentiment.

"I was a mere five feet away from the soldier. When I fired the gun, it did not go off. I had played with it so frequently that the top chamber in the clip had become empty. There was so much noise in the street that the sound of the click went unnoticed. No one had noticed me either. I pulled the trigger again, automatically feeding a bullet into the empty chamber and firing it. I fired at him again and

61

ran down the street heading for the school, which was a few doors down. Everybody else ran too. They knew the British police and army units were going to be there in force. I don't know what I did with the gun. Maybe I dropped it or threw it on the ground. Maybe someone took it from my hand. At any rate, I got to school and mingled with the other students in the yard. Because I was a child, a mere two years into my teens, I was able to take the tension of what had happened as if it had not happened at all. I was calm. Even jovial. An hour later, while we were in class, the British came to the school. They told the principal that a soldier had been shot and that they had a witness with them who saw a girl student do it. All the girl students were to come out into the yard, that very minute, in groups of ten, for viewing by their witness.

"Their witness was one of the local shopkeepers or peddlers, I presume. They had his face covered with a hood because he was afraid of being recognized by someone and consequently subjected to beatings or *el thaer*. They even had him stand way away from us behind a screen. This went on for over an hour. When my turn came, I experienced no remorse, no fear, no notion of the kind of terror I might suffer if I were picked up. But the poor fellow kept saying no all the time.

"When he couldn't pick anyone, the British officer screamed an order and the witness came forward: 'I want you to stand here, right here, three feet away from those students as they pass by you,' the officer shouted at the man, 'And this time I want you to pick the person who did it.'

"Someone translated all this for him. And he nodded repeatedly, looking more ridiculous each time because of his hood.

"The show went on. And on. And the man kept shaking his head. In the end they took him away. And that was the end of it. At the school, that same day, I confided to a friend that I was the one who had done it. And boasted to another, and yet another about it. I explained what had happened, in detail, exaggerating a lot. But I discovered that at least half the girls there were conspiratorially saying that they had been the ones who had killed the soldier.

"In later years Akram came under the influence of activists from the various *nadis*. *Nadis* ostensibly were social clubs for young people but by then had evolved into political centers. The *nadi* he went to had activists who had studied in Damascus, Paris, and Cairo. Some of them had even been to Russia and seen or participated in the Bolshevik Revolution. Akram became a Communist and joined the party, which remained underground in Palestine at all times. I joined the *Ansar* of the party, the youth league, because I always competed with my brother and because I was a great reader. Often, out of a desire not to allow Akram to know more than I did, I read the pamphlets and books he brought home. By that time, your mother, who was the youngest of us and not much concerned with anything except marriage, had already married your father. And poor Akram! At times he couldn't take the idea of my being at the *nadi*—an exclusive domain for men. Then after he got over that, he couldn't take the idea of my training in the use of weapons with men. I was his sister. I was part of his *aard* [womanfolk] and what if someone violated his *aard*. Those were different times from yours. Women were not able to do the things they do now. Yet, in Palestine, we established the first women's union in the Arab world, just as our Communist Party was the first in the Arab world.

"Lord, all the work we did. All the diplomatic efforts we exerted, with the naive expectation that something might result from them. All the fancy delegations we sent to Britain to appeal for independence. And all those commissions they sent to 'investigate.' Those little savages would leave their depressing little island nation and show up in India and Palestine and Malaya saying that they would grant *us* independence in *our* country when *they* judged us ready for statecraft.

"And then the Jewish settlers started coming. They too had a claim on the land. Only theirs, unlike the British, was messianic. And of course there was a lot of killing and death and hangings and violence. During the general strike. During the Revolt. Even during the 1940s. Right to the end. As the British increased their repression, the *mojahedeen* increased their attacks. And every time there was an explosion, a bombing, a shootout, an ambush, the people would start running. There was a logic to the way people responded to urban violence by the *mojahedeen* by 'running.' When an attack took place and a *mojahed* was running from the scene of the operation, chased by British soldiers and police, people would know what had happened and start running themselves. The whole street, the whole neighborhood would swarm with people running. Café patrons, shoppers, pedestrians, everybody would be running so the *mojahed* could get away by making it impossible for the pursuing British soldiers to know who was who. This went on so often that after a while when a bomb went off, people instinctively ran in all directions. No one knows how agreements like that are made. They just develop and emerge. The occupiers write their laws, and the occupied write theirs."

My aunt falls silent for a long while, then mumbles something about being tired. She gets up to leave. As I walk with her to her room she asks, "Do you remember much of Palestine?"

"Not much. Just fragments of memories."

"What? What do you remember? Tell me." The way she asks that question, it is as if she wants me to recall something pleasant, happy, childlike, something without violence, without nobility. Just something light and flippant. But I cannot think of anything like that.

"I have a graphic image of what happened in the village, when we were still there in Balad el Sheikh."

"What?"

"When the Stern Gang attacked. And there was a hut on fire. A woman came out, her body burning. She was clutching onto a pillow."

"A pillow?"

"Yes."

"Why a pillow?"

"Because she thought it was her baby."

My aunt looks at me reflectively. "The baby, whether dead or alive, is on the land of Palestine. That is a better fate for it in the long run, than to be dead or alive in the land of others."

I tell her that the baby's mother subsequently went crazy.

"Without their land," she adds with finality. "all Palestinians are crazy."

I think of how my mother, tending her house plants on her balcony in Beirut, would tell me solemnly how they would grow only if they face south, only if they got the southerly wind from the land of Palestine.

What is this land of ours? Why have we so readily fought for it, died for it, sang for it, these last seventy years? Why have we immortalized, in our literature and active mythology, the names and the memories of those who have struggled for it? Why have we accepted nothing short of return to it and looked with contempt upon schemes that have attempted to estrange us from it? It is doubtful that raising these questions will help. Every time we speak of our relatedness to the land, our words are always accompanied by the habitual discomfort that accompanies our description of the mystery of God's creation. Land. *El ard.* That's what we have called it over the centuries. If ever a common center held us all as Palestinians before the— essentially Western—concept of nationhood was added to our repertoire of historical consciousness, surely it was *el ard.* Over the centuries, in the summative process of infinite individual adaptations in our social system that we call communal meaning, a notion has emerged—a notion whose origins are buried by time—that there truly exists a mystical affinity between people and their land or environment, an interactive relationship that touches on the very core of every impulse in their human and social condition. Everything, in the end, came to be seen as emerging from the womb of *el ard*: the origin of our mythology of hope, the vivid immediacies of daily life, metaphoric meditations on meaning, associative context of reference, as well as acoustic and tactile sensations. At every point of development, from childhood to old age, Palestinians lived on the land. Lived on it. Lived with it. Lived off it. From it they acquired their memories and their moods and their ego ideal and their core concept of their place in existence. The land always contained the actuality of the past and the potentiality of the future, and hence the intimate center of the present. Without it, very simply, a Palestinian could not establish his or her identity.

The foundation of Palestinian culture and inner history, as expressed in literature, poetry, rhetoric, folk tales, song, dance, and political theory, is rooted in this worldview of man and land as two components of the same system, expressing the life process. In this worldview, *el umma*, the community, and *el ard*, the environment, are two interdependent subsystems, never separable in their functions—for they, together, make up a unified, biospheric system of life-facts that can be separated only by abstraction. A man estranged from his land is, in effect, repudiated as a human being. This exquisite nexus binding man to environment is reflected in and energized by Palestinian idiom in starkly imaginative ways. In

Palestinian everyday speech, if you want to ask for the whereabouts of a certain person whom you have not seen in a long time, as in "Where is Ibrahim nowadays?" you say, "Where is Ibrahim's land nowadays?" An awesome challenge or abuse you may direct at an adversary could be "*Biddi ahrek ardek!*" That is, "I shall burn down your land!"

In the 1920s, when the British Mandate authorities, in a characteristically bureaucratic move, tried to introduce the concept of the identity card, the people scoffed at the idea. In contemptuous response, Abdel Rahman Mohammed, the popular Palestinian guerrilla leader of the day who fell in the battle of the *Shajara* (the tree) in 1932, issued a communiqué in which he used the common Palestinian phrase, "*Ardi hiya hawiyati,*" that is, "My land is my identity."

To Palestinians, no phrase—perhaps one should call it a metaphrase, for its penetrative grasp, its complete recreative apprehension of consciousness—is more familiar than *ardi-aardi.* The literal translation, "My land is my womenfolk," masks the unvoiced intent, which is, "My land is my nobility."

To see Palestinian peasants on the land, or those remnants of them left on the West Bank of the River Jordan, or in Gaza, is not to see men and women working or tilling the land, but men and women making love to it, possessed of it, possessed by it, in a sensual absorption at once erotic and spiritual—and to have a glimpse of the outrage they would carry within them at its loss.

But why is my generation of Palestinians, now living out its last teen years, growing up in exile, with virtually no memory of the land, going about its business as if Palestine carried even more subtle, more enhanced nuances of meaning than it did to the generation that came before us? Why are we forever surging toward a sharpened sense of Palestinianness in our everyday lives? Why are we lavishing on what, in effect, is to us an existential homeland such refinement and elaboration of national meaning? Where are we going to go when we go from here, our national being encountering its anti-being in the world of nations around us, our charged environment encountering its anti-environment in the world of men around us?

Like other people who have had a glimpse of God and His wanton ways, we shall translate His text into our context. Who the fuck is God anyhow? The manifold space that contains our coexistence is

one, and translating His language into ours is merely a transfer of
meaning across time.

   Ibrahim, my old shoeshine friend, stands on the podium to deliver
the commencement speech. My old friend who used to have his
head shaved because his father was so poor. My old friend who
attempted to kiss a *zaim*'s foot once because he was too hungry
to care. My old friend who had defied the Lebanese prime minister and interrupted his public speech. My old scrawny little friend,
who had doubled up with laughter in a prison cell at age six-
teen because the Lebanese authorities had threatened to deport
him. Ibrahim today graduates at the top of his class and gives
the commencement speech, which he begins with "In the name
of the Revolution, in the name of the people, in the name of
Palestine." He dwells almost exclusively on the imminent role that
our generation of Palestinians, as well as all other Arabs, is to play.
This, he says, is nothing other than our struggle for freedom and
independence in Palestine, as well as the elimination of all vestiges
of imperialism, Zionism, and Arab reaction in the Arab nation. He
names names of Arab leaders and Arab movements responsible for
the plight of the Arab and Palestinian peoples. There is a great deal of
resentment against Ibrahim among the Lebanese in the audience.
Many later asserted that Ibrahim should have begun his speech with
the traditional "In the name of Allah, the Merciful. . . ." They did not
say that they were threatened by his politics. It would have been
considered bad taste then, almost a blasphemy, to criticize a call for
the liberation of Palestine. As it would have been considered an
affront to the sacrosanct Arab concept of *mabrook* to voice resentment that ten of the twelve graduating students who had won
scholarships to study at Arab and Western universities were Palestinian. These students' parents were told politely, over and over
again, "Blessings, blessings, thanks be to the Lord for your son's
endowments."
   All those years no one knew how hard we studied at the camps and
in the Palestinian ghettos; how dozens of Palestinian kids could be
seen walking, almost in unison, up and down the streets or dirt
tracks, reading by street light because we either had no electricity at

home, or because, where we did, it was constantly being turned off by the authorities.

Ibrahim has a scholarship from an American foundation to study in the United States and an acceptance from Berkeley. Ibrahim, my old friend from Bourj el Barajneh and Awlad Falasteen. Will he play a role in the Free Speech movement on campus? What will be the impact of the collision between his Palestinian environment and the American environment? What will he, and the rest of us who will soon be leaving, do? What will happen to each of us as we bring the charged field of force from our culture to an alternative order of meaning in alien cultures? Will we be annihilated and ultimately go from statement to silence, committing class suicide? Will we come up with an idiom of thought that would belong to neither our culture nor to theirs, an idiom charged with a penetrating current of meaning, of interpretative audacity, speaking of a nation larger than the territorial Palestine we have known all our lives? Or will there be silence, a kind of living darkness in our collective soul?

The American embassy in Beirut is giving Ibrahim a lot of trouble over his application for a visa. Is he sure, they want to know, that he is not going to the United States "to get married and stay there permanently"?

Every day he runs back and forth from the American embassy to the Aliens Department, to UNRWA, and to all sorts of people in between, to get his *document de voyage pour le refuges Palestiniennes*, his blood test, his character references, and a clean police record. He grows used to sitting around the waiting room at the embassy, outside the consular office, day in and day out. He catches up on his reading. When he is finished, he comes over to the Corniche and joins us at Bee-Jay's cart.

"Today," he tells us, "I learned something about Americans, and by definition about ourselves."

"You learned," says Bee-Jay as he busies himself roasting corn on the cob, "that they are a bunch of dummies who can neither ride a mule nor write poetry."

Ibrahim ignores the flippancy. "At the embassy today a Lebanese fellow walked in, actually just barged into the consul's office and closed or banged the door shut behind him. A few minutes later, I hear a lot of shouting going on inside, mostly by the Lebanese fellow. Something about a son or a daughter he had in the States by an

68

American woman, and how he wanted his child brought forthwith, without any delay, to Lebanon. This went on for something like five minutes. Then suddenly the door opened and he and the consul came out, still talking heatedly. 'I want my son here, and I want him without any lip from you,' the fellow was saying. The consul responded: 'I would suggest that you treat me as politely as I'm treating you.' The man would not have any of that. Rather, he was getting progressively angrier. 'We beat the fuck out of you in Korea,' he hollered. The consul told him to watch his language in a place like this, but the fellow did not seem to like the reminder. 'And you are in Lebanon now,' he told him, 'so you watch *yourself.*' Then he walked away, out of the waiting room, mumbling obscenities even as he headed down the corridor into the street. The consul turned to the people in the waiting room, focusing his attention mostly on me, and said: 'I could of course have hit that man, had him kicked out, but that's not the way we do things in America.' Maybe it is and maybe it's not. But this Lebanese fellow walked into the American embassy, told the consul off, and blew off steam, over some family issue that was beyond the control or jurisdiction of the consul, and walked out. He was able to do it, and get away with it, because he was a *national* of Lebanon. And here I was, sitting in the waiting room like a mendicant, treated like one by the consul, reduced to begging for a visa to go to the United States to do something perfectly innocuous and appropriate."

Ibrahim, the former shoeshine boy with the glasses; and Bee-Jay, the peddler with the street-tough, cynical look about him, and I, the old Chiclets boy with secret, escapist plans to run away from the Arab world, from Arabism and from my Palestinianness, talk about the incident and laugh. With a kind of bitterness.

I know Bee-Jay himself will soon take off—now that his younger brother is old enough to work—to join the underground of Fatah, the new organization whose paper he had given me.

One day three thugs working for one of the local *zaims* stop by to argue with Bee-Jay about the incident in the café when he attacked the proprietor's picture of King Hussein. They tried to look menacing, but failed. Most men who work for *zaims* are essentially weak individuals who seek to disguise that by being *zaim's* men.

"Are you the one they call Father of the Beard?"

We stiffen. Bee-Jay reaches for something in the lower compartment of his cart. Probably a knife. The three men look at us. They know we are students—in the streets students are considered weaklings—but they also know we are Palestinians from the camps and that makes us, in their eyes, street toughs."

"I am Samir Salfiti. What's it to you fellows?"

"The way you behaved at Abu Wazzan's Café the other day, he feels that you fucked his womenfolk."

"Are you here to fuck mine?"

"No brother, just to ask you not to go there again, you or any of your friends."

Bee-Jay relaxes his grip on the weapon. He's probably telling himself that if that's all they want, it's not worth a feud.

"Abu Wazzan has a lot of relatives and we are some of them."

Bee-Jay says nothing.

"*Zaim* Abu Taha is also one of them," they add, naming a well-known *zaim* from the neighborhood.

"I am with you, father of all youth," Bee-Jay says, now totally at ease, "I get your message."

They too are now totally at ease. In fact, one of them sits down and starts asking Bee-Jay, *sotto voce,* where he bought his stock of corn, cigarettes, peanuts, and the rest of it, saying he was sure he could get it cheaper for him.

When Bee-Jay's customers stop by to bargain, our conversation is interrupted. Sometimes he waves hello to one of the many people he knows around the Corniche or invites one to come sit with us. Late one afternoon a man in his middle twenties comes by. He and Bee-Jay hug each other and kiss on both cheeks. He is introduced to us simply as Khaled. For a long while, he sits with us without saying a word, just nodding from time to time. Only when Bee-Jay assures him that Ibrahim and I are Palestinians, "brothers in the struggle," does Khaled relax.

"Khaled is a *Fathawi*," Bee-Jay tells us. At that time, before 1967, an obscure term, *Fathawi* means "he who belongs to Fatah." Bee-Jay explains that Khaled was from "the crowd of 1948" who went to live in the camps in Gaza then in Syria, and recently, like himself, joined Fatah.

"Fatah," explains Khaled, "is an acronym for the Palestine Liberation Movement. Brothers, Fatah is us. Fatah is all of us." He tells us

Fatah has cells anywhere where there are Palestinians, individuals who believe the Palestinian cause should no longer remain in the custody of Arab governments and, above all, who believe it is time to stop talking and start fighting.

"Khaled fought in Gaza," Bee-Jay tells us proudly; "he has been on many operations."

The man snorts. "When we fought in Gaza, we thought we were fighting as *fedayeen*. In fact Nasser was using us as a tool to further his inter-Arab feuding. Today we take no orders from anyone. Brothers, I tell you, Fatah is it. A Palestinian has no business assimilating himself in anything, at this point, other than Palestine."

Khaled exudes a quiet intensity, the special elusive tension in his voice and gestures associated with a man who is totally convinced that, having tried everything, seen so much, involved himself in struggle, he has found, at last, an idiom of action singular to his needs. Despite that, his arguments are made with the modesty, and quiet resignation, of a man who has lived his life at a higher pitch of awareness than others.

"We have a program in Fatah," Khaled explains, "tailored to those men who are sole supporters of their families. If they fall in battle, their parents will be supported till they die and their children, or brothers and sisters, educated till they finish high school."

The sun is setting. Bee-Jay lights his kerosene lamp. As on other days when it is not raining or cold, when there are enough strollers around, Bee-Jay is staying open until 10:00 P.M. The spot where he has his cart is a second home to him. And by now, indeed, to us.

When a customer arrives, or a waiter from one of the nearby cafés bring us tea (in Beirut cafés commonly cater outside their premises), we wait till they have gone before we continue talking. We are aware that the subject of our discussion is irreducibly private, secret, and subversive. When I now look back upon it, I realize how normal it was for us, children of the Palestinian diaspora, to sit and talk privately, secretly, and subversively. And how strange it must seem to a Westerner that we, mere teenagers, had nothing to talk about but Palestine. We had no inflated currency of social conversation. Everything we dealt with, in one form or another, in a direct or indirect way, had to do with politics.

Khaled tells us about his father, whom he describes as *sharess*, a savagely committed fighter, who died in Palestine. His land had been

71

taken away from him around 1932 through some kind of manipulation of papers by the Osseirans, a Lebanese absentee landowning family who controlled capital and real estate inside our country and sold it to the Jewish Agency. In the Palestinian Revolt that began in 1936, Khaled's father became a guerrilla who sold his wife's gold bracelets to buy a gun. A year later he lost his leg and was *hors de combat* for the next four years. A year after the revolt collapsed, after being fitted with a wooden leg, he joined those guerrillas who refused to give up and died in a confrontation with the British army around 1946.

Khaled admits that Fatah is still in its early phase as a fighting force. It is operating totally underground from Syria, Jordan, and Gaza with no more than a couple of hundred committed armed cadres, who are perpetually hunted down by the Arab governments and their secret police.

We order more tea from the café across the street as Khaled continues. "I live in Damascus now, and may the lord destroy the house they built and burn down their religions. My entire family has lived there since we left Gaza four years ago. Our cadres go on operations from there. We have to elude Syrian security police on the way to Palestine, fight Israelis in it, and again elude the cursed Syrians upon our return. Many of the brothers are falling that way. I remember the first operation I came back from. I still had a gun on me. I need not tell you, brothers, that everything has to be done secretly. Getting caught by the Syrians means certain death. When I got home that night, my grandfather, in whose house we lived, found the weapon under my coat. He immediately kicked me out. He said he knew I wasn't amounting to much in the first place and now I surely was getting him, my mother, and my brothers and sisters in trouble with the Deuxième Bureau. So I went to my older brother's house. Adeeb was married and much older than me. I knocked on his door late at night. Well, I swear to you, I swear to you by the blood of our fallen patriots, that he turned me away when he realized I had a weapon on me. I pleaded with him. I said I had nowhere to go. He kept saying no, he didn't want any trouble with the police, that we were just Palestinian refugees, we should wait till we returned home. That all this was not necessary now. It was dangerous, he said, since as Palestinians we were suspect anyhow, and why aggravate our problem with the Arab authorities."

72

A few snickers greeted this. We were very familiar with the older generation's anxieties, its subservient obedience to the law, its preoccupation with feeding and educationing its children, and its language of defeat—a language that we found progressively more difficult to understand.

"We've learned to have our comrades wait for us at the border to hide our weapons when we return and take care of our wounded. I swear to you, to be caught by the Syrian police is much worse than being shot. I swear to you by Palestine and the spirit of my dead father that the torture is even worse than anything you people in Lebanon can imagine. Virtually all the brothers who fought with me in Gaza and later in Syria have fallen. So few of us are left that when Abu Salman, our commander who visits us from Gaza once in a while, meets one of us he hugs him and breaks down crying. So few left."

Bee-Jay, as if for relief, says to Khaled, lightheartedly, "Hey, tell them, tell them about Abu Izz." They both laugh.

"Oh yes, perhaps I should tell you about Abu Izz. This was some time ago, on an operation the brothers mounted from Syria. They had to go through the mountains along trails and paths they were not familiar with. So they needed Abu Izz, a man in his late fifties who had fought in the 1936–39 revolt and knew the area like the back of his hand. He was leading a group of six brothers from Fatah along a mountain trail that was so narrow and so dangerous that everyone had to be careful, carrying a heavy load and a weapon. Falling over meant sure death. It was already early evening and the men following behind Abu Izz were anxious to hurry so they wouldn't be caught along that trail when it got dark. All of a sudden Abu Izz stops in his tracks. Everyone thinks they've been spotted by a Syrian or Israeli patrol—there's no difference for us between the two. They tense up. But Abu Izz seems relaxed. He just says, after a long pause, 'Listen, do you think we will ever return to Palestine in our lifetime?' Hearing this, the men tell him not to worry. *He* may not return to Palestine, they say, since he is already old; but *they* certainly will."

Khaled's voice acquires a somber edge to it as he continues. "Do you know, since that operation all the six brothers have fallen, at different times and places. And Abu Izz is still around."

It was dark at the Corniche. We stood up to leave and thank Bee-Jay for the tea. "Next time in victory," we mumble. "Next time in the homeland."

73

3

Australia. This is the land where pioneering Anglo-Saxon culture begins anew, with its uncompromisingly destructive drift against nature, against time, and against brown men—to be respectively tamed, killed, and conquered. Australians will tell you with a straight face that this is the best country in the world. Who am I to say if this is true or not? When I arrive all I care about is that I am in the quintessential whatnot land. And I will like it here because of that. I will enjoy anonymity in a social reality that is the complete opposite of mine. I can be invisible. That is what I want to be at this point in my life. I am now just a nineteen-year-old immigrant cutting sugar cane north of Brisbane. There are many others like me around. Whose names are difficult to pronounce. Whose patrimony is difficult to locate. It is peaceful here. I begin to think less about who I am. It feels good to be away from me, to discard those profoundly painful connections I had carried all those years on my back, connections between selfhood and nationhood that had shaped so much of my history, culture, and landscape of being. I am just here. Waiting. For Godot. For the Return. For an Idea. Yet nothing in this country can fill the vacuum I have so created.

I leave Queensland.

After a while I get tired of moving from state to state. From one construction site to yet another. I feel humiliated at my core when I commence my day hearing the bundy clock punching my time card. I spend the day, every day, operating a simple machine. I stack cartons on top of each other. I load a truck with goods of one kind or another. I get my wages at the end of the week. It had been good in the early days, in the sugar cane fields, when I first arrived and wanted so much to feel nothing that there came a point when I no longer felt. But now, I'm beginning to feel emptiness and despair and unease. Another week, another month, another year. And I'm still helpless. Still unable to comprehend how long I have to wait for Godot, for the Return, for the Idea, for my wretched Palestinian consciousness to finish communicating with itself, in accordance with those awkward rules of antithesis I have set for it, so that I may emerge from this mesmerizing limbo.

In Sydney, where I now live, I go to work at Tooth's Brewery early in the morning. At 5:00 A.M. Why do I hate my work? they want to know. In this country, no one has to work under duress. I can always return to where I came from, they add. This country belongs to those who want to endure it, not to those who want to change it. It certainly does not belong to those malcontents like myself who come from strange lands to settle here with foreign accents, existential complaints, and radical ideas. This is the best country in the world, mate; show some gratitude at being allowed to live here.

Two weeks before, I had gone to the Personnel Department of Tooth's Brewery with a form from the Commonwealth Employment Bureau saying please employ the "New Australian." He speaks the language real good.

"You sound like one of them blokes on the telly," my supervisor says, "you talk like Perry Mason, that's who."

My job is in the basement. The heat is intense. The work is incessant. The noise is deafening. Beer kegs rush down toward us on a conveyor belt. We take them off, sit them on their sides, and roll them toward the dock. Trucks are waiting to cart them away. Trucks are lined up outside. Trucks come in with empty kegs. We do the same job in reverse. Men and kegs. All are moving simultaneously. All are uttering or making sounds of different decibels. Kegs lifted. Kegs falling. Kegs being dropped. Kicked. Hated. Cursed. In one corner kegs are being stacked. In the next, men are operating a machine to insert stoppers in kegs. Men are operating other machines. In other corners. Inserting other stoppers in other kegs. Noise, sweat, fatigue. I'm becoming a beer keg. I'm becoming interchangeable with one. It handles me all day. All night. It rules my life. It is an extension of my soul. Of my humanity. I ache to get away.

I did not know anything about rugby, cricket, or automobiles, so I couldn't "get away" with my fellow workers to discuss them. One day, I went to a pub with an English boy—an immigrant like me—with whom I worked at the brewery and he burst into tears because his team, back in England, had lost some soccer match or other.

"For heavens sake, man," I say, "it's only a game."

"Yes I know, it's only a game, but . . . "

"Only a game, for fuck's sake!"

I didn't let him finish, though, did I? If I had, he would have convincingly explained to me why winning a soccer match is as important to his internal psychic economy as winning the right to be in Palestine is to me.

I have not yet developed a liking for pubs in this country, where they serve beer out of a hose and the place looks and smells like a lavatory.

The only place left for me to "get away" is the public library in downtown Sydney, where I spend hours every day. Then I discover Gino's, a little Italian brasserie tucked away in a sidestreet, complete with checkered table cloths and wine carafes, to which gravitated a pathetic little group of Australian Bohemians—for that is what they called themselves at the time—who discussed literature and philosophy, Sartre and Kierkegaard, *On the Road* and *L'Etranger*. In effect, what they thought their counterparts in Western Europe and the United States were discussing. They were lost souls who sensed—but could not yet articulate—their deep sense of alienation from the social and cultural reality they inhabited. They became, at any rate, the first people in Australia that I felt at ease with. And it was there, at Gino's, that I met Gillian, the first woman I ever shared my nakedness and myself with. One day she says she wants to know who I really am. I say I have a real name and a language and a culture and a history. I belong to a people who have a unique way of translating their basic impulses and emotions. I say I have an ache to be home, except I don't know where our home is. Maybe somewhere between dream and nothingness, somewhere in the geography of my soul. When I was there, at home, I was close to my own myths, I tell her. The reality of these myths once again becomes tangible because I am sharing them with her, talking about them to her. Before I met her, I confide, the sound of my idiom and the consciousness of my culture were beginning to seem alien, remote, and strangely unconnected to everything I touched in this world, in this country, in this room. People here, as elsewhere, may reduce my potential for growth, but I still possessed my sense of freedom and my sense of worth. I am only waiting here. Waiting. This is just an escapist haven from the world's intolerable hostility, till the Return. In the meantime, I just want to know how I can disconnect myself from this world and create another habitable one, because I am afraid of talking to myself, of spending myself in a useless, impassioned soliloquy.

I don't know why I'm telling Gillian all of this. I don't even know that I'm saying what I'm saying. It all comes out by itself, as if my ideas have a free existence all their own, independent of me. And in response, she just smiles at me and assumes a look of pensive tenderness.

We live together. One day she tells me she has to go home to Melbourne to celebrate her twenty-first birthday. I am twenty-three and I remember my twenty-first birthday only vaguely. I had been in the cafeteria of some factory where I worked, having lunch and reading a book, when a woman who worked with me came to my table and said "Happy twenty-first." I looked up at her, momentarily destabilized and embarrassed, said thank you and went back to my book. I didn't know what else to say. I was not used to birthdays or to the idea that one's twenty-first is significant. Where I grew up you come of age at ten and you celebrate that birthday by joining a demonstration and getting locked up in jail. Or something approximating that.

When I see Gillian again, she tells me her dog was run over by a car. And she is crushed. I laugh at her sadness. And she is sad at my laughter. What is happening to me, she asks. Will I, like all those other revolutionaries, expend my humanity in the fire of political sophistry, leaving it charred and skeletal? But I am not concerned with politics nowadays. I don't even read the papers. In the Arab world, there are military coups, assassinations, civil wars, and border clashes. Elsewhere in the world Cuba is invaded, Kennedy is assassinated, the war in Vietnam is heating up, and hundreds of thousands of Indonesian leftists have been slaughtered *en mass* in the wake of a coup. But I am *sama'an bide'a*, out to lunch.

At work, my supervisor asks his supervisor what to do about an unpleasant job.

"Well, put the wogs on it, man, put the wogs on it," he responds, in my presence.

At the University of New South Wales, where I am taking a few humanities courses, professors teach their students about homeostasis in "primitive cultures," about the conflict between "love and thanatos" in consciousness, and about the "exceedingly tiresome" views of Karl Marx.

So one day I give my supervisor's supervisor and my university professors the finger and go on the dole. I also agree to do something that Gillian has been urging me to do for her ever since we met: I go down to Melbourne with her to visit her mother and her mother's boyfriend.

Though only in her late forties, Gillian's mother looks awful. She is an outright alcoholic. Her boyfriend, Phillip, a boorish Englishman forever dressed in blazers and cravats, is also an alcoholic, and a racist to boot. They are forever drunk, morning, afternoon, and night—in splendor: Gillian's father had been truly wealthy, and Phillip had "made his money in the colonies."

When our cab stops outside the family house in Toorak, a fashionable neighborhood, I am shocked by the spectacle of where my girlfriend had grown up. I had never seen a house that big before. Or, at least, once I went in and inspected it, I could say that I truly had never been *inside* a house that big before. There were living rooms and lounge rooms and family rooms and game rooms and sun rooms and guest rooms and dining rooms. There were large bedrooms and small bedrooms. There was a room called "a study" and a room called "a library" and rooms that were called "servant quarters" and rooms that had not yet been named.

Gillian's mother, her eyes drooping, her speech slurred, tells me that she is happy that her daughter had finally brought me to visit.

Phillip is aloof and cold. I have, after all, an accent. In the evening, on the way out to dinner at the Tok.H, an expensive local restaurant, Gillian's mother stumbles all over the place as she walks down the garden path and has to be helped to the car. She is complaining loudly that she has left her purse behind.

"Where is my purse, where is my purse?" she demands.

"Mom, you're carrying it," Gillian says. "You're holding it in your hand. Right there."

At the restaurant Phillip insults the waiter, who is a Greek, because he brought him the wrong kind of soup.

"Why don't you people learn to speak English?" he says haughtily, placing the emphasis on "you people." "If you want to live in this country, you have to learn to speak English, do you hear?"

The whole time I am in Melbourne, I remain just a hair short of killing Phillip.

"Why do you allow your mother to hang out with a pompous fool like that?" I ask Gillian.

"He's good for her," she says, "because he doesn't drink as much as she does."

On a later visit, my fifth and last, the four of us are sitting in a living room (I don't recall which one) when Gillian's mother turns to her daughter and says, "Gillian dear, why don't you bring that ever so polite boy, the dark, handsome boy you met in Sydney, to visit anymore?"

Gillian asks her mother if she means me.

"Yes, him."

"But Mom, he's right here."

She looks up, opens her eyes with great effort, momentarily unsure what direction to focus them in, and says, "Well, my goodness me. He is at that. He is at that. How are you dear?"

"I'm fine, thank you," I reply painfully.

"You are the nicest boy that my Gillian has ever dated, you know," she continues.

Phillip looks in my direction and then at the ceiling, as if to address it, not me. "I don't much care for wogs myself," he says.

I stand up. "Listen, shit-head, you're too old to get into a punch-up with me, so shut the fuck up!"

And Phillip—poor, pathetic, English Phillip—actually responds by asking, "How dare you use that kind of language around here?"

Poor, pathetic, English Phillip comes from a country that during its colonial heyday legislated laws against kicking dogs while sending its troops to enslave, murder, occupy, and torment millions of brown people, black people, and yellow people around the world.

"I'm pregnant," Gillian says to me one day in Sydney.
"I'm not ready to be a father," I answer despondently, "I don't want to be a father."
"I'll take care of the baby when it's born. I want a baby. I'll bring it up myself. I can afford to do it. I'll be the best mother in the world."
"Be that. You just go on and be that."
Gillian goes on to be a mother and I go on to the bush.

The Old West is not so old here. In the bush, men work with road gangs, in iron ore mines, for sheep stations, and for geophysical firms exploring for oil. On Saturday nights they drive to the nearest town, still dressed in their work clothes, cowboy hats, and boots, get drunk in the local pub—whose owners recognize no closing time—and get into fistfights. If they work way out in the bush, they work seven days a week, up at dawn to beat the heat, finishing by early afternoon. At the end of the month they get flown by Cessna to Darwin, Perth, or Brisbane, where they have a whole week off to spend all their money, get drunk, and get into fistfights. Nobody could take the aimlessness of bush life, the snakes, the centipedes, the 120-degree heat, the brawls, the alcohol, the volcanic passions of men in combat with nature for very long. Nor the timelessness of the way time asserts itself in the bush, moving not in chronology but in melancholy.

How long have I lived in the bush? There are so many stars here and it seems as if they all come out at night. All of them. Together, they mock our perception of time. I am sitting outside the tent one night with half a dozen men from my work unit drinking beer. We are so far away from the outside world and I am so far away from my own world outside that world. One of the men, a youngster in his late teens, is trying to write a love letter to his girlfriend in Tasmania, and I'm thinking about that world I left behind.

"You want to help me write this letter?" he asks me. "I mean, I want to ask Janice to wait for me. I want to say I love her. I want to tell her that my being here isn't a rejection of her."

The other men, long since brought together by the rugged camaraderie of shared isolation and shared hardship, are in an engaging mood. They tease the boy about his love letter and loudly urge me to dictate it to him.

"I'll help you, Nigel," I say.

Laughter and applause greet this. I too want to write a love letter, to that world I left behind. I miss it, and I don't know if it will still want me when I get back. I'm thinking so intently of my land as I knew it when I was a child, I am thinking of my father and the way he died, I'm thinking of the Corniche, of the boys from Awlad Falasteen, of the refugee camp I grew up in. I'm thinking of all this and I'm dictating Nigel's love letter to him. At the beginning the men snicker and shout "Ya, mate, you tell her," but I'm so consumed by the pathos of my thoughts, and by the emphatic awareness of whom I'm addressing, that the words just keep pouring out. And pouring out. After a while I realize I am surrounded by total silence. Even Nigel has stopped writing to listen. Words—ostensibly addressed to Nigel's girlfriend—burst forth from my mouth as if they have an independent will, a life, of their own, divorced from me, words of joy and anguish, words celebrating love and lamenting separation, rhythmic words invoking the coherence of the sea and words of a heightened lyric form affirming the union of one body to loved ones—words that I never thought I knew or was capable of stringing together. But the words came out, independently of me.

In Darwin I stand in a pub and debate with myself whether I have lived in the bush for two or three years. What year is this anyhow? Should I look for another job in the bush, on a station, in an iron ore mine? Where am I? I am broke again. I am unemployed again. I am spending my day in a pub again. I am getting into a fistfight again.

In the pub, middle–aged men line the bar drinking beer and arguing with their bookies. They too are half drunk, unemployed, and unsure.

Where you from, fellow?
Where you from?

Like them I have a sweaty body and a dirty T-shirt and anger at the world, but this is not enough. I do not have their pattern of unconscious cultural behavior. Their turn of phrase, their nuance of response. And I have been so eager all these years to carve out a life here modeled on theirs, in their own image. And I am dying here. I am a thing. An object that fell from space, from another world.

How'd you be mate?

Where you from, fellow?

Thump him Riley.

Riley is the small man with bloodshot eyes drinking at the bar. A familiar current runs through my spine. Outside the pub the sun is shining and the traffic passes along the street. I am aglow with alcohol.

Thump him, Riley.

Ya Riley, thump the dago.

Come on Rile, old mate, thump the wog.

Don't fuck with me, Riley. Where I come from we never weep for our fallen patriots. We celebrate and dance when they fall. The vestiges of their passion are implanted here. Everywhere around the world. Around the universe. They are like stars shining at night and you watch them eternally as you sit on the sand by the Mediterranean, or on the roofs of houses in our villages or near the vineyards reclining on the land.

Thump him Riley.

The tension is instant as I stiffen. It is urgent. And I thump Riley. I thump the man to the ground. It is as if I am watching myself do it. I am suspended aloft, resting, alone, on a cushion of fluff, happy. Outside the pub, in this distant city, I watch the mother outside, in the sun, pushing a baby carriage along the street. Her baby is protected against the elements. Against the cold and against hunger and against disease. And I am full of alcohol thumping Riley to the ground. Suspended aloft, I think of when the mother in the village ran out of the house, her body on fire, carrying a pillow. She had thought it was her child. When did she find out it was only a pillow?

Not only am I broke again, unemployed again, spending my day in a pub again, and getting into a fistfight again, I am drifting again. I have drifted to Perth this time and on my first day there an improbable thing happens to me. I actually meet two people I know in the street; but not just two people I know, two people I know who are Palestinian. Two people from my part of the world who live normal family lives in this Australian coastal city. They are a couple in their forties pushing a shopping cart in a supermarket and speaking Palestinian–accented Arabic to each other. I meet them now, just when I am ready to leave Australia. To go elsewhere and wait.

"*Salam Alleikum,*" I say.

"*Wa Alleikum al Salam,*" they respond tentatively.

I looked too weird for them, with my cowboy hat, bush outfit, and boots, to be a Palestinian.

"Are you Palestinian?"

"We are."

"So am I."

I am dying in this country, I say to them when I go to their house. They were married in Lebanon and their daughter was born here. Are all other Palestinians dying like me? Our home and homeland no longer exist, I say. We are scattered around the world. I must leave this place. Many places are as distant as this, as remote from my reality as this, and I could go to one of them. Couldn't I? We talk in our language. I have forgotten, I find, some of the words, some of the idiom, some of the phrases. But I use the language with gusto, as if to assert myself, to assert the totality of my intellect and emotions. When I hear my name mentioned, it is pronounced in that same manner, in that same intonation that identified me as the being I was. The being I wanted to remain.

Everything is familiar here in this room, in this house, with these people. I explain to them that I cannot impose harmony on the confusion of my life. I cannot come to terms with my political reality and existential discontent.

In the evening we sit in the room overlooking the yard. They ruffle my hair playfully and remind me of well-known political incidents in my youth, such as the many times when King Hussein's troops, known for being universally illiterate, were sent to quell student demonstrations on the West Bank, and how they would stop boys and girls in the streets and ask them if they were students.

"The students always responded by saying they were not students, but pupils, and of course the Bedouins, not knowing there was no difference, would let them go," he narrates.

The three of us slap our knees with laughter till the tears fall down our cheeks—only I don't know if the tears were those of laughter. Where will I go? they want to know.

When I see her one last time, in Sydney, Gillian looks much more beautiful than any woman I had ever seen in my life. She has acquired the beauty of emotional maturity and self-assurance, the beauty of a woman who is being precisely what she wants to be at that time in her life and is confident she has the means to be what she wants to be at a later time. And she exudes that beauty in her body language and her gestures and her voice.

"This is Malcolm," she says. "He will be three next March."

I stay with them for a week.

I tell her I am leaving Australia.

"You sound . . . I mean you don't sound like you did when I first met you. You sound like an Aussie now. Totally. You even, I mean, you even look like one. I can't explain it," she says. "And you want to leave now?"

I say yes. Perhaps that was the purpose of my being here to begin with. We all have an assigned place in the world and to find it we have to look where it cannot be, to live where it is not. Only then do we know where to go. And once we do, no one can tear us from the moorings of our "placeness," because if we were severed then we would be thrust into anarchy, into a void of meaninglessness.

Where will you go? she wants to know.

It is almost dark when I go off with my bag and wait for a bus. I get off at North Sydney and walk over the Harbor Bridge and get to the Quay. I board my boat. The coast line recedes from my view and I know that though I do not now understand what these six years in Australia have taught me, or meant to me, they will be among the sediments of experience that my mind will finally have to crystallize. Stretches of time will give them meaning, just like a stone that has lain in a river is given a defined shape and a softness sensuous to the touch.

It was 1967. Some months before the Arab regimes and Israel had gone to war. The whole of Palestine was now under Zionist occupation and there was talk of "Palestinian *fedayeen*" who were beginning to ensconce themselves in Jordan and to create a state within a state. It all lit a light inside my brain. But I didn't see it. Not yet.

4

In the Arab world, starting in Jordan, the time of Palestinian exceptionalism had come. The energy of a whole generation, accumulated over the previous twenty years, was slowly coalescing, slowly coming to a critical mass, slowly projecting itself outward into its final concentric circle of reference. The time had come for the Palestinians to wrest control of their political destiny from the Arab regimes. In the June War of 1967, in six days the Arab armies had been destroyed and with them all the secular beliefs from which the Arab world had derived its vision of itself. The Arab masses felt betrayed, crushed, and helpless. They reeled at the unbelievable spectacle of their armies, their leaderships, their political values, and their long-held assumptions about their sense of historical worth crumbling around them like a house of cards. It turns out, they concluded, that all along our armies have been inept, our leadership corrupt, our political values mendacious, and our self-definitions incoherent.

85

In the wake of that cruel revelation, the inhabitants of the Arab world were never to be the same. Their whole associative context, from emblematic invocations about Pan-Arabism to the *argot* of Western scientific materialism that many had embraced, was to drastically change or be swept away. A vacuum in the heart of Arab nationalism was created, a gap in the soul. It would take a long time to fill it.

In the meantime, all those little Palestinian organizations that had been hunted down by the regimes because they called for, and to a certain degree practiced, armed struggle, were emboldened by the chaos around them and began to emerge from underground. Their message was simple: the Palestinian people, and the Arab masses in general, will achieve liberation through people's war, or national armed struggle—where a whole community's human, military, economic, social, and political resources are mobilized to fight the enemy—and not through dependence on traditionalist, corrupt regimes and classical armies. Fatah, the largest of these groups, with cadres that had been trained in guerrilla warfare in Algeria, Vietnam, and China, and indeed had mounted limited operations against Israel in defiance of the Arab regimes, began to establish footholds in Palestinian refugee camps in Jordan and to recruit volunteers. One of Fatah's first slogans was *Fidaye wa ma'of baroudeh*, A freedom fighter with his weapon.

The *fedayeen* (patriots who sacrifice their lives for the cause), as these guerrillas were known, were adulated by the bulk of Palestinians. Their youthful daring, their self-assurance, their revolutionary élan, and, above all, their message of hope—that all is not lost, the Palestinians must seize the moment—struck a responsive chord in Palestinian society as a whole. As time went on and more recruits joined the movement, control of Palestinian camps progressively passed from the hands of the Jordanian army and police to the *fedayeen*. The regime did not like that; but not only was it unable to do anything about it, it was unable to do anything about the almost daily *fedayeen* military operations against Israeli settlements and patrols across the Jordan River. The fame of the *fedayeen* was spreading beyond Jordan to the entire Arab world. Soon it would spread to the whole world.

The Arab regimes, vulnerable as they were in the wake of their humiliating defeat in the June War, and standing in contempt as they were in the eyes of their masses, were helpless to check this phenomenon—the phenomenon of a people who, in the environment of defeat and mortification that the June War created for the Arabs, were standing up and fighting the enemy; and in process showing up the Arab regimes as corrupt systems whose muscle all along had been used exclusively to repress their masses.

No less than the Arab regimes, the Israeli regime was highly disturbed by the reemergence of Palestinian nationalism. Though not a threat to Israel, the Palestinian struggle represented, by its sheer presence, moral and political imperatives that destabilized hitherto comfortable assumptions about the very legitimacy of Israel in the eyes of the world. For if these people fighting against it are *Palestinians,* then where did they come from? And if they came from *Palestine,* why aren't they allowed to *return?*

The Israeli army, freshly established across the Jordan River following its occupation of the West Bank, began to study plans for its first major attack on *fedayeen* concentrations in Karameh, the refugee camp closest to the border. The Jordanian army, which had its Badya battalion ready in a military base a mere two miles away from Karameh, was preparing its own offensive.

The Jordanians moved first. On January 19, 1968, the Badya troops, who were famed throughout Jordan for their brutality and their primitive ways (their commander, Kasseb Sfouk, was perhaps the only illiterate commander in any army in the world), surrounded Karameh from three sides (the fourth being the Jordan River) and demanded that all Palestinian fighters there surrender their weapons and leave the camp within five hours.

At that time, Salah Ta'amari, a twenty-three-old from Bethlehem who had been with Fatah since the age of eighteen, was commander of the *fedayeen* forces in Karameh. When he radioed for orders, he was told that he should evacuate, since the guerrillas at the camp were outnumbered ten to one by the Bedouin forces, and worse yet, the Palestinian weapons were no match for the tanks, rocket-propelled grenades, cannons, and the like that the Jordanians had marshaled. Ta'amari asked for another hour to assess the situation. In that hour he used his intuition in a way that was to affect the history of the Palestinian movement and its relationship with the masses—without which it could not exist—for years to come.

Ta'amari knew the people in the camp and knew the kind of mood they were in at that point in their history. After years of repression by the Jordanian regime and feelings of helplessness about their condition, the presence of the *fedayeen* in their midst—most of whom were their own sons and daughter, brothers and sisters—had given them their first opportunity since leaving their homeland two decades before to hold their heads high. He knew that evacuation of the *fedayeen* from Karameh that day would result in great demoralization not only among the people at the camp but among Palestinians beyond it. So this young fighter climbed to the top of the mosque minaret, in the middle of the camp, to speak to the people directly. Thousands gathered to hear him. He explained what was happening and said that the fighters of Karameh were being given a few hours to evacuate. He finished his speech by saying that the decision on what to do was theirs, since the *fedayeen* were in the camp to protect them and fight on their behalf. Within minutes, virtually the entire population of the camp converged on the three entrances to Karameh and threw their bodies on the dirt tracks in front of the Jordanian tanks. Old men stood up in their midst to narrate stories about the heroism of the *mojahedeen* of the 1930s inside Palestine and declare that they had not given their lives so the young generation could surrender its right to struggle on. Young girls and boys who had been part of the *ashbal* movement, the youth brigade, fired the people up with speeches declaring that if the Jordanians wanted to take Karameh, they would have to do it over their dead bodies.

As the deadline approached, it appeared obvious to the Badya Brigade that they really would have to kill hundreds, maybe thousands, of people if they were serious about entering and occupying the Palestinian camp.

Meanwhile, Ta'amari, fully aware of Bedouin customs, ceremony, and traditions of hospitality, grabbed three of his officers and walked up to the main concentration of the Jordanian troops in the southern entrance to the camp, taking with him no weapons but a pot of tea and a dozen tea-glasses.

"*Salam Alleikum,*" he and his comrades said to Kasseb Sfook, the Jordanian commander and his officers.

"Peace be unto you too, brothers," responded Sfook and his men carefully.

"We are here to share our tea with you," Ta'amari said.

"Blessings be unto you brothers, but is our uncle so immoral that you have to bring your own tea with you," the Bedouin commander replies, chiding Ta'amari, in traditional Arabic idiom, for suggesting that the Jordanians came from inhospitable families.

"No brother," Ta'amari says, "but we are of the same family, together people of the Book and speakers of the letter *da'ad,* and our tea is your tea."

After more exchanges about Arab hospitality, dignity, and the like, they get down to business. The Palestinian fighters were not going to evacuate the camp under any circumstances, nor were the Jordanian soldiers going to lose face by backing down. The *fedayeen* knew that if they left, they would be betraying the people, and it would take a long time indeed to regain their faith, not only in Karameh but elsewhere in Jordan. The Jordanians realized that if they attacked the camp, they would end up massacring thousands of people.

A compromise was reached. A platoon would enter the camp and establish a base in an unobtrusive spot, without interfering in the affairs of the people or the fighters.

After the agreement was made, the people of Karameh went wild with excitement. They had maintained control of their camp. The presence of the Jordanian platoon represented no threat to their dignity or the mobility of the *fedayeen.* In fact, soon after the soldiers moved into their base inside the camp, camp residents often visited with them, bringing along pots of tea, hot meals, and fresh fruit. A warm relationship developed between at least this one platoon and the people of Karameh. Less than two months later when the *fedayeen* battled a major Israeli invading force in what became the key turning point in modern Palestinian nationalism, these soldiers fought side by side with the Palestinians.

This inevitable, predictable, and decisive battle with the Israeli army, which took place on March 21, 1968, henceforth was celebrated by Palestinians as a national holiday. Israel and its allies argued that if the Jordanians could not stem Palestinian nationalism in its form as a liberation movement with growing mass support among the populace and the world at large, the Israeli army would have to do it.

Actually, it wasn't only the Jordanian regime, intelligence, and army that had failed to block, even impede, the Palestinian *intilak* (or renaissance, as that period came to be known among Palestinians themselves); the initial Israeli tactic that sought the same objective had also proved unsuccessful. This tactic was direct and brutal. Its goal, very simply, was to empty out Karameh, leaving the *fedayeen* without mass cover or mass support. To compel people to move, the Israelis mounted weekly, sometimes daily, bombing raids designed to terrorize them and destroy their community centers and means of livelihood. Every raid, for example, left an UNRWA center in ruins. UNRWA would then build a replacement school or clinic *outside* Karameh, which in turn would encourage people to resettle where the schools and clinics were. Even the main market place in Karameh, the Hisbeh, was bombed periodically, so buying and selling agricultural produce and other necessities of daily life there became a risky business. The agricultural land around Karameh was also subjected to bombing raids so that employers would move their packaging plants to Amman and their laborers would have to follow with their families. Even Palestinian peasants who had purchased or leased their own land were finding their lives impossible under these conditions. The Jordanian regime itself began to pull its business and social centers out of the camp. Even the police station was closed down, leaving law and order in the hands of the *fedayeen*—who, of course, had no facilities or experience for the job. In effect, the Jordanians and the Israelis were colluding to tell the Palestinians of Karameh that their support for the *fedayeen* would cost them, and cost them dearly.

The *fedayeen* commanders, though lacking experience at the time, were not unimaginative in their response to these challenges. They knew that the people of Karameh did not want to evacuate their homes, and leave their fighters behind, in response to these crude pressures. Ways were found to make life at least tolerable, if not comfortable, for the mass of Karamits. If UNRWA officials decided to move their clinics or schools from the camp, the *fedayeen* would immediately confiscate them and run them with the aid of student doctors or teachers from their own ranks who were volunteering to join them from all over the Arab world. Peasants who contemplated moving or landowners who contemplated suspending work "till the situation settled" would be told that the *fedayeen* would supply them with *ashbal* and other volunteers to till their land for them. A special corp of volunteers from the camp, called *Hamat el thawra* (Guardians of the Revolution), was formed to act as a provisional police force. Whatever community service was suspended they proceeded to restore. Whatever building was demolished they proceeded to rebuild.

Tension mounted daily. The *fedayeen* knew, as the people did, that a massive land invasion from the West Bank of the River Jordan was imminent. Reinforcements poured into the camp. Most military commanders and the top cadres of the various guerrilla groups, most prominently Fatah and the Popular Front for the Liberation of Palestine (PFLP), moved their headquarters there and made up their minds to disregard, in this instance, their guerrilla tactic of withdrawing when the enemy attacked and attacking when it withdrew, despite the overwhelming enemy superiority in military hardware. They told the people, and each other, correctly as it turned out, that the coming battle was a battle of destiny.

"It is no shame to us," Salah Ta'amari proclaimed from the minaret two months after the Jordanian siege, "that the Israelis should invade our camp. The shame would be if they leave alive because we did not stand up to fight them."

Abu Tayeb, another Palestinian commander the same age as Ta'amari, also took to the minaret and expressed what turned out to be the mass sentiment of the people of Karameh: "We shall stand and fight. We shall protect every house, every hut, every tent, every tomato patch in this place," he shouted to sustained applause. "We know the Zionists are coming. We shall stand and fight them. No one will make us leave. Ever again. We are men and women who bring with us a whole tradition of struggle stretching back to a hundred generations. We say to the enemy, here we are. Let him come. We shall stand and fight."

This was suicidal talk, of course. Even if the militia and the *ashbal* were added to their ranks, the *fedayeen* were going to be outnumbered and outgunned by the Israeli force, with its tanks, helicopter gunships, air cover, and deadly arsenal of napalm, rockets, and the like. Karameh, however, had the best fighters, and what they lacked in weapons they made up in courage and determination—in this case, very simply, the courage and determination to die. In addition to that, it seemed in those days, on the eve of battle, that every man, woman, and child who could fight walked the dusty lanes of the refugee camp with a weapon. A communal sense of historical reference, a collective sense of shared destiny, gripped the inhabitants of Karameh, as if everybody itched to see the battle through or die in the process. Two decades of nothingness, of internal combustion, were about to reach a flash point.

91

Forty-eight hours before the invasion force came, Salah Ta'amari and two other Palestinian commanders, Abu Sabri (now dead) and Ahmad Jibril, who led the PFLP forces (and later split from them and formed his own Popular Front for the Liberation of Palestine–General Command) went to meet with Kasseb Sfook, the commander of the Jordanian troops around the camp. When Sfook asked them what kind of weapons they had and they told him, the Jordanian laughed in their faces.

"You're going to fight the Israelis with semi-automatic weapons, handguns, kalashnikovs, and World War II anti-tank guns?" he asked incredulously.

"That's roughly what we have, plus a couple of Dorschkas that we haven't had time to test," he was told.

"You people are crazy, you're all stark raving mad," the Jordanian said, and he sent the Palestinians six armored vehicles, manned by Jordanian troops to support them in battle.

At five o'clock in the morning on March 21, 1968, the Israelis arrived—in tanks, in helicopters, in armored personnel carriers—attacking from the north, south, east, and west. They kept coming, falling from the air, rushing across the river, shooting, bombing, strafing, and shelling as they did so. The six Jordanian armored vehicles pulled out after forty-five minutes, and with them a small group of Fatah fighters led by Abu Faisal.

"Where do you think you're going?" Abu Faisal was asked by Ta'amari.

"I'm taking my men to follow the Jordanians. We're changing our position together."

"The Jordanians are liars. They're withdrawing. Go back to your position."

"My position is exposed."

"The PLFP fighters are protecting your rear. Go back to your position."

"But the Front people left two hours before the battle started!"

Ta'amari and some of his own men went there and discovered he was telling the truth. PLFP fighters had been given orders to withdraw "to fight another day," when the fighting favored guerrilla tactics.

The main Israeli force was comprised of three brigades, numbering 9,000 armored troops, using mainly M-48 tanks, followed by

1,200 infantry. They crossed the Jordan River at two bridges, the Allenby and the Hindassa. A paratroop force of approximately 5,000 men dropped in the hills to the northeast. These 15,000 soldiers engaged in the attack represented, at least quantitatively, an awesome force indeed. Still, a very unpleasant surprise awaited them.

The Jordanians, believing that the attack was the beginning of a full-scale war, decided to fight the invaders. Units based near the Allenby Bridge used their artillery to stop a major segment of the tanks from crossing, crippling many of them. To the west, in banana groves next to the river, Palestinian guerrilla commander Abu Sharif ambushed several tanks and armored personnel carriers and decimated them with ease. When Israeli reinforcements arrived, a fierce battle ensued; Abu Sharif and many of his comrades were killed, but the minefields they had planted wreaked havoc on enemy forces. Now the invaders, using heavy artillery and reinforced by commando troops airlifted by helicopter into the battle zone, began to move into the camp itself from the southern side. They were met by no more than three hundred Palestinian fighters, who put up the fiercest resistance the Israelis had encountered in any military confrontation with Arab forces since 1948.

Before their hasty withdrawal in late afternoon, still under fire from both the *fedayeen* and the Jordanians, the attackers had been engaged in hand-to-hand combat in the muddy lanes of the refugee camp by guerrillas, militias, *ashbal*, and even civilians.

The Palestinians had fought valiantly, indeed in places heroically (many *ashbal*, carrying grenades, threw themselves under enemy tanks, blowing up the tanks and themselves), not only because this was the first major military confrontation between them and the Israelis since 1948 or because they were defending their homes against an invading force, but rather because the Palestinians—both civilians and fighters—knew the significance of that battle in their history. As Yasser Arafat had said when he was warned by his military strategists that the engagement would result in terrible losses to the Palestinians and the *fedayeen* would not be able to win, "That may turn out to be the case, but our military defeat by the enemy is irrelevant."

What mattered, above all, was that the *fedayeen* stood up and fought, and they did it with the eyes of the whole Arab world on them, the same Arab world that had just been humiliated militarily the year before because its soldiers, lacking training, political consciousness, morale, and love for the regimes that sent them to war in the first place, always ran away in battle. It was the first time since 1948 that a group of Arab fighters stood up and fought back with such suicidal tenacity. The impact of this would be everlasting. Its political, social, and national consequences for the future of the Palestinian movement would be irreversible. Karameh would become both an example to Arabs and a magnet to Palestinians. The reemergence of Palestinian nationalism, the day after the conclusion of the battle, would be assured. All of which was, of course, the opposite of what the Israeli army had set out to achieve with its invasion.

The Israelis claimed that "only twenty-one" of their soldiers were killed in the battle. The *fedayeen*, displaying the bodies of six enemy soldiers left behind and three abandoned Patton tanks, one with its driver incinerated within it, insisted the figure was close to three hundred.

In the late afternoon, after the hasty Israeli withdrawal, the smell of death was overwhelming. The price the Palestinians paid for standing up and fighting was heavy indeed. More than five hundred fighters, militia members, and civilians had been killed. But what they got in return was a place in history from which it was going to be hard to dislodge them. After the battle, throughout the Arab world no one was unaware of the "Revolution," the "Resistance," or the "Movement," as the guerrillas came to be collectively know, and there was no one who did not respond to the name *fedayeen* with respect and adulation. Just as the few survivors among the *fedayeen* were burying their dead in mass graves, the camp was mobbed by thousands of Palestinians who had come from as far away as Amman. They brought food, blankets, money, medicine, promises of total support and pledges of *talahom*, "everything for the homeland."

In the weeks that followed, Palestinian students from every corner of the world dropped their studies and came to Jordan to join the *fedayeen*. Volunteers, both Arab and Palestinian, poured in so rapidly that the *fedayeen* movement could not absorb them. Pregnant women from the various refugee camps in the country visited Karameh and stood in front of the *fedayeen* commanders with their hands over their stomachs, proclaiming "This is yours. I swear to you by the Holy Book and the blood of our fallen patriots that when he grows up, he is yours."

The Arab press, in the wake of the Karameh battle, spoke glowingly, even mythically in places, of "the heroism of the *fedayeen*"; Arab folk singers composed and sang songs extolling "the heroes of the Return."

There was no going back.

The *fedayeen* themselves were well aware that their *military* victory (especially when coupled with the mass support they now enjoyed in the Arab world) could easily be translated into *political power.*

The Palestine Liberation Organization, the only Palestinian institution extant in the Arab world at the time, had been established by conservative Palestinians at the urging of some Arab governments as their instrument to contain Palestinian nationalism. The political cadres of the *fedayeen* were now ready to take it over and transform it into the organization that was formally introduced to the world at the Rabat Conference and the United Nations in 1974.

In the early 1960s, the discontent of the Palestinian people at seeing their cause taken custody of by the Arab regimes, who did no more than pay lip service to it, was becoming evident. The trust that various Palestinian activists, theoreticians, and underground organizations had put in the concept of Pan-Arabism, or Arab unity, as the only vehicle available to them to struggle for liberation of their homeland had begun to erode in the early 1960s following a series of events that included the collapse of the United Arab Republic (a highpoint of Pan-Arab aspirations). Moreover, the victory of the Algerian national struggle against the French in 1962 convinced them further that Arab unity was not a precondition for an Arab people to liberate itself from settler colonialism.

The Arab regimes, sensing the upsurge in Palestinian national sentiment, had hastened to contain and redirect it by siphoning off whatever nascent revolutionary energy existed in Palestinian society through an institution subject to the dictates of the Arab League.

In September 1963, the league appointed Ahmad Shukeiry, a hothead of the old school, as the representative of Palestine at its headquarters in Cairo with a mandate to tour Arab countries where Palestinian communities resided (including the West Bank and Gaza, the 21 percent remnants of Palestine that had not been occupied by Israel in 1948) and announce that a Palestinian parliament-in-exile, to be known as the Palestine National Council, would be summoned in Jerusalem in May 1964.

In the intervening eight months, committees were set up to nominate a list of members. In all, 422 were selected. Though the committees were careful to ensure quantitatively precise representation for the various geographical locales, and even to include representatives of refugee camps, women's organizations, trade unions, student associations, and the like, the large majority of the 422 members turned out to be Palestinian "notables," older men of conservative bent, and public officials such as mayors and presidents of urban councils who were not likely to rock any Arab monarch's boat or challenge any tenet of the Arab League.

Acting as a legislative body, the Palestine National Council in its concluding session on June 1, 1964, elected an executive branch, the Palestine Liberation Organization, with fifteen members and Shukeiry himself as chairman. The Palestine National Charter was approved, to serve as the constitutional basis of the council; the Palestine National Fund was established to solicit and disburse funds in Palestinian society; and the Palestine Liberation Army was created as the council's military arm.

Immediately, the council and the PLO came under severe criticism from nationalists as being too tame and too institutionalized within the framework of the Arab League to be anything other than an instrument to contain, co-opt, and debilitate Palestinian nationalism. Significantly, the first session of the council was pointedly boycotted by the two major Palestinian organizations, Fatah and the Popular Front for the Liberation of Palestine, as well as other commando groups.

After the bold emergence of the *fedayeen* organizations from underground, the PNC's new chairman, Yahya Hammoudah, a Palestinian patriot but still of the old school, made contact with their leaderships to bring them into the council. Indeed, it was only a question of time before the *fedayeen* organizations sat in the council and took it over, especially since its membership had been trimmed down to one hundred representatives, most of whom were sympathetic to the new national mood sweeping Palestinian society that the *fedayeen* themselves had fostered by their military activities before and after Karameh. (After the battle, not only did the guerrillas resume operations inside the occupied territories, they shelled the settlements there daily with mortars and rocket launchers.)

By 1969, the structure, function, and objectives of the PLO as it came to be known to the world in later years had been established.

The *fedayeen*'s popular support in the aftermath of Karameh coupled with the backing, albeit reluctant, they received from the "progressive" Arab regimes forced Jordan to ease restrictions on their training camps, recruitment activities, and military operations in the territories occupied in 1967.

Predictably, this *modus vivendi* did not last long. The *fedayeen* extension of control over the areas they occupied and their mobilization of the country's Palestinian population politically and militarily put them on a collision course with the Jordanian state. King Hussein, heading one of the most conservative monarchies in the world, where the divine right of kings was still enshrined (the Hashemite Kingdom of Jordan is named after the ruling family in the manner of a seventeenth-century fiefdom) could hardly be expected to tolerate any curtailment of his government's authority—or the loss of prestige suffered every time it was shown to be powerless to defend its citizens from the Israelis, who were by then mounting almost daily "reprisals" or "preemptive" attacks on villages, towns, and vital installations in the Jordan Valley. More than that, the *fedayeen*'s claim to being the only official representative of the Palestinian people cut deep into Hussein's own claim of being the King of Jordan, which formally included not only the Palestinians on the East Bank but those on the West Bank of the River Jordan as well. Shorn of this population and the West Bank, the Hashemite Kingdom of Jordan would be reduced to the desert kingdom that Churchill had established in 1926 to reward a Hashemite who fought on the British side in World War I.

As the tension mounted, major clashes erupted between the two sides in November 1969 and the following June.

The Jordanian regime read the mood of the other Arab regimes at this time as favorable to an all-out Jordanian war to either destroy the *fedayeen* or cut them down to size. These countries, Nasser's Egypt notable among them, had accepted the concept of a negotiated settlement with Israel along lines spelled out in UN Resolution 242, packaged by the United States in June 1970 as the Rogers Peace Plan. The Palestinians adamantly rejected the plan. Moreover, they were becoming, if not too much of a threat, at least much too revolutionary for any of these governments' liking. Marxist rhetoric, such as the call of the PFLP and other radical groups for "the overthrow of all reactionary regimes in the region allied with Western imperialism" did not go down well in Arab capitals.

Thus, when several units of the Jordanian army were redeployed around Amman on September 16 and Hussein appointed a military government with orders to take all "necessary" measures "to restore security, order, and stability," Arab rulers sat back and washed their hands with invisible soap.

Yasser Arafat, by then chairman of the executive committee of the PLO and supreme commander of all Palestinian forces (13,000 guerrillas, 30,000 militia members) called a council of war at his Amman headquarters in Jebel Hussein refugee camp.

The attacks by Hussein's Bedouin troops began at 5:00 A.M. the following day. The tanks they had moved into the capital and other cities with high concentrations of Palestinian fighters began to pound not only guerrilla positions but civilian areas in refugee camps as well. The shells were falling indiscriminately, taking a heavy toll in death and destruction. The brutal Field Marshal Habes el Majali (he had ordered his troops to take rocks and smash the heads of two Palestinian guerrillas captured by his soldiers the day before in Ma'an, a town 250 kilometers from Amman), military governor and martial law commander of the new military regime, imposed a twenty-four hour curfew and ordered anyone in the streets shot on sight. Hundreds of houses in Palestinian neighborhoods and refugee camps were destroyed by artillery fire under the pretext that there were snipers in them. Fires raged uncontrollably in the camps. The dead and dying lay in the streets. Hundreds died of unattended wounds. Children died of dehydration. Civilians who ventured beyond the confines of their homes, neighborhoods, or camps in search of food and water were mercilessly cut down in the streets by the Bedouin soldiers. Injured guerrillas, or suspected guerrillas, rescued by ambulances that somehow evaded the crossfire were finished off in hospitals by soldiers who hacked away at them with bayonets and the butts of submachine guns.

The savagery practiced by the Bedouin troops against the civilian population was unspeakable. The vindictiveness of the regime, as expressed in the ruthlessly inhuman orders it gave its army commanders, was beyond all rational understanding.

The president of Iraq had promised that the 12,000 Iraqi troops in Jordan since 1967 to aid in the war effort against Israel would fight alongside the Palestinians in the event of hostilities with Hussein's army. When the assault came, they folded their tents and moved away from the war zone. President Nasser of Egypt largely ignored radio messages from Arafat appealing to him to "intervene."

The *fedayeen* fought tenaciously, in places suicidally, knocking out advancing tanks with bazookas and rocket-propelled grenades. But they were running out of food, water, and medicine.

On September 27 a truce mediated by the Arab League, at the urging of Egypt's Nasser, was signed by the *fedayeen* and King Hussein.

Again the smell of death. Again the mass graves. Again the irrepressible will to go on.

The confrontations with Hussein's troops in September 1970 were the most traumatic experience in modern Palestinian history. It came to be known among Palestinians as Black September. Among its consequences was the emergence of an underground group with the same name that dedicated itself to pure terror.

The man considered most to blame for all of these brutalities was the newly appointed, fanatically anti-Palestinian, 52-year old prime minister of Jordan, Wasfi Tel. Throughout the ten-day war he made highly provocative statements about the need to do away with the "Godless Communists in our midst." (In October, less than a month after the conclusion of hostilities, he sent bulldozers to the Wahdat refugee camp, with orders to destroy a monument the people had erected to commemorate the dead and to desecrate the mass grave beneath it.)

Even before the war was over, the Revolutionary Council of Fatah had passed sentence on Tel "in the name of the Palestinian people": death. The two men later chosen to execute him, Munzer Khalifa and Izzat Rabah, both twenty-one, publicly proclaimed "We shall suck his blood." They meant that literally. They were promising to commit *thaer*, an act of revenge. If they failed, they would be dishonored for the rest of their lives.

On November 28, 1971, Tel was in Cairo leading his country's delegation to the Arab Defense Council. He was staying at the

Sheraton Hotel downtown, a mere three blocks away from Anwar Sadat's presidential palace. In the early afternoon when Tel was driven back to the hotel, Khalifa and Rabah were in the lobby waiting for him. As he walked through, accompanied by three of his own guards and Egyptian security police, they pulled out their guns and fired five shots into him. An accomplice, a young Palestinian woman studying at a Cairo university who was in Black September, was waiting in the background a mere dozen feet away to throw a hand grenade at Tel if her companions' effort was foiled. She was not needed.

After the Jordanian prime minister fell dead on the floor, one of the Black September youths walked over, bent over the body, and sucked some of the blood that poured from the wounds.

"Our *thaer* has been fulfilled," he exulted.

With such emotional vehemence and lunatic rage was my generation of Palestinians projecting outward two decades of inner history. With such force was the soul seeking vengeance on those that had crippled it. And with such anarchic grammar of human perception were we emerging from behind the blackened walls of our world of nonbeing to present ourselves to the world outside.

The language of our darkness, with its twists of feeling and subterranean notions, makes no sense in the world of their light.

5

When I arrive in Paris it is August 1970. I have sixty dollars in my pocket and the idea for my first book in my head. I find a small room with a stove at a *Hotel Residence* in the 14th *arrondisement*, rent a typewriter for ten dollars, and begin work on the first chapter of a book eventually titled *The Disinherited: Journal of a Palestinian Exile*. I finish it in seven months, with hardly any revision, and is accepted by the first publishing house it is sent to in New York. While I am still on my first chapter, merely a week after my arrival, I meet an American girl who had just moved into the room across from mine.

"Hi, I'm Caron," she offers. She is dark, with long hair, and looks like my sister, Jasmine.

I introduce myself.

"What kind of a name is that?"

"I'm Palestinian."

"Really, you mean like PLO Palestinian?"

"That's right."

"I mean, I've never met a Palestinian before. I'm Jewish. Palestinians don't belong to a nation, do they?"

I tell her that it is more complex than that.

That afternoon when I go back home from the café where I always do my writing in longhand, I sit back and think about her words for a long while. *Palestinians don't belong to a nation, do they?* Before the afternoon is out, I find I have written a long, impassioned article that I mail the following day to the *International Herald Tribune*, which I was convinced would not accept it. A few days later the editor in chief, Murray Weiss, calls me at the *Hotel Residence* and says that not only would his paper publish it, they would run it without a single word edited out. It appeared on August 10, 1970, taking up a half page, with the title "I Belong to No Nation, but Damn You All, I Belong to a People." (It was later picked up and translated by other European papers.)

Caron knocks on my door. "I'm glad I was the inspiration for your piece in the *Trib*," she says coyly.

"That's how it always is, isn't it?" I respond. "People in struggle don't operate in a vacuum when they go about creating their self-definitions."

I take Caron to political meetings at the Mutualité and the Cité Universitaire, and to demonstrations organized by students, unionists, leftists, and others in support of the Palestinians. When the events of Black September erupt in Jordan, she is with me at the Boulevard St. Michel (or Boul'-Mich' as it was engagingly known to those who made the street their second home) distributing leaflets and shouting with gusto: *Soutenez la revolution Palestinienne contre le régime fantoche du roi Hussein.* By that time Caron and I have moved into a studio on the rue St. Jacques in the Latin Quarter.

I publish more articles—though less impassioned and not as lengthy—almost on a regular basis in the *Herald Tribune*, attracting the attention of the small Palestinian community in Paris. Before long I am meeting with them, taking Caron along, and holding forth about politics and national life. Other Palestinians passing through Paris on their way from or to their various host countries in the Arab world also become accessible to me.

It is like a dream, living in Paris; not only because the city is so kind and inviting and hospitable and responsive to the *deracinés* of this world, be they alienated writers or revolutionaries or political fugitives; and not only because its daily life is expressed in a language understood by anyone, from anywhere, who relishes a city that has autonomous *quartiers* for every rebellious form of outsiderness; living in Paris is a dream world because it is so easy, as in night dreams, to make quantum jumps, to turn becoming into being, to transform action into words. For elsewhere men are engaged in going from being to becoming, from words to action—and that is so easy to do, so ordinary, so mundane. This city has returned me to my original, genuine core of Palestinian selfhood. I am again engaged in national politics, in revolutionary ideas, as I had been when I made that original leap to a maturing consciousness back home in the streets of Beirut so many years before. I'm now speaking in lecture halls, at rallies, at demonstrations and other political gatherings. I am again dissecting our political universe, with fellow Palestinians and European revolutionaries, as if it were an extension of our soul, nourishment to the heart, an antidote to the poison of oppression in our age. My Palestinian rage, though now tempered by my years of wandering and rationalized by a kind of systemic frame of reference, returns to haunt my days, especially after the events of Black September. Various Palestinians stop in Paris to visit with me and share their views of Black September, others to narrate their participation in it. It is so crushing, yet, mysteriously, so exhilarating to be part of a movement so forcefully edging its way to the center stage of the historical arena.

One of these individuals, Suleiman Ammouri, probably the first Palestinian student ever to be deported from Britain for his political activities, was a man who truly possessed style, a cool man-of-the-world hipness that few Palestinians had. Suleiman had two passions, the *yarghoul* and politics, both of which he played well. He was outrageous in both and the British Home Office, offended beyond endurance by the way he played the latter, determined that he should be deported. But not just deported; they actually sent a cop—one of those polite British cops, and British cops were still that in those days—with official papers ordering Suleiman to accompany the man in blue, within twenty-five minutes, to the airport, whence he was to be put on a plane and sent packing back home to Jordan.

"Sure, come on in," Suleiman says, as if addressing an old friend or neighbor from next door who had just dropped by for a cup of tea, and resumes watching a game show on television. He puts his feet up, puffs on cigarettes, and giggles at the funny parts of the game show.

"You have fifteen minutes left," the cop says nervously.

"I'm fine, don't worry about me."

Then he is told, by a progressively bewildered policeman: "You have ten minutes, you know. You ought to be packing, oughtn't you?"

"No, I'm fine," Suleiman responds, his eyes glued to the screen, still laughing at the game show and acting as if the Home Office order for his deportation was too trivial, or too contemptible, an issue to warrant any undue attention on his part.

"You have two minutes," he is warned again. "This is most highly irregular, you know!"

Halfway through his last minute, laughing uproariously at something the game show host was saying, he stands up, turns off the television set, grabs his passport from a drawer, and says: "Well, let's go, old fellow."

When he arrived in Amman, it was January 1970. Seven months later he was in the thick of Black September.

Today Suleiman is in Paris on his way from or to some other European capital. Caron and I invite him to our place for dinner: he arrives with his Jordanian lover, Hala, a beautiful woman who was a half-dozen years older and a good dozen times crazier, and three other Palestinian friends, two men and one woman, all active participants in the Black September war. I had cooked a *mansaf* dish that we are eating communally with our hands. We are sitting on the floor, talking politics—even through dinner—but mostly in an abstract fashion: what the dialectic of Black September is, the relationship of the Palestinian movement to the Arab regimes and the Arab masses, where we can move our revolutionary tents to, now that we have lost our base in Jordan, what changes in Palestinian strategy and tactics are imperative in response to the new challenges facing Palestinian nationalism, and so forth.

Later on in the evening, after Suleiman has played his *yarghoul* briefly and we have finished off five bottles of wine, we Palestinians return to our social-gathering traditions: singing folk songs and reciting poetry. After a bottle of Calvados everyone finally loosens up enough to talk about what they had witnessed or participated in during Black September.

The two fellows that Suleiman brought with him, Boutros and Sami, were in their early twenties; they had grown up together in Amman. Both were in the Revolution, attached to the Fatah militias. Boutros, who had earlier been talking about how our culture was conservative but our ideology was radical, and how sexual mores in our society had been determined by the repression that characterized our various political systems in the Arab world, was now waxing poetic about the heroic symbols Black September had already created for our nation—which leads him in the end to a narrative of his own involvement in the war.

Whenever a person describes an individual event, he is describing an individual event plus a setting. And the setting is familiar to Sami and Salwa, and to Suleiman and Hala. So when Boutros begins to talk, everyone feels his or her *own* story is being told, though from a different angle.

Boutros begins evenly, telling us how he dropped his schoolwork in Beirut and reported for transfer to Jordan so he could join in the fighting.

"There were about two hundred of us being taken in trucks to Ramtha, the border town between Syria and Jordan. The president of Syria then, Attassi, was a progressive man who supported us in our struggle and certainly facilitated the movement of our troops to the Jordanian border. The closer we got to Ramtha, the louder the sound of rockets, bombs, and firing of all kinds became. The whole area there, around the Jerash and Ajloun mountains, was a liberated zone. As we went through, we could see *fedayeen* on both sides of the mostly dirt road walking around in groups, or constructing something, or driving their jeeps or building sandbag positions and the like. Some of them waved at us with the revolutionary clenched fist, shouting something that we would catch only in part. Men from the Palestine Liberation Army who had been stationed in Syria and had filtered into the area were there too. It was funny, though, to see Palestinian fighters in *uniforms,* for heaven's sake. I mean it's odd, it goes against the grain of everything we stand for. Everybody in my truck was getting agitated, excited about the prospect of finally being there, finally being part of all the sounds, all the action, living every moment of that historic time. When we got to the Ajloun Mountains we were broken up into smaller units and despatched to virtually all guerrilla detachments fighting in the hills, particularly the ones around the Aquabi camp and the Gaza camp further away. Ramtha, the border town, was a major base for the Resistance and very strategically located. From there we had access to both Syria and Iraq, from which our food and ammunition came. Ramtha, in turn, supplied the two major fronts where we were fighting the Bedouin troops, Amman and Jerash, as well as other regions such as the town of Salt and the area around it—liberated zones the *fedayeen* had turned into soviets, which Hussein's troops assaulted from time to time.

"In Ajloun, the commander, a tough-looking middle-aged man with a *hatta* and baggy pants, was acting both sweet and tough at the same time. He stood there and stared at us. I don't know why he singled me out, but he just walked over to me and looked me up and down.

" 'So you are *gada'a*, hey, baby face? You want to fight, hey?'

" 'Yes brother,' I said.

" 'Where have you just come from?'

" 'Beirut, brother.'

" 'Beirut!' he says, roaring with laughter. 'Beirut is a great place to learn to be a revolutionary, in the cafés off Hamra Street. You know, brother? You know? You'll go to fight like a little bird. All of you. You understand that? If you go to fight without knowing what you're fighting for, you're not coming back, like little birds.'

"I was tired and hungry and did not respond. Then the commander gives us all a look of incredible tenderness, the like of which I had never seen on the face of a *fedayeen* commander before, and says, 'But may God bless you all, God bless us in our struggle to be free men in a free Palestine.'

"That night I slept as I had never slept before. At dawn, just before we all had to get up, I dreamed that King Hussein was going around the country turning out the lights and leaving us all in pitch blackness. And when we tried to light candles, he buried them in the ground with their flames still burning. I was angry when I opened my eyes. Someone from *Hamat el thawra*, Guardians of the Revolution, was telling me: 'Watch your *klashen*, brother.'

"In the morning, we were out of the base in less than fifteen minutes, after eating a breakfast of black olives, *labni*, and tea. There were twenty-one of us on the truck, which was to take us to Jerash. Before it pulled out, someone ran after it shouting at us and gesticulating with his *klashen* to stop so he could climb aboard. It turned out to be none other than Sami here."

"Yes, well I had been with my unit since January, when I first began my training in Amman," Sami volunteers.

"So I said to Sami," Boutros continues, "You, you who are damned by your religion, what are you doing here? We hug and kiss and he tells me that he's around the neighborhood with a bunch of Godless Communists, which is what King Hussein's troops called us at the time.

"Already we were in the midst of it. Dorschkas, Katyushkas, rocket-propelled grenades, *klashens,* AK 47s, name it. When we got to the base, Sami disappeared and we were separated again. A young fellow called Izz el Deen seemed to be in charge. 'Okay brother, you're in supply,' he said, and told me that I'd be driving a truck to the Aqabi refugee camp everyday and make stops on the way to deliver ammunition, food, medicine, water, and whatever else was needed from and to the camp, and from the camp to the fighters in the hills.

" 'There won't be any fighting? No engagements with Hussein's troops?' I asked.

"He said maybe, maybe not, depending on whether I'd be at Aqaba when they attack, for surely they will be attacking, strafing, with tanks, artillery, napalm. Izz wasn't much older than me, twenty-three, but he had been a fighter since 1965. We found time to talk about personal things, like where he was from in Palestine, and how I was a Palestinian who was born in Jordan, grew up in Kuwait—where my parents lived and worked—studied in Beirut, held a Syrian passport, and did not believe in anything other than Palestine.

Izz told me that the next day we would drive to Jerash together.

" 'What's there?' I asked him. 'I thought Jerash was leveled.'

" 'It was, but some houses are still standing. One of them belongs to the prostitute king.'

"I smiled. He laughed out loud. 'We store some of our ammunition there,' he said still laughing, and put his right hand out palm up for me to slap.

"At three or four o'clock in the morning, I woke up with a start. The other four people in the tent with me woke up too. Someone from *Hamat el thawra,* who is on guard, was shouting 'Cover me, cover me' to someone. But before any shooting started, they realized no intrud-

107

ers were around, just a squirrel maybe, running around in the bushes. It was pitch black out. We couldn't see anything but fireflies. I couldn't get back to sleep. It was cold. I dozed for a few minutes and got up again. My eyes were staring at the opening between the flaps of the tent door.

"My God!' I said out loud. 'Phantoms. Israeli Phantoms heading this way!' Fortunately, before everyone woke up, I realized that I was just seeing fireflies in the sky.

"In the morning I drove off to Jerash with Izz and two other men. On the way, he received a message on the radio that he was needed at the base. So he drove us to town and dropped us off outside a big, partially demolished house, saying he'd be back in two or three hours. In the meantime we were supposed to pile up the boxes of ammunition we needed. The two other guys were tough kids from the area whose families lived at the camp. One of them was in his early teens with a patchy beard—well, a sort of a beard, and some fluff for a moustache. The other was a bit older and didn't say much the whole time, but every now and again he hummed a tune to some folk song or other about how he and his comrades were *dabki* dancers, tough *dabki* dancers, and whoever picked a fight with them would get really fucked, and how he wanted his girlfriend to pile scotch over their cognac so they could get really drunk. At other times he looked bored, as if he'd been through it all. Both kids had peasant accents.

"After we got all the stocks piled neatly on the pavement, we sat and waited. Izz didn't come in two hours. He didn't come in three. By noon he still hadn't come back. Nor by the evening. Then all hell broke loose. A formation of Jordanian Skyhawks and Hawker Hunters strafed the Aqabi camp and the guerrilla concentrations in the mountains. And out of nowhere and everywhere in the mountains, anti-aircraft guns fired at them. Then the planes broke up into three groups and disappeared into the sky. They came back minutes later and headed in three different directions. Some flew over the Jerash area and dropped their bombs. One fell on the outskirts of the town with deafening fury. Then there was dead silence for a few seconds as the planes disappeared behind the mountains. Before they came back again, one solitary Dorschka at the foot of the mountain was shooting at the empty sky.

" 'That must be Abu Murad,' Abu Omar, the kid with the almost-beard, said. 'He does that when he's mad at someone. He shoots rockets at heaven before he goes to sleep every night.'

"When the planes came back they dropped their load directly on the town. We took cover behind the rubble of one of the houses. I couldn't figure out why the hell they were bombing the town; it was dead already. Then we heard a terrifying explosion in the air as one of the jets received a direct hit and plummeted incredibly fast, incredibly, frighteningly fast, into the thick woods and exploded again. We started applauding and hollering, '*Bravo, bravo aleik Abu Murad!*'

"But it wasn't Abu Murad. He had been killed the day before.

"The stray dogs and cats in the town were running back and forth in a panic. We drank some water and ate up the little food we had—sitting and waiting. We were speculating on when the Jordanians would be attacking the Aqabi and Gaza camps. Abu Omar said that Hussein's troops had been bombing this town for the last seven months but had never once hit this house. 'Bombs have fallen everywhere, everywhere around here,' he gestured with his arms, 'but never on this house. Because we have ammunition here. God is with us. How else would you explain it? Our cause is just. God is with us, I tell you. Think of all the explosives in there brothers!'

"Around two o'clock in the morning we woke up to the sound of singing coming from down the hill. Jordanian army songs, for heaven's sake. A Jordanian army truck was driving up the dirt road with its lights on. Obviously lost. I mean, what the fuck were they doing there at two o'clock in the morning? The sound of the singing had assimilated itself into a dream I had been having, which now turns into a nightmare. I was at the Aqabi camp and it was being attacked by Bedouin tanks. I wasn't part of the action, just observing it, sort of from every direction. The camp was all rubble and the Jordanians were burying bodies in mass graves. On top they were placing branches brought there for the purpose from the Mountain of Fire outside Nablus.

"The three of us were up simultaneously, running inside the house. Using our flashlights to guide us, we came out with an RPG each and picked up our kalashnikovs, which already had full magazines as well as a spare one strapped on with masking tape, upside-down, for easy reclipping. The army truck was driving down slowly and its occupants were still singing.

"Abu Omar, lying in the middle of the road, adjusted the RPG over his shoulder and shot. Immediately a flame shot through from the back end of his weapon. Then he ran off like a frog from one spot to another, one side of the road then the other, crouching with the RPG on his shoulder and shooting at his target till he had fired all six of his grenades. And we, in the meantime, had emptied our magazines firing on automatic, thirty-two bullets in each, into the truck. If our target had been tank, not a mere truck, I'm sure it would have been pulverized by the amount of fire we pumped into it. Truly a case of overkill. We approached cautiously, as we had been trained to do, and found the bodies of three soldiers there, bodies I don't want to describe to you.

"We stayed up all night in different spots around the street, expecting other army vehicles or tanks or even a whole column to turn up. We couldn't imagine any reason why Izz hadn't come back for us other than that he had been killed. He hadn't been. He arrived at dawn, threw a cursory glance at the truck, and told us to load the arms and get moving. We were needed at Aqabi. When we started describing what had happened, he absent-mindedly said we'd done well, and we had to get moving right away. A major attack was expected soon. On the way down the mountain road we passed a lot of *fedayeen* trucks driving in the other direction, obviously to pick up more matériel. The attack, of course, didn't come till eight months later, long after the truce was signed in Amman, which committed us to evacuating all our forces from the cities into Jerash and Ajloun.

"We delivered our load at the Fatah headquarters and waited around for an hour or two to pick up fresh bread from the bakeries. There were so many bakeries at the camp, each one a hole in the ground where a woman stood putting dough into another hole at chest level filled with burning coal. The dough went in, bread came out. Little girls grabbed it and piled it in neat stacks in straw baskets. From time to time, a *shibil*, a little boy from the militias, walked in with a kalashnikov over his shoulder, showing off a lot of authority in his gait. The woman in charge of one bakery told us as we carted bread baskets away, 'My sons, you are like petals. May the Lord protect you.'

"We left the camp just before noon and made a few stops on the way, going into the forest to deliver our bread to the *fedayeen* at the anti-aircraft guns. We stopped to talk and they made us tea and lentil soup, which is what everybody was living on. The tea was donated by Bangladesh and the lentils were expropriated from UNRWA.

"Keep in mind that, at this point, the American government was pouring massive amounts of arms into Jordan. Our front in Amman and just outside it, sealed to the world, was no longer receiving arms of any kind. The brothers there were running out of ammunition, food, medicine, and water (the water mains servicing the camps had long been cut off by the government). Yet they didn't show any signs of giving up. Most of our military and political leadership was inside the Wehdat and Jabal Hussein camps. A week after that the Jordanian troops leveled them to the ground, killing thousands of civilians and fighters with what they called arc shelling, as opposed to level shelling. In level shelling, you see, a shell can knife a building in half and level it, but the people who have taken shelter in the basement survive somehow. In arc shelling, the shell falls *on top* of the building, and whoever is inside, whether in the basement or elsewhere, is killed. Literally hundreds of men, women, and children died that way, under the debris of their own homes.

"Bedouin troops were finishing off wounded *fedayeen* on stretchers with their bayonets. They were lining up guerrillas or suspected guerrillas who surrendered to them against the wall and massacring them. They were raping, killing, and torturing Palestinians they picked up in the streets, and I mean ordinary people looking for food and water. But we didn't find out about all that till the truce was signed and the brothers from Amman started arriving in Jerash.

"One day, the three of us were driving back from the camp. It had been raining all day and there was mud all over the truck. And we got bogged down halfway. At the camp, life is misery, with everybody wading in the mud, slipping, cursing. Tents had fallen down. Women with babies and water buckets were slipping all over the place on their way to or from the water pumps. And the rain kept falling. All day. It never stopped.

"So we were sitting and waiting for someone to drive by and help. The rain eased a bit. About an hour later, we heard the sound of people singing. It got closer and closer. Then in the distance, taking the turn in the road, on foot, we saw about fifteen men. I took my binoculars out and looked them over. God! I gave the binoculars to the other two brothers to check out this weird scene."

Boutros stops talking for a moment and looks at Sami, who is

111

sitting next to me. Sami just bursts out laughing. "Those were the days, weren't they, hey, father of all youth?" he says to Boutros, still laughing.

Boutros continues: "So by God, we just grabbed our *klashens* and waited to see what the devil was going on. I mean, the men in the distance were singing. We couldn't tell whether they were singing *fedayeen* songs or maybe something else. Some of them, however, were loosely dressed in Jordanian uniforms, the others were wearing the regular *fedayeen* headdress and fatigues. Those in Bedouin uniforms were also wearing *hattas*. They were laden with arms—G3 Kalashnikovs. Seminiovs, name it. We wondered, are they defectors from the Jordanian army? Are they Jordanian soldiers who are lost in our zone? Are some of them prisoners? Whose prisoners?

"The three of us took positions on either side of the road behind bushes and trees. The men got closer and closer. A disheveled mob of fighters, whoever they were. They were singing *fedayeen* songs. Finally we saw them. They were our people. And one of them, right there in the very front, singing his head off, was none other than our friend here, Sami. We came out of the bushes and asked them what the hell they thought they were doing. They told us they had been on a road near the Gaza camp and had ambushed a Jordanian army patrol. I asked Sami if there were any prisoners and he said, 'What for?' He just said, 'What for?'"

Sami is no longer laughing. "Yes, right, what for? I mean the sons of whores rape and kill and napalm and practice their savageries on us, and then they want to be taken prisoner and be put up in comfort till it blows over. *Kiss imhum sharmoota!*—Fuck you, motherfucker!"

"Yes, *Kiss imhum sharmoota*" repeats Salwa, who had walked into the apartment holding hands with Sami. She doesn't appear self-conscious repeating the rough language of her boyfriend. She is a very intense, even taut person, her face projecting rage of a kind that had not yet been rationalized. Fierce, burning rage.

"These people don't belong to any human group on the face of this globe. Nor do they belong to any era in its history. Not the Dark Age. Not the Stone Age. To call them animals would be an insult to the animal kingdom. And the social system they've created in Jordan— the little entity that Winston Churchill, that super-racist and cold warrior, created with the stroke of a pen to repay a debt to his agents in our midst—is not fit for beasts of burden to live in.

112

"You know," she went on, "around the same time Sami and brother Boutros were in Ajloun, I was in Amman, less than half a mile from the Wahdat camp, in a Palestinian neighborhood. Some of the king's troops gathered there on afternoon and began rounding people up and shooting at anything that moved. My father, mother, two sisters, and I crouched on the floor in the kitchen, because that was on the far side from the firing. For a while it would stop and then, I guess just for the fun of it, the soldiers would shoot at the buildings again. It was too late to leave the house, because the Bedouins would have shot us dead as we walked out. Bullets went through the windows but none of us was hurt. Then they started going into all the houses, one by one, looking for people and snipers. It was already dark and the sniping had stopped. The Bedouins had completely subdued the neighborhood. Then about eight o'clock at night, we heard them coming up the stairs. Soon they were shooting at the lock and the hinges on our front door. A soldier kicked the door and it came crashing down. At that moment, Randa, one of my sisters, panicked and started screaming with fright. She was screaming and screaming. And before anyone could stop her, she stood up and rushed toward the soldiers. To plead with them to spare our lives. Or whatever she was going to do. She was hysterical. Hysterical. Randa was hysterical. Just . . . hysterical. And the Bedouin shot her dead. Then my mother started screaming.

"I have no recollection of what happened after that except that we were led to the area where the other people were. Men, women, and children. Most of the men were old. Some were middle-aged. There were hardly more than half a dozen young men there—that is, young men of fighting age. We all sat there on the ground, about two hundred of us, in a kind of semi-circle. I may have been dazed, but I was angry too. I was determined to tell them, if they questioned me, that I was indeed part of the *fedayeen* militia. And I was going to spit in their faces as I told them that. Then I became conscious of the smell. The smell of bodies. Of people killed and then bayoneted by soldiers who shouted at the corpses, Godless Communists, Godless Communists. But the real horror didn't start till about ten o'clock, when the Bedouins had finished eating by the light of kerosene lamps. The soldiers closest to us were roaring with laughter at their own jokes and at how they all playfully aimed their machine guns at a dog that strayed close and turned it into bits of flesh strewn all over the road.

"Then two or three soldiers left the group and came over to us. Maybe they were drunk. I swear to you on the Holy Book they were swaying like drunks. They stood over us, two of them with their arms slung over each other. They grabbed a woman by the hair and she began to scream as they touched her. Her daughter, who was no more than ten or eleven, stood up and coiled herself around her mother's waist. The girl was crying. As the other two soldiers tried to subdue the woman, the third took the girl away from her mother and proceeded to undress her.

"The people began to murmur, and then to shout, in unison: '*Allah akhbar. Allah Akhbar. Allah yifdah Hareemak.* God is great. May the Lord punish you.' And the mother was shouting, 'No, no, no, please God, no. Please. I beg of you. She is only a child. She is my only child. Please God. God no. I appeal to you, by the Holy Book, by the Companions of the Prophet. Please God, no. My child. Don't, please.'

"One moment she was screaming all these entreaties. The next she was dead silent. One of the Bedouins had slashed her throat with a bayonet. And she lay there. Just a corpse, a few feet away from us. I'll never forget how she lay there. In death, she lay there hugging her knees.

"I couldn't see well what was happening in the dark. Only shadows. They took the child away. When they came back, they were naked from the waist up and laughing. They waded through the crowd, probably to look for someone else to rape. Then a man still chanting incantations of *Allah Akhbar, Allah Akhbar,* stood up. He was very tall. And even in the dark I could see the look on his face. I have never seen a look like that on anybody's face in my life. I know I never will again. A look of such savage, such fierce fury. The look of a man who knows he must kill, before he does anything else. In this case, before he dies. A man who knows he had marshaled enough strength to split a rock in two. Even while he is standing up, he lurches forward, grabbing the soldier by the neck and the testicles. The soldier screams and then whimpers with pain as he goes down. The man takes the gun off the Bedouin's shoulder and hits him on the skull with the butt till pieces of his brain spill onto the ground."

Everybody in the room sits motionless with tension, almost paralyzed by the revolting image we have been called upon to recreate in our minds.

"All this took no more than thirty seconds. Perhaps less. As two other soldiers climbed over people to aid their comrade, the man had finished the job. Then suddenly, the two Bedouin had fallen, or been tripped by the people, and everyone was over them. The other soldiers rush over in our direction and everyone was running off into the darkness, hiding in the bushes and screaming. All the men, women, and children. And the Bedouin were after us, firing their weapons blindly in the dark. I got separated from my sister and parents and went crawling in the bushes on my hands and knees. And the Bedouin were close by, shouting orders to each other in their ugly accents. I hate their accents. I hate their voices even more than I do them. They are the ugliest animal sounds in all of creation. Like pigs. I hate them. I hate them. God in heaven, how I hate the *ben sharmootas*. I kept crawling and half-walking away from the area till I got to the main road leading north to Jerash, which was a long way off, but I walked and walked till it was dawn. I did not know that I had walked that long, or that far. I had been as if in a dream, as if I was still back with those people and the naked soldiers, in the bushes, raping the child and slashing her mother's throat. Then I was crying. I didn't know it till I had to duck when I heard army vehicles coming up behind me and I felt the tears. I was crying when I thought about Randa and how she suddenly went mad and they killed her in the corridor of our house. Maybe I wasn't thinking about all this, all night. Maybe my mind was blank. Because when it got light, I was surprised. It was as if I had just woken up. I was nowhere. I just knew I was in a spot with thick forest on both sides of the road. Then suddenly I heard the sound of army vehicles behind me. A couple of personnel carriers and a tank. I ducked behind the trees. When they got about a hundred yards from where I stood, *fedayeen* pounced on them, coming out from everywhere in the forest. The tank was knocked out immediately by a couple of RPGs, and the Bedouin soldiers—there were just a few of them—were jumping off their vehicles with their arms up. They were rounded up by the *fedayeen* and dragged into the forest. The whole operation took no more than a few minutes. I just crouched there, transfixed with fear, anxiety, and fatigue. I also knew that unless I joined our fighters there and then, they would disappear into the forest and I would have no chance of

115

remaining alive. I would have died of thirst and hunger. So suddenly I started running down the road shouting, *fedayeen, fedayeen,* and just as suddenly, they were shooting in my direction. But that didn't make me stop running. Then, realizing I wasn't a soldier, they held their fire till I got to where they were standing.

" 'Sister, who are you, and what are you doing here?' they kept asking. I told them briefly what had happened in Amman and also that I was part of the Fatah militia. Before I knew what was happening, someone had thrust a *klashen* in my hand. It felt good. It felt so good, oh, ever so good, to hold that weapon in my hand."

"What did the *fedayeen* do with the Bedouin prisoners?" I ask Salwa.

"They killed them," she responds with finality.

"How many of them were there?"

"Brother," she says, with weariness in her voice, "who cares? Who cares?"

I don't. I, for one, don't.

Caron is pregnant. She is homesick. And she wants, though a Marxist, to find her Jewishness in a paradoxical way linked inextricably to Israeli statehood in Palestine. She flies to the United States. I stay in Paris a short while, think about it, and then catch a flight there too. The October War has just broken out and I am on a plane heading to the United States. What the hell am I going to do there? What am I going to do in the United States? Do people there hold demonstrations every day the way they do in Paris? Do they read the *International Herald Tribune,* drink *grand crème,* sit in cafés and talk all night, walk the streets, kiss in the metro, eat an *assiette de fromage* with a *ballon* of red wine in the afternoon, go to political rallies every other evening, and live in a city that gives shape to the poetics of an outsider's life, and throws its shadow against every line he has written and every word he has uttered?

6

I arrive in the United States in the fall of 1973. The Arab regimes and Israel are about to conclude their fourth war, and in its aftermath the conservative Arab right will emerge, for the first time since 1952, into a position of power and prestige. To this new power block in the Arab world, the Palestinians and their movement will become both an embarrassment and a threat. With their own separate vision of a political settlement that they feel sure the Palestinians would object to, the Arab regimes will be determined to finish the job they started in Jordan in Black September. The attack will come in the cities and mountains of Lebanon, three years hence.

A friend who picks me up at the airport drives me through the vast, undefined spaces typical of American highways. Suddenly I feel the need to define my own space. And I talk bitterly about both the October War and MacDonald's. The one is about real estate, the other is a fragment from the vacuousness of the American Dream.

117

My friend gives me a grin and concentrates on his driving. Like my other *ghourba* friends he has the cynicism of the rebellious outsider and the counterpolitics of the disinherited acquired by all Palestinians who have spent their late youth in the West. They see themselves as hip activists to whom the traditional concepts of the Arab nation and Arabism are a camp joke, and America and its dream are issues mockingly remote from their vision, their reality, and their aspirations. To these Palestinians living in the United States, America is not the land of opportunity but the land of whatnot. To them, Americans are naive, uninformed, hick.

In the car, I am railing against the Arabs and their October War. I am convinced, I say, that this war will inevitably create space for a political settlement that will be signed at our cost. They will screw us.

We talk about the war incessantly. Even when we stop at MacDonald's, we continue to talk. When there is a gap in the conversation, we fill it with furtive, absent-minded remarks about our personal lives and plans for the future.

Then we go back to our impassioned discussion of the war, interspersed by the chaotic images of our condition that most Palestinians insinuate into their political conversations.

"Do you know?" I say, leaning closer over the table, "in this war, the soldiers who are killed are being buried in their own countries. But we have no cemeteries to bury our own dead. Do you know that? Do you know that? We belong to a generation of Palestinians that has no cemetery to bury its dead. Everybody has a cemetery. Everybody. Everybody visits their dead during the *Eid* with flowers in their hands. But we have been denied everything, including the right to bury our dead in our own country . . . to raise our children there . . . in one place that is our own. Do you know that?"

He tells me that he visited Geneen, his home town, five months ago. I ask him what happened. He says he was confronted, at the border between Jordan and the West Bank, by Israeli police.

"I mean they are all brothers of prostitutes, I tell you," he says angrily. "There was this fucking Israeli soldier, with a heavy East European accent pushing me around. Pushing all of us around. This guy with a two-day stubble was checking my passport and the whole time he's looking indignant like, the *ben sharmoota*, it was me, not him, who was there under duress. The whole time I was saying to myself, What are you doing here? Who sent you here? Where did you come from? What are you people doing around here in our world, dictating to us, indignant even at the presence of our shadows? After a while he wanted to know what I had in my suitcase. I told him clothes. Then he started shouting obscenities at me for not having had my bag open and ready for inspection. When I opened it for him, he threw its contents on the table. And the whole time, there were hundreds, yes hundreds, of Palestinians, traveling back home from Jordan, standing around, pleading to be let through. There were kids and old people sitting in the shade or milling around aimlessly. Some had been there for days, unable to get through. I wanted to shout at the soldier that it was too late for them to be doing this sort of thing in our part of the world. A century too late. I wanted to shout that it's best that they understand that, for they will never know peace here till they understand this one cardinal truth. But what the hell. We and they cannot hear each other."

He does not, or forgets to, tell me about his family and the time he spent with them. Instead we talk briefly about some mutual friends at Bir Zeit University. Who was in jail. Who was free. Who had left to study or work abroad. Who stayed behind and how active they are. And who left Palestine permanently to join the revolution in Lebanon.

We hop back in the car and head up to Cambridge, a three-hour drive. My friend, whose real name is Suleiman, had, like most Palestinians, a nickname reserved for the use of his close friends. Suleiman was known as el Amid, the dean, a name he acquired because of the various leadership roles he had played over the years in the student movement, in community affairs, in Palestinian institution-building in the United States, during his time in an Israeli jail. (He was later to be the principal figure behind the founding of the 5,000-member North American chapter of the General Union of Palestinian Students.)

Amid was born in Geneen, a town of 40,000 to the north of Nablus on the West Bank. Like most Palestinians from there he was grappling with what it means to be Palestinian while dismissing the Jordanian aspect of his citizenship. For, ironically, the national identity of Palestinians from the West Bank is not as sharply defined as that of Palestinians who were born or grew up in exile. Whereas we, in Lebanon, Syria, Kuwait, and elsewhere, had no problem retaining our identity—even enhancing it by adding on attributes that had not existed before—our counterparts inside Palestine lived

119

under material conditions that destabilized their associative context as Palestinians.

The subordinate status that Palestinians in the West Bank were relegated to and the marginal role they played in determining their destiny go back to a time long before the Israeli occupation of 1967. After the November 29, 1947, partition of Palestine by the United Nations the two remnants of Palestine not grabbed by Zionist forces, the West Bank and Gaza, were occupied respectively by the Jordanian army (led by British officers from Sandhurst) and the Egyptian army (led by decadent officers from the aristocracy). The Arab Higher Committee, the political leadership of the Palestinian people at the time, proceeded to create what came to be known as the All-Palestine Government (in Gaza, in September 1948) with the aim of exercising "national authority" over the territories, leading potentially to statehood. But with their military presence in these same territories, the Egyptians and Jordanians were in a position to decide, even dictate, Palestinian affairs—and neither welcomed the establishment of a Palestinian state. King Abdallah's government in Amman in particular was violently opposed not only to the idea of Palestinian independence, but even to the idea of Palestinian representation through the All-Palestine Government at the General Assembly.

When the Arab League, and umbrella organization representing the Arab states in the region, adopted resolutions in support of "the soundness, legality, and necessity" of Palestinian independence, which is a "natural right" of the Palestinians, King Abdallah responded by convening the so-called Jericho Conference near the end of 1948. This gathering of Palestinian notables, quislings, landowners, and others met with Jordanian representatives and passed a resolution calling for "unification" of the West and East banks. This unification was formalized in late 1950, when the Jordanian Chamber of Deputies was dissolved to make way for "elections" (rigged, with voting restricted to male property owners) for a new parliament with deputies from both banks. In effect, the West Bank was annexed.

Though the Arab League expelled Jordan for this move and Britain was the only country in the world that recognized it, in time the annexation became a *fait accompli* and Amman was rehabilitated into the Arab establishment. The Jordanians could afford to proceed with their plan with no serious challenges from any of the forces of the surrounding countries, which were just emerging from their colonial experience into "independence." They were backed by Britain and the muscle of the oldest and best-trained military force in the Arab world, an army that possessed a sophisticated system of mechanization and communication and efficiently served the interests of the ruling classes just as the British, who had established it, intended.

Thus the curtain fell on the Palestinians' first attempt to achieve statehood, though on a small segment of their land, stifling the development of Palestinian national identity in that part of Palestine. For not only were these Palestinians now regarded as Jordanian citizens, but they came under the pervasive influence of every state institution in the land, from education to the media, whose goal was to "Jordanize" them.

For two decades, the West Bank was left to rot. Industrial projects were diverted to the other side of the river. Banks were based in Amman. Industrial development efforts were so aggressively concentrated in the East that, by law, all major industrial projects with a total capital of one million *dinars* or more had to be set up there. Government subsidies were more forthcoming to industries on the East Bank. As a result of this policy, by the mid-1960s most industry was located on the East Bank, a dramatic change since the annexation. Since the Palestinians were not allowed to establish a single university on their land, those seeking higher education went to Jordan. Those seeking employment went to the Gulf States. Those who resisted were subjected to long imprisonment and torture. (To be caught with a penknife, in those days, meant long incarceration coupled with beatings.)

Though for twenty years they were hit at their most vulnerable point of self-definition, the Palestinians of the West Bank still retained a sense, though fragile, of who they were.

This sense of identity was constantly reinforced by the political repression of the regime, the most stark example of which came in the wake of the assassination of King Abdallah (whom Palestinians on the West Bank never ceased to refer to as the "agent king") in Jerusalem in 1951, when the Jordanian army and police went on a vengeful rampage of arrests, torture, and killing that was not checked for half a dozen years.

Whereas Palestinians in exile had no restrictions on defining their identity, indeed were compelled daily to contemplate reminders of it, the Palestinians of the West Bank had to wait till 1967, when they came face to face with Israel. Their identity was then literally brought home to them, in the form of its antithesis, by Zionist occupiers. They were, however, desperately ill-prepared to resist occupation of any kind. (The Palestinians of Gaza, who had chafed under Egyptian civil administration, had had that identity similarly driven home to them back in 1956, during the comparatively brief occupation of the Strip by the Israeli army.)

"What the hell are we doing in this country, brother?" I ask Amid.

"I'm going back as soon as I finish my dissertation."

"You can't go back to the Bank," I say in alarm, referring to the occupied territory the way Palestinians always do, "or they'll put you behind bars for the rest of your life."

"They're not going to be there for the rest of my life."

Amid has spent a total of fourteen months in the prisons of Ashkelon and Ramleh and was released around the end of 1970.

"I mean since your release you've been to Lebanon, you've been active," I say, "surely they'd know about that."

"Let's not overestimate their intelligence. They know far less than we imagine. They didn't question me on my last trip. I can't choose not to go back. We belong there."

"I understand."

"You know, ever since 1968, ever since the battle of Karameh," he says, "an incredible mystique has developed in the Bank about the *fedayeen*. We all wanted to be *fedayeen*. The occupation unlocked forces within us, social forces, emotional forces I can't describe, that had been repressed ever since we acquired a consciousness. But we were so unprepared to deal with them. You know, by the time the Israelis came six years ago, the Jordanians had turned the West Bank into a place fit for habitation only by old people and children. All able-bodied men and women were on the other side of the river or in the Gulf. We used to joke about how the West Bank was good enough only for the newlyweds and the nearly deads. But something happened when the Israelis came. It was as if we were freed of the paradox of being Palestinians *and* so-called Jordanian citizens. We could now fight them as *Palestinians*. Mind you, there were a lot of cadres from Fatah and other factions already in place when the occupiers came, but by early 1970 most of them, or most of their cell leaders, had already been picked up. Arms were smuggled in to us then, almost daily, but we were not as smart, as organized, or as trained as the brothers in Gaza. I mean the Gazans had been at it since the 1950s. Still, the recruits were there. Virtually everybody on the Bank was young. And they all wanted to fight. Some youngsters were doing it freelance, without being attached to any faction.

"I remember Dayan once made a statement in which he said that, for all intents and purposes, the Palestinian resistance on the West Bank had been wiped out. There were no more terrorists left in the land. Well, the following day, there were these two kids from Geneen, first cousins they were, who had gotten hold of some hand grenades and had been walking up and down the streets of the town for a week waiting for an Israeli patrol to pass by. The day after Dayan's statement they came across a jeep with four Israeli military men in it, one of them an officer attached to the military governor's office, and they threw the grenades at them, killing the officer and wounding the other three soldiers. Well, the people of Geneen went crazy, saying that the operation was the response of the Resistance to Dayan's statement. Of course it wasn't. But those were exciting days, when everyone wanted to join the Resistance, one way or another. Yet it was difficult to do that because most of the top people had been arrested earlier on, and there was little coordination. The vacuum had to be filled, though. I remember when I graduated from high school, which was the very year the occupation started, I and some of the other kids from my class—Riyad Awad, the Hantoli twins, and Mohammed Lutfi Abdallah among others—went around, in our primitive way, putting out stenciled leaflets and defacing the walls with political graffiti calling on the people to oppose the occupation and beware of collaborators. This was a cell, if you wish, but with no physical connection to any faction, though we identified ourselves as PFLP. But when we got together it was as if the fate of the Bank depended on us. We also read Che and Fanon and Mao.

"In 1969 one of the boys with us, Mohammed Said Dein, left Geneen and joined the movement in Jordan. He was with the brothers there for four months, then they sent him back to operate underground. When we got together, he told me not to worry, weapons were coming in soon, and we should prepare ourselves. For us, this was like a letter from our beloved. We figured, that's it, now we can start doing some real work. Mohammed even assured us that the weapons were arriving on the *Eid*, either the first or the second day after Ramadan. We were all on cloud nine. We could hardly wait. By that time, mind you, our cell had become officially recognized as PFLP by the brothers and we had contacts with other cells from other factions. The night of the last day of Ramadan we got together with some fellows from Fatah and some from the Palestinian Communist Party, there was a whole bunch of us, to talk about the weapons. We got into all sorts of heated arguments over who was supposed to do what, and who was to lead whom, and so on, till we were all exhausted.

"I got home just before dawn. When the dawn *Izan* from the mosque started, I had just gotten into my pajamas. That's when the knock on the door came. I ignored that. You see, my mother is a midwife and I thought it was someone who needed her to make a delivery. So I went to sleep. It was Captain Barsli, from the occupation police, whom I had met when he interrogated me for two hours because I had led the funeral cortege for a slain Resistance fighter three months before. He walked in waving his handgun at me in the manner of someone saying 'naughty, naughty' and said, 'Last time we talked, I told you I was convinced you were a terrorist. You insisted you weren't. Now who is right?' I told him I was no terrorist. As I got dressed, he said to my mother, 'Your son is delicate.' My mother got insulted and responded by saying that no son of hers was delicate. At any rate, the first thing she'll do tomorrow, I say to myself, will be to go around bragging to our neighbors, friends, and relatives that I had been arrested as a member of the *fedayeen*.

"When Captain Barsli got me to the station, one of our comrades was already there, a fellow called Ibrahim Kirsh Jiryis. He was of Assyrian background. A real Palestinian patriot. I didn't recognize him. He had been beaten senseless. One of the men who participated in the beating was, believe it or not, an Israeli-Abar prison official, a fellow called Jaber Ahmad Jabareen. He comes from a family of collaborators. Way back in the 1930s, his father, who was also a prison official, had helped Dayan escape from jail, or avoid being jailed, I forget which, and Dayan, after 1948, returned the favor by appointing him mayor of Um el Fahem in the Triangle, in northern Palestine. I served fourteen months."

"What happened? Who had betrayed you?"

"We found out. A boy called Fahmi. In jail, where all the prisoners were organized by their own faction leaders, Fatah, PFLP, PDFLP, and the Palestinian Communist Party, we had gotten together with Tawfik Zakani (who was incarcerated with his son), the faction leader of Fatah and known by them as Abu Saleh, and with Abu Baaker, who led the PFLP brothers, and we voted to send word out to the street that Fahmi should be offed. He wasn't, quite. The brothers hit him on the skull with a pipe and left him for dead. He survived, but he was never the same."

"But the word went out about the fate of collaborators."

"It did. But as I say, we were so ill-prepared, in resources and in background, to face the demonic forces the Israelis brought with them to destroy our history," Amid says reflectively, concentrating on his driving.

Some say that prior to their occupation Israeli leaders had not conceived of a master plan to alter the economic structure and social life of the West Bank. Whether this is true or not, the impact of occupation on West Bank and Gaza Palestinians was profound.

Though even before the occupation the West Bank had suffered grievously from limited natural resources, lack of capital, marketing outlets, and an entrepreneurial class—it had long since been driven to seek employment in the Gulf or the East Bank—these problems were all aggravated even further under the occupation.

By 1973 the West Bank economy was completely subservient to and dependent on the Israelis. With no national government to protect their industrial goods against competition from highly subsidized Israeli commodities, the Palestinians of the West Bank, like those in Gaza, lost their own production and became a protected market for Israeli industry. Even before the October War, the occupied territories came second only to the United States as an Israeli export market, absorbing 17 percent of Israel's total exports. By 1980 the proportion was up to 25 percent. And there was nothing Palestinians could do about it. Rather they found themselves passive victims of developments in the occupiers' home economy, such as inflationary stress, currency devaluation, and economic slumps, as well as a source of menial labor.

In agriculture, the situation was equally bleak. Through confiscation, land became steadily less available to Palestinians, and, where they clung to it, increasingly less cultivatable, since the necessary water was no longer the prerogative of the landowners. The marketability of their produce was curtailed, and the number of laborers needed to work the land diminished.

Palestinian agriculture encountered even more serious problems in later years. It is estimated that the total annual water supply in the West Bank is about 850 million cubic meters. Of that only about 120 million meters were allotted to the Palestinians population. By the time the Israelis had drilled some twenty-five artesian wells to depths of 100–600 meters, ground water levels were so low that wells in neighboring Palestinian villages dried up. To make matters worse, Palestinians were prevented from drilling their own wells, on their own land, for their own agricultural purposes.

The ferocity of the policy of pauperizing the Palestinians (with the aim of driving them to seek their livelihood, and ultimately their residence, elsewhere) is evident in figures on land expropriated for Israeli colonies on the West Bank. By 1973, long before Menachem Begin's Likud Party came to power and made land robbery even more fashionable, 94 percent of the land Israeli settlements were built on had been privately owned by Palestinians, some of it the most fertile areas in the Jordan Valley, the bread basket of the West Bank.

The first of these colonies was established in July 1967. By 1973 forty more had been added. In almost all cases, they were initially established under the auspices of the Israeli army, as "paramilitary outposts," only to be turned over later to civilian settlers. As the colonization program accelerated after Begin's election, it became clear that the underlying intention was to plant Israeli communities all over the territories so that the West Bank and Gaza could easily be incorporated into *Eretz Israel*. In Jerusalem, starting in 1968, the occupation authorities expropriated huge areas of Palestinian-owned land within the municipal boundaries and built housing projects for Israeli settlers on it. These multi-story apartment blocks were carefully arranged to form a ring around Palestinian neighborhoods. In the minds of those developing the Zionism-is-racism UN General Assembly resolution at the time there could have been no clearer

126

proof of the nature of the Zionist experiment than that ring of concrete buildings, located on expropriated Palestinian land in a "united Jerusalem" but open only to Jewish tenants.

The rush to Judaize Jerusalem had been going on since June 29, 1967, when the assistant military commander of Jerusalem sent a hand-delivered letter to the Palestinian mayor of the Holy City advising him that he "had the honor to inform" the mayor that his municipal council was dissolved. Weeks before that the effort to make Jerusalem what Housing Minister Zeev Sharif described as "an emphatically Jewish city," began when bulldozers came almost immediately behind the Israeli troops to demolish what was, in effect, an expression of seven hundred years of Arab history.

The Magharbi quarter—adjacent to the Wailing Wall—which was founded by Saladin himself, was inhabited by pilgrims, scholars of Islamic studies, and functionaries of the Moslem Trust, all of whom had originally come from the Maghreb countries, hence the name. On June 11, well over a thousand people living there were turned out of their homes on a few hours notice.

After the municipal council was dissolved, municipal property and records were seized. The city's economy was Judaized. Palestinian banks were closed and their funds appropriated. West Bank products were banned from entering the city. Local businessmen had to obtain Israeli licenses and operate under the Israeli taxation system. Israeli currency became the legal tender. Palestinian schools followed the Israeli curricula. Civil courts worked under the Israeli judiciary and municipal departments under Israeli jurisdiction.

The rush to colonize and finally annex the West Bank and Gaza depended for its success largely on three elements. First, the Palestinian population had to be rendered submissive, without hope of liberation. Second, Israel had to use its role as the guardian of U.S. imperial interests on the western flank of the Middle East (just as the Shah's Iran was on the eastern flank) to win support for its denial that the PLO deserved any credibility as the official representative of the Palestinian people, and that the Palestinian cause had any legitimate national component. Third, through intensive propaganda, Israel had to disseminate the myth that its occupation of the West Bank was the most benign in modern history and that the Palestinians living there had never had it so good.

The occupation, of course, has been far from benign; it has been characterized by the detention and long incarceration without trial of suspects; the demolition of homes inhabited by suspected members of the Resistance; punitive curfews; collective punishment (imposed on whole villages); land confiscation; burning of crops and trees; deportation of prominent activists; population transfers; razing of whole areas of refugee camps ("for security purposes"); censorship of media and artistic expression; repeated closure of institutions of higher learning; and torture of prisoners.

No occupation of a people by another can ever, of course, be characterized as benign. Occupation is, by definition, vile and scurrilous. It also goes to the heart of the human dialectic: for the venomous consciousness of the occupiers turns inward in time as they subjugate their victims by the rule of the gun, thus destroying for themselves what there is of humanity in humans and restoring in them what there is of beast. For brutality has a way about it of seeking vengeance on those who unleash it. Conversely, the struggle of the occupied draws into its orbit men and women whose consciousness is penetrated by a sense of the value of freedom. Whereas Zionism, as a colonizing ideology, has become the code of the bully, tyrannizing people through contempt of their humanity, an encounter with the Palestinian national liberation movement, already a central force in the Arab world and the third world, has marked the consciousness, the work, and the thought of the best writers, theoreticians, ideologues, and bellettrists of the region.

"It's a long, grim duel," Amid tells me.

"We've been at it for half a century already. Who do you think is winning?"

"I'll tell you. You know, before I left the Bank, I was on a bus one day. It was full of workers. Many of them coming back from work inside '48-Palestine. Well, the bus was stopped at an Israeli checkpoint. The soldiers asked all the passengers to get off and leave their belongings on their seats. We stood out there in the sun for half an hour and some of the passengers were muttering under their breath and cursing the day the Israelis came, cursing the Arabs, cursing the United States, and so on. Some even started complaining to the soldiers. But two guys, two workers, responded to the indignity in the most eloquent way, in the most historically cogent way. They sat by the side of the road, took out a deck of cards, and started playing, showing total indifference, even contempt—the way they giggled and talked to each other—for the ritual terror of their situation. To me, that spectacle was nearer the mainstream of Palestinian feeling, of the Palestinian temperament, than any I've ever seen. These two fellows were saying, in effect, here we are, our roots here sink deep, we'll wait you out if need be. We're not going anywhere. We're not going *anywhere*. You see, whenever we and they come together, as colonized and colonizer, we regroup."

"We're not going anywhere." I repeat.

"Where are *you* going, brother?" Amid asks, with sudden somberness to his voice.

I say simply I am going to Cambridge because the woman who is carrying my child has already come here and I wanted to be with her and with the child when it is born.

I don't tell him more because I don't know more. It seems like I have been able to pick up and go "elsewhere" with impressive ease all my life. I have never felt any loyalty to any one place. It is as if being homeless has been my homeland, a kind of transnational place where I, along with other Palestinians of my generation, have felt the same sense of at-homeness that other folk, with a state of their own, have had.

I don't know though, I tell my friend, if when I arrive in Cambridge, I will be able to stay one step ahead of starvation. And madness. And irrational rage. Who wants to read what I write in the United States? Who wants to read, in this country, about why a people's history has been constantly linked to death and suffering and exile? Who wants to read, as it were, obituaries everyday?

No sooner do I begin living in Cambridge, where I had thought I would somehow escape the noise of pain, inside the bowels of middle-class-intellectual United States, than everyone is repeating to me the litany that Palestinians are the outlaws of the international community. Terrorists and killers all.

In Cambridge—no halcyon zone either—I cannot begin a chapter with my half-sleeping child inside her mother's womb, and the sounds of my Palestinian past rattling in my head. I cannot turn what I see around me into metaphor. An expression someone else can understand. Like the brown, peasant face of my father and the images I retain of the Palestinian ghetto in Beirut. My wife Caron, who is Jewish, whimpers in her sleep about our child, who is full of time from within. She holds it, in a kind of hemisphere, inside her belly, and thinks of what will be coming into the geography of her future. A crazed dream to speak to her, perhaps.

In Cambridge, I meet a lot of Palestinians. Students, immigrants, travelers, visiting professors. Reactionary Palestinians, progressive Palestinians, young Palestinians, old Palestinians, reflecting the many ideological currents with which our little society is imbued. They all meet, at all hours of the day, at the Algiers Café, a basement coffee shop off Harvard Square owned by an emaciated Palestinian from my home town. At first I am delighted and grateful to be around so many people from my country, who speak my language and pronounce my name the way it should be pronounced. Though I have long since begun to define myself as the native son of a nation larger than Palestine—encompassing all people who share with me a commonality of political consciousness and aesthetic sensibility—I feel with fellow Palestinians a nexus I do not share with others. It is as if their words, their gestures, their anger, their plaints, hit a sensitive chord in me, an inner likeness of the childhood I had lived around the refugee camps and the streets of Beirut. Every day, I sit in the Algiers Café and write bad poetry, drink strong tea, and wonder how I will pay the rent on my apartment so that I, my wife, and my child will not be out in the street. And I talk to fellow Palestinians, who talk about nothing but Palestine every minute of every hour of every day. Soon I begin to tire of dissecting the universe with them, as if it were a watermelon, looking for the seeds to chew on at night.

At home, the woman I live with begins to reject me soon after our child is born. Her hostility is disguised as hostility toward my "sexism." It seems all these four years together, in Paris as in Cambridge, she has gradually come to define her Jewishness in response to my Palestinianness, just as I too had become more sharply defined through her responses. My identity has begun to acquire a subtler nuance to it and, when interacting with her, a defensiveness. Now on the eve of our breakup, we have become paranoid.

I am betraying my proclaimed revolutionary ideals, she says, by divorcing them from a "liberated" mode of interaction with her as a woman. And I retort that she is copping out on her Marxist commitment to anti-Zionism and socialist ideals by hobnobbing with reactionaries and participating in their meetings.

What about the Jews, don't they deserve a homeland too?

The distance widens. I spend less time at home.

It is of no concern, or consequence, to me what they deserve; it is not with us that their accounts have to be balanced. Don't you see?

Cambridge has all manner of political people. All manner of political groups. I have very little patience with them, especially with "left-wing" groups calling themselves by high-sounding names who, when debating the Palestine question, sound like they are playing university politics. And liberal Jewish groups that called themselves "non-Zionist," whose members debated whether they were "Jewish radicals or radical Jews."

Is this the American left? Is this all there is to it? Having just arrived from Europe, where the revolutionary left is a movement with a genuine ideology and established party politics—drawing on a long intellectual tradition—I was shocked by my encounter with its American counterpart.

After all, they say, in the long talks I had with them, how do you expect Israel to recognize your rights if you do not recognize Israel's right to exist as a Jewish state in Palestine? After all, what guarantees can the Palestinians "offer" in the event Israel were to "offer" the Palestinians a separate state? And so on with that litany that has not changed since the days the British could not "offer" the Kenyans independence because the Kenyans "were not ready for it," and the French could not "grant" the Tunisians self-government because the Tunisians "could not govern themselves."

For many years to come, we will remain to them, I say to myself, nameless, faceless gooks, niggers, and wogs. That is, so long as we continue to refuse to go to them with hat in hand and produce iron-clad guarantees that we would not destabilize the status quo that they have established around us. These people did not seem to realize that to the Palestinians, like the slaves before them, it is the status quo that is at question and on trial.

The Palestinians were chipping away, tentatively, at that status quo back in Lebanon. If they had not yet scored any military gains against Israel or succeeded in liberating any part of the homeland, they had, nevertheless, convinced the Arab world, and the rest of the international community, that they were there to stay. A force to be reckoned with. A force that could neither be controlled nor destroyed.

Convincing the world that their movement was not finished after the clashes of 1970 in Jordan was a major challenge for the Palestinians. Jordan was, after all, as some Palestinian leaders described it metaphorically, the "heart" of their national struggle. Jordan had the highest concentration of Palestinians in exile and the longest contiguous border with Palestine. Though Lebanon already had a population of 400,000 Palestinians and a small presence of guerrillas in the south (formalized by the so-called Cairo Agreement of 1969 between the PLO and the Beirut government), the country seemed out of reach as a place for the Palestinian movement to rebuild in.

At times soon after Black September, it was difficult for the Palestinians to convince not only the world, but themselves, that their movement was not finished—elements within the PLO itself were arguing that the era of armed struggle was over and it was time for the "political struggle." Though stricken and in despair, the Palestinians still had to answer the question: Where should we go? By the winter of 1971, remnants of guerrillas from Western Jordan and Amman and others from the Ajloun Mountains had begun to arrive in Lebanon and establish formations in the most barren areas in the south, by Mt. Hermon, as well as in the Bekaa Valley to the east. Immediately, isolated clashes started with elements of the Lebanese army. The Israelis initiated massive air raids. At times the Israeli air force would mount saturation bombing of a Palestinian base, and, in obvious coordination, the Lebanese army would arrive soon after to besiege it.

Many Lebanese, however, were beginning to lean heavily on the side of the Palestinians. The Shiites supported the Palestinian movement because they, like the Palestinians, were at the bottom of the socioeconomic ladder in Lebanon. The Sunnis, who had never approved of the sectarian division of their society, saw hope in the secular values of the PLO. And all the progressive elements in Lebanon, Moslem and Christian, from Nasserites to Baathist, from the Communist Party to the Syrian Nationalist Party, formed alliances with the Palestinians.

What alarmed the Lebanese establishment above all about this swelling movement was the degree of support for the Palestinians among peasants and workers in the south. It feared that the presence of the PLO there would catalyze an upheaval by a population that had long chafed under feudal conditions imposed by the indigenous landowners and the central government. Barren, with no paved roads, no electricity, and even no guarantees by the authorities for the sale of its products (mostly citrus and tobacco, the latter needing thirteen months from planting to harvest), the south had been so neglected by the ruling classes in Beirut that the region was known as a "different country," linked to Lebanon only by abstraction. Though since independence Lebanon was considered a "tourist country," drawing Arab tourists in the tens of thousands, no area in the south was developed as a tourist attraction.

In April 1973, the Lebanese army besieged the major Palestinian refugee camps around Beirut and subjected them to heavy bombardment. In response, the militias of the Lebanese National Movement (the coalition of groups favoring a secular and democratic state) came out with their arms and fought alongside the Palestinians. At various checkpoints along the main highway between Sidon and Beirut, soldiers seized recognized Palestinian guerrillas and executed them on the spot; among those killed was a high PLO official, Riad Awad. At one point during the hostilities, twenty-four unarmed Palestinian guerrilla leaders stopped at an army checkpoint were about to be shot when an army commander, Ahmad Khatib, threatened to order his unit to shoot at the checkpoint soldiers if they fired at the Palestinians. (Two years later, during the civil war, Khatib led his troops in a breakaway from the General Command, precipitating the final breakdown of the Lebanese army as a national entity.)

The Palestinians in Beirut were running out of ammunition, from anti-tank missiles to bullets. Their comrades in the south and the Bekaa Valley had enough of both, but the highway along the coast and the mountain roads from the east were blocked. So was access to the camps by sea. There was no apparent way the Palestinians, with the comparatively limited resources they possessed at the time, could break the siege.

At this point a young Palestinian commander in the northeast, Sharif Hassanein, who had recently gotten married and bought himself a Renault 15, took to driving daily from Masna, where he was based, to Beirut, accompanied by his wife and mother-in-law—with grenades hidden under the seats. In Sidon, another young commander came up with an ingenious idea. Mobilizing dozens of adolescent Palestinian boys and girls, he would give each of them about twenty bullets, to stuff in their pockets, and send them by public transport to Beirut. Each of these kids would make the trip at least four times a day. In time, virtually every Palestinian child in Sidon wanted to be part of the scheme. Among them was Nabila Nasser (the niece of Kamal Nasser, then poet laureate of the Revolution), who was later killed during the 1982 siege of Beirut; and Aida Slaman. During the bullet run, Aida became so bold and reckless that she took to smuggling handguns, beginning with one gun, then two. When she started carrying three, her handbag bulged, and at one of the checkpoints a soldier asked to search it. She was arrested, and stayed in prison till the end of the hostilities. (In 1979, three months after marrying one of Yasser Arafat's bodyguards Aida was killed in an Israeli bombing raid on Bourj el Barajneh.)

Sharif Hassanein was saved from arrest, or death, by the incredible sixth sense of his elderly mother-in-law. One morning, as their Renault was being loaded at the arms depot, Sharif's mother-in-law barged in and demanded that all the weapons be taken out of the car.

Sharif tried to reason with her; but Um Kassem would not be dissuaded. She just breathed heavily and waved her fists at them all.

"I have a sense," she exclaimed, "I have a feeling, I tell you, that today we're going to be stopped."

The weapons were taken out of the car and Sharif, his wife, and mother-in-law began driving to Beirut. Sure enough, their car was not only stopped but searched thoroughly at every checkpoint.

Gun running to the guerrillas under siege in Beirut was not confined to these individual acts of daring; as the fighting intensified, pro-PLO forces in the Lebanese army itself used their own military vehicles to get weapons through to the camps. The notion that two people in the Arab world would fight *together* and raise threatening slogans about social justice and freedom was without precedent in the Arab world. The reactionary camp in the Arab world and those who were underwriting it wanted to make sure this couldn't happen again. They were determined to prevent the emergence of a secular, democratic, progressive Lebanon, much less a kind of People's Republic of Lebanon.

Toward the end of 1974, the Arab states, meeting at a summit in Rabat, proclaimed the Rabat Resolution, designating the PLO as the only official representative of the native people of Palestine. Soon after that, Islamic, nonaligned, and socialist countries followed suit. A major segment of the world community began to invite the PLO to open bureaus in its capitals. Around the same time, the United Nations General Assembly invited the Palestinian movement to send the chairman of its executive committee, Yasser Arafat, to address it in November of 1974.

This was a time of great excitement for Palestinians. Not only had the movement survived the upheavals of Black September; it was transforming itself into a robust and cohesive organization recognized by most of the globe. National unity was at its peak. Palestinians, though still without home and homeland, were *proud.* For the first time since 1948, they were being recognized as a people, as a nation, as a movement. There was cogent symbolism in the idea of the United Nations, the very international body that had caused the dispersal of the Palestinian people by partitioning their land in 1947, inviting them back to address it on their aspirations.

The Arab-American community in general, and the Palestinian-American community in particular, was galvanized by the event. Truly, November 1974 can be taken as the starting point of the proliferation of Palestinian activist groups in the United States and the emergence of those Palestinian figures who over the years became "spokespersons" of the Palestinian cause to the U.S. public. Certainly, political life in the Middle East in the wake of the October War and the tenor of Palestinian exceptionalism in it contributed to the desire of the media and the academic world for information about Palestinians by Palestinians. It was becoming increasingly clear that though Palestinians were Arabs, they were *Palestinian* Arabs, with unique problems. Who else, the argument went, is better qualified to speak about the Palestinian problem than Palestinians themselves? Neophytes in public relations, inept at the art of the quotable quote and inexperienced in the trick of the short answer during a two-minute interview, Palestinians did not do well initially. For many years hence, Palestinians disseminating information about their cause in the United States would assume a defensive posture, preoccupied with pleasing their audience. We are really, honestly, the injured party in the dispute and we are really, honestly, a nice, peaceful people once you get to know us. Then you'll realize the justice of our cause and your government will correct the wrong committed against us.

After many of my own encounters with the American public, in appearances on the Martin Agronsky show, the MacNeil-Lehrer report, and other national TV and radio programs, in articles I wrote for the op-ed page of the *New York Times,* the *Christian Science Monitor,* and other national papers, in lectures I gave on innumerable campuses, and in statements I made to the press, I would always be approached by Palestinians with the complaint that I was a bit too harsh. Too blunt. Too radical. How are we going to *niksab,* to gain the sympathy of Americans, with such intemperate language? How are we going to have the United States on our side if we *binzael,* alienate, Americans? Who was *niksab* and who was *binzael* Americans became a touchstone for determining the usefulness or uselessness of Palestinian activists in the United States.

There were, however, some of us who could not, because of our political background and social experience, drop that implacable harshness of tone we had set for ourselves as revolutionaries and adopt in its place the rhetorical sophistry of people aiming to please. We could not become Uncle Ahmads.

In the Arab world, however, appearances are deceptive. Despite their consensus at Rabat, the Arab regimes were very uneasy about the emerging power and influence of the PLO. They saw the Palestinian movement as a destabilizing force acting as a magnet to Arab revolutionaries and as a potential trigger for upheaval throughout the Arab world. Yet the Arab League resolution to accept the PLO as the sole, legitimate representative of the Palestinian people—thus frustrating King Hussein's ambitions to speak on their behalf and the American government's plans for the region—had a certain logic. The Arab governments realized that the Palestinian movement could not hope to secure their support for the cause without a corresponding abnegation of its freedom to pursue revolutionary goals. The level of support the PLO received from the Arab states varied inversely with the movement's level of maneuverability. This was consistent with the new order that was fast emerging in the Arab world in the wake of the October War.

Every major war in the Middle East between Arabs and Israelis has created a vacuum in the Arab world that was soon filled by forces in dialectical opposition to the ones that created the vacuum in the first place. The defeat of 1948 was soon followed by the emergence of Nasser and Nasserism, of Baathism and of a confrontationist Arab nationalism that toppled the monarchy in Egypt and Iraq and came close to doing so in Jordan. The Suez War of 1956 reinforced Pan-Arabism and Arab unity, as manifested in the emergence in 1958 of the United Arab Republic, the union between Egypt and Syria. The June War of 1967 brought to an end the twenty-year era of Pan-Arabist aspirations, which the Arab masses had put so much of their trust in and by which they now felt betrayed. The vacuum was filled by the emergence, from underground, of the Palestinian movement—no small event in modern Middle Eastern history.

And now the October War, seen as a "victory" by the Arab regimes and people, triggered its own dialectic. For the first time in a quarter century, the conservative Arab right was able to come out of the closet into a position of ascendancy and prestige. And this Arab right, centered in Riyadh, Cairo, Damascus, and Amman, formed a power bloc of awesome dimensions whose influence surpassed anything the nationalist camp of Pan-Arabism of the 1950s had ever achieved. Here was Saudi Arabia, with virtually all the capital in the Arab world; Egypt, with virtually all the population; Syria, with virtually all the mystique of the "heart of Arabism"; and Jordan, with virtually all the land border with Israel. A formidable power bloc indeed, with its own designs on the region, its own political values, and its own vision of conflict resolution. If the PLO, by being integrated into the Arab League as a member with the lofty title of "sole, legitimate representative of the Palestinian people," could be contained, the ability of the conservative Arab right to etch its dictates on the region would be greatly enhanced. "Containment" of the PLO would not, as some Arab states had hoped, liquidate the Palestinian movement, but surely it would stultify the PLO. And surely if the PLO deviated from the Arab League's charter and played revolutionary as it did in Lebanon in 1976 by siding with the nationalist forces against the Phalangists, it could be hit, as it was by the Syrian army that June, better when stultified than when vitalized.

In November 1974, when the Palestinian delegation was about to arrive in New York for the UN session, there was no PLO office in the United States, or anywhere else in the world for that matter. We were still a revolutionary, or at least a national liberation, movement, not dependent on the Arab states, not consumed by the image we projected to the West, and not weighed down by a vast bureaucratic elite and network of mediocre official representatives.

In downtown Manhattan, as I walk the city's grimy streets on my way to the United Nations, I hit the spot where a large demonstration of 60,000 Zionist Jews and their supporters are protesting the PLO visit. They are shouting racist slogans and venomous rhetoric at the Palestinian movement as Abba Eban and others address them. Do they really look upon the suffering of the Palestinian people as a moral or political gain for themselves? Do they wish, like Golda Meir when she said "the Palestinians do not exist," to reduce us and our homeland to fire-water, a substance that does not exist anywhere in nature? Do they want to use cash-and-carry brutality to deny us the right even to be heard?

As I stand at a street corner and contemplate the throngs and their barroom machismo, I have a formidable urge to scream, "You've got it all wrong. You've got it all wrong, do you hear?" Instead, I just continue standing there and, in frustration, point my middle finger and utter an expletive. At one point I look down and realize I am wearing a button calling for the release of Palestinian political prisoners form Israeli jails. I know the madness of crowds; they are the story of my life. I reach to cover the button, to pull it off, to hide it. But then I say, hell no, and my hand slowly moves down away from the button and I involuntarily again thrust my middle finger at the crowd in the obscene gesture I had learned in my own streets back home.

How do I convey to a crowd such as this the quality of my national experience and its roots in oppression? The pain of my father's death is alone enough to make me clutch them all by the throat. What do I say to a crowd like this? Come and live as Palestinians for just twenty-four hours, that's all. Our suffering is sixty years old, I'll begin. It is twenty years old. It is two minutes old. It begins and ends right here as I stand before you with a past bleeding memories and words bleeding colors. And as always they will begin by asking me to drink their strange sorrows and I will respond by telling them how I came into this life. But in the end, the gulf between us remains.

Some in the crowd are holding banners demanding "Arafat Go Home." That is fine with me. Those are the banners that we hold in our own demonstrations.

Unable to lay myself open to this crowd, I join another—directly outside the UN building. About six thousand Palestinians and their supporters were gathering, many just arrived on chartered buses from cities all along the East Coast. Old women in their embroidered Palestinian national dresses ululating to heaven. Men from Atlantic Avenue in Brooklyn who have closed their shops for the day. Children everywhere. Students, workers, teachers, accountants, and newly arrived Palestinian immigrants of peasant background whose English is still pronounced with the accents of the Arabic vernacular. But this is not a demonstration; it is a happening. There are no political speeches; just music, dance, and poetry. Here is a group dancing the *dabki* to the music of an improvised band of four youngsters playing the *oud,* the flute, and the *tablas.* And on a podium in another spot stands Rashid Hussein reciting angry poetry about how we are enraged not only at the whorehouse that the Arab world has become but at heaven, whose God has no one to punish Him for His sins as He goes about punishing ours.

Hussein was a truly tragic figure in our community of Palestinian-Americans. To begin with, he was an alcoholic. And his sense of guilt for having left Palestine voluntarily (he grew up as an "Israeli-Arab") was consuming him. His wife, who was Jewish, had left him some three years before and he was having problems even supporting himself. He lived in a small apartment uptown where he wrote prodigious amounts of poetry that he kept in shoeboxes. One night, not long after the UN demonstration, he burned to death when a fire started in his place while he was asleep and presumably drunk. When his body was returned home, no less than eighty thousand people turned out to march in the funeral cortege.

As Hussein descends from the podium he sees me in the crowd, waves his arms extravagantly over his head in warm greeting, and comes over to hug me.

"How are you, how are you lover of the masses?" he asks in a typical Palestinian greeting.

"May your tongue always be safe for the struggle," I respond in kind.

"And where are your *aradeek*—lands—these days?" he wants to know.

"In Cambridge, but I'm moving to Washington."

"May he who built that city be damned by both his parents."

I tell him I have no choice. It is not working out in Cambridge. He asks me if I want to have a drink after the demonstration and I say that I can't because I'm supposed to be part of the delegation—doing press releases, editing, and the like. Maybe later on in the evening, I add.

Behind us Palestinian women of peasant background are trying to shout in unison "Welcome, welcome, PLO." But the "k" sound is pronounced "ch" and "PLO" is a mouthful, because the letter "P" does not exist in our language. What they come up with is "Welchome, welchome beagle-go."

After the chanting dies down, one of the women walks up to us and says, "By the Lord, sons, it was different in Palestine in my day. We were fighting *inside* our homeland."

Security inside the United Nations is as intense as it is outside. I have never seen so many FBI agents and policemen concentrated in one place before. On my way to the escalator I am stopped by an agent who asks to see my special UN ID card (issued to me even before I arrived in New York). I fumble in my pockets but I cannot, for a moment, find it. Before I know what is going on a half dozen FBI agents are all around me asking who I am. Happily, I find my ID after fumbling nervously in my tote bag.

"Oh, PLO, ha?" one asks.

"Ya!"

"Go ahead, sir, you're clear," he responds, looking at me oddly, as if I were some strange, antigravitational creature from outer space. I suppose he couldn't reconcile the fact that a young man with a corduroy suit and a beard, who looked no different from many other Americans, could be, could *really* be, Pea-El-Oh.

I was introduced all around; to Farouk Kaddoumi, head of the foreign affairs department of the PLO; to Shafik el Hout, responsible for the Lebanon Desk; to Mahmoud Darwish, soon to become recognized as the national poet of the Palestinian people; and to the other dozen PLO journalists, writers, and officials attached to the delegation.

"We need you—now!" Nabil Shaath, head of the PLO delegation proclaims. "The PLO gets its right to rebuttal at the General Assembly tonight at 7:00 P.M. Can you draft a response to Tekoah's speech and have it ready by then?"

He was referring to Yosef Tekoah, head of the Israeli delegation, who had spoken two days before.

I tell him I haven't seen the man's speech and Shaath says jokingly that maybe I shouldn't bother reading it since I could guess what Tekoah had said about the Palestinians, namely that, in effect, we didn't exist and should seek a homeland in Jordan or one of the other Arab countries, since there were twenty-one of them.

"But of course we have a copy," he adds. "You can have my room."

"Okay, you bunch of terrorists, let's get to work," he says to the gathering mock-seriously.

The legacies of experience particular to our community have made it imperative that we seek inventive ways to endure, survive, and transcend the ravages of our material condition. "Terrorist" is of course the ultimate expression of the sense of otherness that others have afflicted us with since our emergence on the scene as a national liberation movement. Over the years we have unconsciously appropriated the term from those who first coined it, filtered it through some kind of reconstructive logic in our mind, and, not only given the original a withered, lifeless meaning, but turned it, by restatement and paraphrase, into a heuristic term of endearment. It is perfectly normal, at times even hip, to ask the whereabouts of a friend by saying "And where is that terrorist nowadays?" Similarly, in Jordan—that most outrageous of all two-bit police states in the Arab world—where Palestinians are not allowed to call themselves *Palestinian*, since as *Jordanian* citizens that represents "a negation of the legitimacy of the Kingdom," they go around calling themselves Belgians. "Is the brother from Belgium?" a fellow Palestinian would ask you in mixed company, thus defining you and him as sharing an identical posture of sensibility. Other terms, such as *refugee, Arab citizen, Arab government, autonomy, Resolution 242, el hawiya* (ID cards issued to Palestinians by their host states), *el hodoud* (crossing interstate borders in the Arab world), and *UNRWA*, have been similarly penetrated, modified, subverted, invalidated, and finally mocked.

Shaath's room next door turns out to be bare except for a table, a swivel chair, a typewriter, stationary supplies, and a sort of hospital bed. I had heard the man was a dedicated, hard-working revolutionary, but I hadn't thought him so dedicated and hard working that he would sleep on the premises.

"We won't let anyone bother you while you're working on the speech," the woman who shows me the room says.

I read Tekoah's speech a couple of times, underlining some of the outrageous paragraphs in it. Then I spend an hour drafting a response describing how the Palestinian people have developed a powerful relationship with their homeland over four thousand years that cannot be severed now to accommodate Zionist claims. Moreover, I explain that the *national* identity of the Palestinian people is now a concrete fact whose expression cannot be realized in a region other than the one where it originated. Our political program, I write, calling for the establishment of a secular, democratic state in the whole of Palestine for both Palestinians and Jews, represents a humanistic vision of a society that recognizes no oppressor-oppressed, occupier-occupied dichotomies. Palestinian violence, I conclude, is the only weapon left to the Palestinians—a colonized people—to ensure a hearing for the voice of moderation. Besides, I add, the world recognizes that the violence committed by slaves to break their chains is not the same as the violence committed by the slave master to subdue them.

No one spoke of a separate Palestinian state then; we were still preoccupied with convincing the international community that we were the injured party in the dispute.

As I reread what I have written, I realize even before anyone gets to see it that this speech is too literary, too romantic, too un-General Assemblyish. I rewrite it and Shaath seems satisfied. I stay for another hour or two, helping to draft the pathetic press releases the PLO is putting out that are directly translated from Arabic. Then I go to the General Assembly and sit at our six-seat spot in the very front to hear Farouk Kaddoumi read the speech I had labored over all day. Instead, I find he has drastically changed it. Oh, well, what the hell.

There is pitiless irony in our presence here, I say to myself as I look around the huge hall filled with member states representing virtually the whole planet. The majority of them weren't even states, let alone member states, when the UN General Assembly passed its resolution recommending the partition of Palestine twenty-seven years ago this week. We, of course, were neither present nor consulted. But that is how it was done in those days, when the United Nations was virtually a club controlled by the United States and Western Europe, supported by third world governments whose economic and political survival depended on those powers.

Within another week, the Palestinian delegation has done its job, officially etching our presence on the consciousness of the third quarter of the twentieth century and reminding the world of our presence and of our commitment to self-determination, a principle the United Nations holds sacrosanct. The two weeks the delegation spent around the General Assembly—two weeks that altered forever the way the world thought of Palestinians—led to the adoption, by overwhelming majority, of a series of resolutions that, in effect, negated the 1947 partition resolution and affirmed the right of the people of Palestine to statehood, independence, and freedom.

We were about to discover what a movement that originated as a revolutionary uprising by a disinherited people would produce when the pressure of diplomatic respectability is added to the many other burdens that it has traditionally shouldered.

I return to Cambridge and, somehow, go through the agony of the next few months. I am not cut out to be the husband of a Jewish woman who is suddenly rediscovering her Jewishness and her womanhood, or the father of a one-year-old baby who is picking up all the tension around it.

One evening while sitting at the Algiers Café—still writing bad poetry—I meet a Palestinian friend who tells me that a group of Palestinians, all mutual friends, have arranged a party somewhere on Beacon Hill.

What's the occasion? The friend says to celebrate Kissinger's failure to conclude some accord or other with some Arab leader or other. Already Kissinger is being called "my friend Henry" by Sadat of Egypt and getting lovey-dovey with Assad of Syria. The Palestinians are worried, suspecting the outcome of this rapport will be at their expense.

On the way to the party I stop at home. I find a note from my wife saying she's going "home" to Chicago. As I walk back down the stairs to rejoin my friends, just for a moment regret grips me, a feeling of emotional fatigue. I do not let the moment stretch. I do not care that my marriage is breaking up, that I am joining a group of Palestinians who have been reduced to celebrating, not victories, but a defeat for Kissinger's shuttle vulgarities. I feel too exhausted.

I have been in the United States just over a year. Already, I am set to take off again.

At the party, I get drunk and watch my friends dance. And sing. And talk politics. And recite poetry. And tell funny jokes about our condition. There are so many things that populate our space. But we can make peace only with dreams, emblazoned on some tattered rag, washed in tattered memories from a refugee camp. We are still like blind fireflies in the sky.

I return home at dawn and stagger into the living room, talking loudly to myself. On the mantlepiece is a photograph of the three of us, my wife, my child, and myself, sitting on the floor in front of a Christmas tree. Christmas is neither my wife's holiday nor my own, but we celebrated it anyway.

At that point Palestinians had not yet established any of those institutions, councils, and associations through which they were to speak so cogently to themselves and to the American people. Palestinian students, for example, were still integrated into the Organization of Arab Students (OAS). This was established in the 1950s, with chapters all over the world, including one on virtually every major, and some minor, campus in the United States. Its membership mirrored all the ideological, political, and social dichotomies that existed in the Arab world—between the rich and the poor, the powerful and the helpless, the secular and the sectarian, the radical and the conservative, as well as politics ranging from tribal traditionalism to proletarian socialism. To meet with these students, as I did on innumerable occasions in locales from San Francisco to New York to Chicago to Austin, was to encounter a microcosm of the modern Arab world and to get a glimpse of this generation of Arabs. After a while, I began to feel, despondently, that this was not a new generation, just another one.

I am waiting at Chicago's O'Hare Airport for a connection to Columbia, Missouri, where I am to deliver a lecture sponsored by the local chapter of the organization on campus. I recollect from previous engagements in Missouri, or from being told, that the chapter is composed predominantly of students from Saudi Arabia, Kuwait, Qatar, and the Gulf states. I have already made up my mind that I will be addressing students who will not tolerate or relate to my political views. Deep down in my heart, like it or not, I feel great resentment toward affluent people from that part of the Arab world. Though I often succeed in suppressing this resentment, which I attribute to a regionalist or elitist form of Palestinian chauvinism, it recurs every time I am somewhere, lecturing or visiting, and discover how the students from the Mashrek countries of North Africa are forever living on a shoestring, mopping floors in restaurants, waiting on tables, doing the night shift at gas stations, driving cabs, and working in factories to get a degree; yet their counterparts from the oil-rich states of the Peninsula not only drive around in sports cars, live in luxury apartments, and lead an impossibly decadent existence (I remember the case of a rich brat who not only lived in a palatial home with five stereo sets and purchased a new car every other month, he brought his black servant with him from Qatar) they also seemed jealous of their possessions, as if the wealth of the Arab world did not belong to all Arabs, and generous scholarships should not be made accessible to less fortunate Arab students from the refugee camps and the ghettos of the Arab capitals.

I sit in a lounge at O'Hare Airport waiting to board my connecting flight. Suddenly I notice a verbal commotion at the passenger service desk involving the ticket agent and a young couple. I look at the couple and say "Saudi Arabian" to myself—even before I hear their accent with their pronunciation of "people" as if the "p" were a "b." The woman, wearing an exquisite long Arabian dress, is holding a baby on her arm; her husband is in an ill-fitting Western suit and tie. I have never seen an individual more obviously fresh from the Arab world or more ill at ease in the hyped-up, bewildering world of O'Hare Airport than this man.

The man's wife is standing in the background as her husband is anxiously explaining to the ticket agent, in his improbable English, that he had just flown in from New York to connect with another flight from Chicago. Where are his three bags? What happened to them? Why have they not been unloaded? He is worried, he repeats.

The ticket agent is trying to explain that baggage is automatically loaded on connecting flights so passengers don't have to concern themselves with it. When he arrives at his ultimate destination, she says, it will be there for him to pick up, regardless of how many flights or connections he has made. But the man is either unconvinced or uncomprehending. He wants to know where his bags are *now*. Where are they?

Other passengers are in line to check in and the man continues talking. Is she absolutely sure they will be on his flight?

It is also my flight. I walk up to offer my help as a translator. He is delighted that I am an Arab, like him, and can help, although he is initially dubious about my intentions.

I translate for both of them, and he feels momentarily reassured. We sit together in the waiting area and talk for a few minutes. He tells me he has just arrived from Saudi Arabia to study on one of his government's scholarships. Then suddenly, in midsentence, he stops and asks me about his bags again. Are they safe? Am I sure they are safe?

I say they are and explain the system regarding passenger luggage. You do not have to worry, I repeat. Should we ask the woman at the desk *again* if his bags are really going to be on the flight? I say no, that will not be necessary. But he insists that he wants to speak to her and that I translate. And there is no dissuading him.

The ticket agent, still busy, begins to get impatient with him. Because she is talking to me, the translator, she levels her impatience at me.

Again we sit down. And again the Saudi talks about his bags; it is becoming intolerable. I want to tell him what he can do with his confounded bags; instead I just repeat everything the woman at the desk had told him. He settles down only after the flight is announced and passengers are lining up to get on board. All the while, his wife is unobtrusively sitting with the baby, neither participating in the conversation nor, in fact, bothering to listen to it.

We enter the plane and he sits next to me. His wife is sitting behind us. A few minutes before the plane is to take off, he looks through the window and sees attendants wheeling up the passenger luggage trolley for loading. He jumps up.

"I see them. I see them. There they are. My suitcases. I see them!" The man is literally shrieking.

He runs down the aisle and grabs a stewardess by the arm. "My suitcases. I want them. I see them," he tells her repeatedly and excitedly.

When the stewardess does not respond and expresses surprise at his outburst, he walks all the way down the aisle and into the cockpit where he taps the pilot on the shoulder. I watch him from my seat, as shocked at his behavior as the flight attendants and the passengers in the front. He is gesticulating wildly with his arms and pointing in the direction where his suitcases were—and pointing at me, presumably telling the pilot that I am his translator or friend or heaven knows what.

The pilot beckons to me. When I get to the cockpit, he asks: "What's all this about?"

I stand in front of them attempting to seem nonchalant.

"This gentleman is trying to say that he wants his bags on board with him."

"Why is that?"

I translate. The Saudi says to me in Arabic: "Because I have valuable stuff in them."

I translate back to the pilot.

"That's highly irregular," he says.

"But I must have my bags with me."

I translate again.

The pilot gives me a disturbed look, as if I am behind the whole charade.

"What nationality are you sir, anyhow?" he asks me directly.

"I am a Palestinian."

147

"Oh!"

Then silence, for a moment or two. I am a Palestinian. On a plane. Uneasy silence. For a moment. Or two.

"And what have you got in the bags?" he asks me pointedly. He is now no longer even looking at the Saudi.

"*I* haven't got *anything* in the bags. The bags are not mine."

"Whose bags are they?"

"They are his."

"Are you traveling together?"

"No. Not quite. I mean we have just met."

He turns around, walks into the cockpit, and speaks into his headphone, mumbling airline incoherencies to someone at the control tower. Before I know what is happening, nearly half dozen FBI agents and airport security police are swarming all around us, walkie-talkies in their hands and guns on their hips.

"Who is the Palestinian? Where is the Palestinian?"

It seems the question is coming from everywhere.

I am ushered off the plane along with the Saudi and his wife and child. We stand on the tarmac by the luggage trolley.

One agent says to me, "All right, pick up your suitcases."

"I keep telling you they are not mine."

"Whose are they?"

"They are his."

Even at that point, when I am already breaking out in a cold sweat, the Saudi Arab is completely, utterly, and innocently oblivious to the implications of what is going on. He actually picks up his bags and attempts to climb back on the plane, with his wife trailing behind him as he shouts contentedly to her "*Yallah, yallah imshi,* Come on, let's go."

Then we are taken inside the terminal building where we are ordered to wait as the fellow's bags are inspected and my plane takes off.

I am astounded to hear the Saudi utter, in fluent English and with great confidence, a phrase that someone had clearly urged him to learn by heart before he left his country for just such an occasion: "I want to see a representative of my embassy."

I laugh bitterly to myself. Whom do I, as a Palestinian, appeal to in a moment of crisis like this, when people find me fair game for abuse?

Four hours later on another flight, I sit back in my seat and close my eyes. I wonder about the symbolism in what has just happened. I wonder if this incident is not, after all, a microcosm of what has been happening to the Palestinians, all the time, these last sixty years, in our interaction with the Arab world on the one hand and the rest of the world on the other. Whenever Arab regimes lose a war, sign a treaty, search for a settlement, devise international and domestic policies, or simply interact with the West, it is always the Palestinians who suffer.

The most dramatic form of interaction the Arab establishment was ever to conduct with the West, or more specifically with the United States, was already taking place then. It was the beginning of 1976. The so-called confrontation states in the Arab world had already committed themselves to the Geneva Conference that both the United States and the Soviet Union were promoting as a forum through which the Arabs and the Israelis would reach a comprehensive settlement. No event of this kind had ever taken place before, a face-to-face encounter between Arabs and Israelis at an international conference whose objective was to resolve, once and for all, the territorial and political conflict between them.

The Palestinians, who saw themselves as the principal party in the dispute, were predictably insisting on an independent voice at the peace parley. And they were not prepared to pay the price that the Arab governments, not to mention the United States, were asking of them for admission: acceptance of UN Resolution 242. (Resolution 242, adopted by the UN Security Council immediately after the June War of 1967, was shaped to deal with the interstate dispute between the Arabs and Israel. It called for evacuation of the Arab territories captured by Israel in the war, for mutual recognition, and for a "just settlement of the refugee problem." No mention was made of the Palestinians except as refugees. The Palestinians, not surprisingly, overwhelmingly rejected the resolution as a basis for negotiations, and have remained unrelentingly opposed to it ever since.)

In 1976, not only were the Palestinians, by their rejection of Resolution 242, an impediment to the conservative Arab governments' design for a settlement; they were up to their necks in Lebanon's civil war, having sided with the Lebanese National Movement (LNM) against the fascist forces, embodied mostly in the Phalangist militias. By June of 1976, the combined Palestinian-Lebanese forces had for all intents and purposes defeated the Isolationists—as the fascists were known—and dislodged them from their strongholds around the Hotel District in West Beirut and around Damur in the south. Except for their little enclave in Juniyeh, north of Beirut, the Phalangists were on the run everywhere.

In those days it would have seemed odd, even inconceivable, to an observer who did not know the true sectarian, parochial politics of the Damascus regime, often perceived as "radical," to imagine that the Syrian army would invade Lebanon in June to reverse the military and political victories of the Lebanese National Movement and their Palestinian allies. But that was exactly what happened. The events in Lebanon represented a triple threat to the Damascus regime. Hafez Assad, the Syrian president, a man who had come to power in a military coup just six years before and ran a police state to keep that power, did not relish the emergence of a kind of people's republic, controlled by *national* forces, on his western flank. Wedged between that kind of state and a hostile Iraq, his regime would be doomed. Second, Assad feared a revolutionary Lebanon would give the Palestinians a free hand to attack Israel, potentially precipitating a war he was desperate to avoid. And finally, there was the prospect of the Geneva Conference and a peaceful settlement with Israel that his regime had already committed itself to. The PLO, with influence and power in a state ruled by a Lebanese National Movement that shared their ideological and political objectives, could easily torpedo the whole idea of Geneva should it feel the conference did not meet Palestinian demands.

It was not, of course, only Syria that was worried by the prospect of an LNM-Palestinian victory. Their concern was shared by Jordan, Egypt, and Saudi Arabia, who wanted to eliminate a potential threat to their goal of becoming the pivotal states in the Arab world, and to assure their realization of that goal by bringing "stability" to the region.

The Arab League gave Damascus its official green light to invade, under the improbable name of the Lebanon Peace-Keeping Forces. Israel was delighted and, as expected, expressed no objections.

The military resources of the combined Palestinian-Lebanese forces were no match for the massive firepower of the Syrian army.

But the war went on for a good five months, during which the Syrians suffered massive blows in hit-and-run operations, especially in Sidon in the south and around Bhamdoun in the mountains. Assad's army, in turn, showed a fanatic, often barbarous, streak in its attacks on Palestinian refugee camps, where Palestinian guerrillas and militias traditionally operated.

The most savage of these attacks was on Tel Zaatar, Hill of Thyme, a Palestinian camp perched on a hill strategically located between East and West Beirut and thus of importance to the movement of military supplies on the highway between the two sectors of the city and between West Beirut and the mountains. By July, after repeated attempts, the Syrians and their fascist allies had still been unable to penetrate the camp and overrun it. The resistance by the population, the militias, and the guerrillas inside was, rhetoric aside, no less than heroic. The camp was put under siege—and remained so for forty-three days. Its water and electricity were cut off. No food or medicine was allowed in. Thirty thousand Palestinian men, women, and children were trapped inside.

The fascists, with support from the Syrians, pounded the camp with artillery shells, day and night. Day and night, with no respite between the setting of the sun and the break of dawn, between the noon sun and the midnight wind. Big bowflies, and emaciated dogs and cats, fed on dead bodies lying in the lanes, in the front yards of abandoned homes, and around the water wells. Children were dying of dehydration. Fighters were dying of unattended wounds. Civilians were dying of starvation and thirst. Fascist snipers perched around the camp shot at anyone and anything that moved. Their guns were aimed at any structure not already in ruins. Camp dwellers, crazed by thirst, attempted to sneak out at night, crawling on all fours, to nearby wells. Those who made it came back with their water mixed with their oozing blood. Near the end of the siege a building in the middle of the camp collapsed on the people who had taken shelter there, killing over two hundred.

By that time, negotiators from the Red Cross and the Syrians and fascists had resulted in an agreement calling for the evacuation of the camp by all Palestinians in return for safe passage to West Beirut.

But the ordeal did not end there. On their way to the western half of the city, many stragglers were killed off by fascist gunmen who lined the highway. Boys over the age of fourteen were abducted and were never seen again. Fourteen nurses who had worked at the Tel Zaatar hospital were lined up and shot dead. Only their doctor, ironically, survived. Apparently the leader of the fascist gang who had stopped them, recognized him as the doctor who had treated him some years before and spared his life. But he refused all entreaties to spare the nurses.

"It is the duty of every Lebanese to kill at least one Palestinian," one of the fascist leaders, Abu Arz, had once proclaimed.

The children, arriving in West Beirut without parents or relatives, were traumatized. The men and women were in shock. So were all Palestinians, all over the world, as news of the slaughter spread. Tel Zaatar came only six years after Black September, another seminal event in Palestinian history that brought with it images of pain beyond all rational understanding.

The Palestinians in Lebanon began to rebuild, in the wake of the confrontations with Syria, and to rehabilitate, in the wake of Tel Zaatar. They also held a Palestine National Council session in Cairo, which came out with a conciliatory political program accepting not only the principle of a negotiated settlement but, for the first time ever, the idea of a separate state, which they euphemistically called a "national authority" on any part of Palestine "to be evacuated by or liberated from" the Israelis.

Everybody, at least in the Arab world, now seemed ready for the Geneva Conference.

Five months later in January 1977, Jimmy Carter was sworn in as president of the United States. In June, to the shock and consternation of everyone who knew his background in terror and right-wing extremism, Menachem Begin was elected prime minister of Israel. Five months after that, on November 19, 1977, leaving Geneva and the idea of a comprehensive settlement by the wayside, Anwar Sadat of Egypt went on an official visit to Jerusalem. And ten months after that, on September 17, 1978, the Camp David Accords—in effect, a separate peace treaty between Egypt and Israel—were signed.

The Camp David Accords were piously advertised as a major step toward resolution of the core issue in the Mideast conflict, the Palestine question. But the Palestinians saw the accords for what they were, yet another agreement signed over their heads, disregarding their pleas, and in their absence. This time by a former Pole who had moved to Palestine, a former army officer from Egypt, and a former peanut farmer from Georgia. Even those Palestinians who may have had naive expectations that the Camp David summit in Maryland could come up with a workable solution found the accords worse than worthless: mortifying.

The accords promised the Palestinians a "self-governing authority" on the West Bank and in Gaza. The nature of that authority, its modalities, powers, and responsibilities, were left "to be determined by Israel, Jordan, and Egypt." After a five-year transitional period, negotiations on the future of the West Bank–Gaza would start, this time *possibly* with representatives of the authority. Not only was the future of these territories left undefined, but "the delegations of Egypt and Jordan may include Palestinians from the West Bank and Gaza or other Palestinians as mutually agreed." That was the point: Palestinians *may* be included, contingent on *mutual* agreement. (More devastating still, from the point of view of Palestinians living outside Palestine, was the accords' division of the Palestinian people into separate and disturbingly named categories, with a separate formula for dealing with each: "the refugee problem," "the inhabitants of the West Bank," and "those displaced from the West Bank and Gaza in 1967." Mercifully, they did not speak of, assign a different fate to, or confer dehumanizing names on other categories of Palestinians, such as those displaced or deported from the West Bank–Gaza *since* 1967, those who stayed behind in their homeland in 1948 and became "Israeli Arabs," or those who did not, for their own reasons, register with the United Nations Relief and Works Agency as "refugees.")

Israel of course had every intention of vetoing any arrangement that could have led to anything resembling self-government, or ultimately statehood, where Palestinians—even in this tiny remnant of Palestine—could exercise their will, safeguard their rights, and define their nationhood. This was beyond dispute soon after the negotiations between Egypt and Israel started—Jordan refused to participate—and collapsed a year later.

Begin got precisely what he wanted from Camp David: a reincarnation of his own Begin Plan of December 1977. At that time, soon after his election, debate in Israel raged over a major contradiction in Zionism, at least as defined by Begin himself, his party, his coalition supporters, and other right-wing groups imbued with the notion of *Eretz Israel*. To be sure, the debate had started, though not as vehemently, as early as June of 1967, soon after the conclusion of the military conquest of the two remaining remnants of Palestine, the West Bank and Gaza.

The debate centered on the messianic notion in Zionism that the Jews had a historical imperative to control and keep the newly acquired territories, since they formed a part of *Eretz Israel*. The notion, however, represented a contradiction for its adherents, since it came with a demographic imperative: the incorporation of well over a million Palestinians into the social, political, and economic life of the *Jewish* state. This community, together with the 600,000 Palestinian Arabs already living in Israel, would in time jeopardize the majority status of Jews in Palestine, without which Theodore Herzl's Zionist dream of a *Judenstaat* would be rendered unworkable.

The debate over how to keep the land but isolate the people simmered quietly in the late 1960s but more intensely a decade later following Begin's election. (The late Premier Levi Eshkol likened this debate to a Russian story about a would-be groom torn between his strong desire to lay his hands on the dowry and his unwillingness to take the bride.) There were many "proposals" that floated around at the time. Moshe Dayan suggested "an Arab Bantustan" in the *Times* of London on June 16, 1967. Begin suggested as early as an interview published in the *New York Times* on September 4, 1967, simply annexing the territories without conferring political rights or citizenship on the inhabitants. Some right-wing activists sought a final solution to the problem through engineering a mass emigration of the Palestinian population.

The Sadat visit precipitated a compelling need for a formula for reconciling the expansionism of *Eretz Israel* with the exclusivism of the *Judenstaat*. The answer was the Begin Plan of December 1977, offered only weeks after Sadat's initiative.

This plan, which presaged the Camp David Accords in many uncanny ways, separated the fate of the Palestinians from the land. They would have "self-rule," but the land would effectively continue to be ruled by Israel and the military occupation would remain in place. The question of sovereignty would be "held in abeyance" and Israel would veto any competing claims or challenges, in projected negotiations, to its "right" to determine the future of the conquered territories of the West Bank–Gaza.

So much for the widely trumpeted Camp David Accords.

Mohammed Anwar Sadat may have been mocked by his people for his repressive policies, and isolated by the Arabs for being a buffoon and allowing Begin to pull a fast one on him, but he was despised by the Palestinians as no one has been in their modern history. For he, very simply, sold them out—and sold them out very cheaply. It dishonors our Revolution and its fallen patriots, Palestinians went about saying, if we allow this treacherous creature to remain alive for long.

The Palestinians were shocked, scandalized, and enraged even before the Camp David Accords were signed. They could see what was coming not only in Sadat's speech to the Knesset, in which he did not even mention the PLO, but in the increase in brutalities under the occupation and the raids that the Israeli air force was mounting almost daily in Lebanon, culminating in a major invasion of the south of Lebanon in March 1978.

Palestinian institutions in Lebanon sprang up or, if they had been established previously, grew substantially: the Samed workshops, the Palestine Red Crescent Society, the Palestine Folk Troupe, the Palestine Research Center, the Palestine Cinema Institute, and all manner of orphanages, hospitals, schools, and the like. Political organizations, such as the General Union of Palestinian Women, the associations, and councils already in existence, bringing together writers, teachers, workers, and other professionals, were becoming more activist. And this was happening all over the world, wherever Palestinians lived in sizable numbers.

In addition, the war that the Lebanese army launched against the Palestinians and their Lebanese allies in 1973 had never stopped; it had simply expanded, intensified, and become more complex as it drew in the Syrian regime, whose aim was to serve the interests of Arab reaction by recreating Lebanon in its own image; Israel, whose aim was to depopulate the south and terrorize the north, thus turning the Lebanese masses against the Palestinians; and the United States, whose aim was to return Lebanon, through the use of its agents in the country and elsewhere in the Arab world, to the *status quo ante,* when it was free of the PLO and of the revolutionary ferment that the PLO had fostered there over the years.

As one PLO official, Abu Kifah, described these years in an oral history narrative,* "It was like a video game, like Pac Man, you know. There was a battle to fight everywhere. No sooner did you finish one than another would erupt elsewhere, in an unexpected place. The bug was insatiable, inscrutable. You couldn't pin him down. We and the brothers from the LNM would put out the fires of one disaster one place, conclude a battle in another, and settle a dispute in yet another, only to have more disasters, battles, and disputes crop up elsewhere, in the most unexpected place, at the most unexpected time. You see, the forces we were fighting against were not only elusive, coming at you from the three directions [of the imperialist, Zionist, and reactionary camps] but they were smarter than we were, more experienced, more resourceful. You know, these people, I suspect, had read Guevara more assiduously than we had. They knew the first step on the road to disarming a revolutionary is not to take his gun away from him, but to take the people away from him."

To disarm the Palestinians and their allies in Lebanon, for example, the Israelis mounted massive and repeated air raids on the south, deliberately targeting civilian centers. The population, in terror, would flee their homes and seek refuge to the north. In July 1979 alone, it was estimated that no less than half a million people from South Lebanon evacuated their towns, villages, and fields for refuge in abandoned homes, schools, and parking lots in Sidon and Beirut, creating social tension and chaos.

"If Lebanon had been fighting as a *revolutionary state*," continued the PLO official, "then the revolutionary resources of the state, from the media to the police, would've been mobilized to inform the public and take care of its immediate needs. In Lebanon the opposite was true. The resources of the state, owned and controlled by it and by those social classes supportive of it, went to work to mobilize the mass sentiment against the revolutionary forces. 'You see,' they would say, 'if it weren't for the Palestinians, you wouldn't be suffering that way. They are the cause of your plight.' When the blows kept coming, not only in the south but virtually everywhere in Lebanon, there came a point where they couldn't take it any more. Not because they were becoming anti-Palestinian, or because they did not instinctively side with the Revolution, but because there was a limit

*In an unpublished collection of oral history interviews, the Palestine Research Center in Cairo and the Middle East Resource Center in Washington.

to their endurance. The Israelis destroyed hospitals, schools, homes, farms, roads. They disrupted, in a very systematic way, the very fabric of social life in Lebanon."

As more Lebanese found themselves refugees in their own country, not only those from the south who came north but also those who at times fled from one city to another in the same region, indeed at times some who sought refuge in one neighborhood from another, tension mounted. Refugees, in a pitiful bid for shelter, would break into homes, or squat in schools and mosques. Hospitals were occupied. The unrest intensified as refugees arriving in a region to escape the bombing would find it as much of a killing zone as the one they had fled, compelling them to take off again to become refugees for a second, third, or fourth time.

The assault against the Palestinian cause came not only from without, in the form of an imposed settlement from Washington, pressure by the Arab regimes "to see reason," defection by Cairo, a distraction by the Arab masses at large from the issue of Palestine and from the suffering the Palestinians were enduring in exile and under occupation; the assault came also from within. The alienation of Palestinian society from the Arab world was becoming a profound metaphysical scandal. Thus the frenzy of institution building— *Palestinian* institutions. The General Union of *Palestinian* Writers, the *Palestine* Research Center, the *Palestine* Folk Troupe, and the *Palestine* Cinema Institute were all established and justified by the Palestinians on the grounds that their nation-in-exile needed institutions that could be transplanted intact to Palestine when the independent state was finally established. Palestinians even had special designs cut for postage stamps in anticipation of the day.

This frenzy of institution building, which peaked around that time, was moving outward from Lebanon in concentric circles to touch every community in exile. It was not long before it reached the Palestinian community in the United States.

So far, the Palestinians in the United States had been satisfied to operate within the context of small, regional organizations in their own cities or, at best, states. The national organizations—if there was ever more than one, the Arab-American University Graduates

Association—were *Arab*-American, not *Palestinian*-American. Many Palestinians felt a need for a truly national Palestinian organization that would institutionalize, and give expression to, the voice of the Palestinian community in North America, a region where the Palestinian struggle for statehood and freedom was both misunderstood and maligned. Moreover, the passions of our North American exiles are equally as authentic Palestinian passions as those of our compatriots back "in the countries."

In early 1978, a few small, local groups in New York had gotten together to discuss the issue. There was unanimous agreement that a national Palestinian organization was an idea whose time had come. To agitate for it, they contacted a dozen or so local groups around the country to canvass their views. The response was, for the most part, enthusiastic. More contacts were made by one group with another. More ideas exchanged. More ambiguities ironed out.

A meeting, called the All Palestine Congress, was held in New York on December 1–2. The two days of deliberations by delegates representing at least one hundred groups nationally—interspersed by poetry readings, guitar singing, folk dancing, and declarations of solidarity by American supporters—culminated in the decision to hold a formal conference, the Palestine American Congress, Constitutional Convention, in Washington, D.C., on August 17–19 of 1979. A committee was established to write a constitution for consideration by the congress. Area conferences were to be held all over North America in the last week of July to elect delegates.

By July it was becoming obvious that Palestinians all over North America were anticipating the congress with both seriousness and enthusiasm. Groups in faraway places in Canada were writing for information. Palestinians in Puerto Rico and the Virgin Islands promptly sent in their application forms. "At last, at last, we're organizing in this country," an old man from Jenin, standing behind the counter in his little grocery store in Charlotte, Virginia, was incessantly proclaiming to his Palestinian customers, "we're doing something."

Palestinians were ready to bring all the passions of their North American exile, all the passions of the sixty years of struggle of which they were existentially the product, to a national organization they hoped would ultimately impose harmony on, and give full expression to, their self-definitions. No mean task.

158

I wonder about all this as I pore over the congress literature in front of me. Why has this idea gripped Palestinians around the country? Why, specifically, now? After all, for the most part Palestinians have been content to be active these last twelve years with other Arabs in Arab-American political organizations. Why the need now for a *Palestinian* one? Has there been a shift—unconscious, deep-rooted—in the political psyche of Palestinians here? And if so, does it reflect an identical shift in the psyche of Palestinians back "in the countries"? Are Palestinians over the years, in their exile, in their different spacial realities, going through different transformational processes, acquiring a different subjective relatedness to their Palestinianness and to their ongoing struggle to define it? Have they become so alienated from other Arabs, at this point in history, that they feel the need to speak separately because they have separate aspirations?

In the middle of 1979 the American government was discovering how much a prisoner it had become to the contradictions inherent in its commitment to Israel. In one breath, American officials, including President Carter, were declaring that the PLO should recognize the right of Israelis to a state and, in another, they were saying that they were against the concept of a state for the Palestinians. At one point, in a display of total nonsense, President Carter even said that "a Palestinian state would not be good for the Palestinians." Moreover, they were saying that only when the PLO "recognized" Israel would the United States conduct a dialogue with the Palestinian movement—presumably just for dialogue's sake, since these officials made it known in no uncertain terms that they would not only oppose Palestinian statehood, but would veto any revised or new version of UN Resolution 242 that included a call for self-determination for the Palestinians.

In the middle of August it was revealed that the American ambassador to the United Nations, Andrew Young, a black American former activist in the civil rights movement, had met privately with the PLO's UN representative to discuss postponement of the Security Council debate on revision of Resolution 242.

The media went mad. The Israelis, with their usual pathological

159

response to anything connected with the Palestinian liberation movement, went berserk. The machinery of the State Department and the White House went haywire. Within twenty-four hours, Young was fired.

"I did nothing wrong," the former civil rights leader stated. "I would do it all over again." He went on to identify his government's attitude toward the PLO as "ridiculous."

I was having dinner that night with an older Palestinian intellectual who had been active in the labor movement in Palestine back in the 1920s and 1930s. Chuckling happily over his stuffed squash, the man said, "The United States is a dumb elephant."

While Israel raved and ranted about a change in American foreign policy; while the White House issued clarifications about the Young affair; and while commentators quoted their sources on the background of the meeting between the U.S. and Palestinian officials at the United Nations, Palestinians, all over the North American continent, were getting on their flights for Washington, D.C., for the Palestine American Congress convention.

There was something beautifully mischievous and defiant, beautifully lawless and outrageous, about Palestinians entering the third quarter of the twentieth century. I wonder if it is *lomo,* that quality of endurance characteristic of a people whose spontaneity in struggle, whose unpredictability, and whose nose for history are beyond the ability of linear thinkers to define or comprehend.

Much of that mischief and defiance, that lawlessness and outrage, was in evidence at the Palestine American Congress, the largest official gathering outside the Arab world up to that time of Palestinians bent on etching a presence and asserting a reality to speak to the world and to each other of the pain and ecstasy of what Palestine is all about.

The Shoreham Americana, a first-class hotel on a tree-lined street in downtown Washington, is a most unlikely place for a revolutionary gathering—or a gathering predominantly tuned in to a revolutionary movement. Yet, that is what the roughly eight hundred Palestinian delegates, observers, and guests were, whether they were young or old, students or workers, old women and men in their traditional peasant dress or middle-class, middle-aged affluent Palestinians who had lived in the United States for many years and carved out a comfortable existence for themselves, or young men and women with markedly ideological leanings determined to ensure that the politics of the congress was responsive to their perspectives.

The congress kicks off with solidarity statements. A representative from the black American revolutionary All-African Peoples Party salutes the struggle of the Palestinian people for freedom and condemns imperialism and Zionism. He is followed by another black American, an assistant to the black congressman from the District of Columbia, who dwells on how unjust it was that "Andy" was forced to resign under fire because of his contact with the PLO. The American government should "talk" to the PLO, he adds. When he finishes his remarks, a trifle too long for a solidarity statement, he is given some polite applause.

The representative from the Lebanese National Movement, a man in his early thirties with an impeccable command of classical Arabic, tells the gathering, "You are not dispersed, because you live in freedom and dignity. It is those who belong to a nation and are not living in freedom and dignity who are dispersed."

A statement of support and good wishes from the PLO representative in New York, who by law is not allowed to venture more than thirty miles from the city, is read to the applause of the audience.

The keynote speaker is the mayor of Ramallah, a handsome man in a neat, well-tailored suit. He is given a standing ovation and the well-known Palestinian slogan, "Revolution, revolution, till victory," is shouted over and over again.

"I come from occupied Palestine to be with you," he begins. "I speak to you as brother to brother, militant to militant." He tells the audience that the American taxpayer is indirectly paying the Israelis to kill, occupy, exile, and hurt Palestinians. The American public should know the facts about occupation. He narrates stories about deportations, torture, land expropriation, collective punishment, political repression, exploitation, and the hoodlum practices of Israeli settlers.

"America is not working for peace," he says. "It has buried peace in the White House, in the Camp David Accords. America talks peace while it arms and supports the enemies of peace," he says, his voice rising a trifle.

Characteristically, the mayor from time to time quotes lines of poetry to make his point, which of course goes down very well with a Palestinians audience.

A chorus of youngsters from time to time shouts out slogans: *To lay down our arms, never; never, never, shall we lay down our arms*, and *Revolution, revolution till victory*.

The mayor loses some of his audience when he gets defensive, claiming that "we are not terrorists, we want peace." He makes up for it, however, by ending on a defiant note. "Jews came to settle in Palestine," he shouts. "We did not ask them to come. They came by force! No to Resolution 242 and no to an amended version of it."

He gets another standing ovation.

Then everybody files out of the big hall, spilling into the corridors. I saw little hint of the fireworks that were sure to come the following day at the first session of the congress.

At eight o'clock in the morning, passions are already raw. Everybody is seated in rows along long tables. Everybody is quiet, neither talking nor distracted. None of the four hundred official delegates is late. From the gallery where I am seated with the other observers and guests, the delegates seem young, earnest, serious, as if they know they are on a historic mission of sorts. The meeting is chaired by a Palestinian lawyer, born in the United States, one of half dozen men and women who in the previous three or four months had spent hundreds of manhours to get the congress together. He speaks no Arabic, but does not betray any defensiveness about it. His voice, however, like his boyish demeanor, does not carry across the hall. Although he does not have a stage presence, he does have, as is revealed later, great reserves of patience and masochistic tendencies.

First order of business. The minority at the congress, which comprises a not insignificant number of delegates representing the Popular Front and the Democratic Front, including less than half a dozen from the Arab Liberation Front, want to question the right of Palestinian "charity" groups, such as the United Holy Land Fund (UHLF), to send so many delegates to the congress—thereby, presumably, tipping the scales even further in favor of the majority, representing Fatah.

"We question the membership lists of the UHLF," a Popular Front delegate is shouting into the microphone.

In defense, an official of the charity organization takes to the microphone in the aisle and explains that his group has always been active, sending medicine to the Red Crescent, bringing the Palestinian Folk Troupe to the United States for a tour, collecting "as much as $2 million" since 1967 for the educational, social, and cultural needs of Palestinians under occupation, and so on. When he says that his organization has sixteen thousand members, the opposition erupts in sustained hisses and boos.

Quite a few individuals are talking at once. Others are standing to shout they have a point of order to make. The Chair recognizes an "independent," who proceeds to ask "for tolerance" saying, "I ask you, I plead with you, not to forget that we are all Palestinians. I plead with you not to forget the major task before us in this congress."

His voice is virtually drowned by sneers from the radical factions and applause from the other side. For a while, it seems that everybody is standing up demanding recognition from the Chair or shouting accusations across the hall. An older man, with a booming voice, grabs the microphone and hollers into it: "Brothers! Brothers, what *is* it with you? Are you going to liberate Palestine from *here*?"

Please be seated, the Chair is repeating over and over again. *Please be seated. Please be seated. Please be seated.* Yet no one heeds the call.

Children are running in the gallery. Many of the women delegates have babies in their arms. From one side of the hall, a youngster from the majority faction shouts across at the opposition: "We are sons of the camps. No one can accuse *us* of being undemocratic." Hurled back at him is the remark, "Yeah? Well, you are also the sons of Resolution 242."

Please be seated. Please be seated. Please be seated.

I wince. Maybe it is a combination of my lack of sleep the night before, my fatigue, and my hangover, but suddenly I feel a formidable urge to walk out. Instead, I just close my eyes. I cannot, so early in the morning, be witness to the passions of sixty years of Palestinian history, sixty years of contradictions in Palestinian society, spilling out here in microcosm. It is too overwhelming.

Please be seated. Please be seated. The Chair's appeal continues to be ignored.

One young delegate, a man who runs a gas station in Chicago, stands up and demands to be heard.

Please be seated.

163

"I will continue talking until I'm recognized," he shouts. And he does exactly that.

Please be seated. Please be seated.

Verbal side fights erupt all over the hall. Some delegates appeal to the fighters for calm; others ask everyone to please be seated.

Please be seated.

The Chair has obviously lost all control of the gathering.

What now? I feel a knot in my stomach. Have I in my writings all these years been overly romantic in defining my people? Is this a case of Palestinians taking out their frustrations and rage against each other because they have nowhere else to go with them? Or is it, most probably, the inevitable interaction of energies flowing from a people debating an issue that is the very core of their life and its commitments?

Whatever answer one may give, all of this is a fragment of Palestinian history and a manifestation of its pain.

The meeting is finally recessed for ten minutes.

Immediately, animated conversations erupt all around the hall. I am sorry I cannot tape some of them (recorders, for some reason, were not allowed) to capture the moment for a Palestinian psychohistorian of the future, studying us from the vantage point of a free and independent Palestine.

Ten minutes later, *Please be seated. Please be seated.*

Surprisingly, everybody sits—and quietly. We are surrounded by total silence and calm.

"I move to accept the credentials of the charity organizations," an older man is saying into the microphone. He adds that if anything, we want to increase, not decrease, their membership figures. "Look at the Zionists, and how they falsify their records."

Someone from the opposition takes the floor and says, "We are a democratic people. Ours is a democratic revolution. We want this congress to be an authentic reflection of our people's wishes. Palestine will be liberated not by fictitious names, but by democracy. We do not want to imitate the enemy."

Another man from the opposition says, "We salute the work done by the United Holy Land Fund, but we question the authenticity of its membership total. We feel that powerful elements among the majority here want to take over the congress. We of course salute our brothers and sisters in Fatah as patriots in the liberation of Palestine, but who are these members of the UHLF and who has elected them? We shall remain in the congress. We are here to contribute to its establishment and not its destruction."

A few individuals, lulled by his calm tones, come forward to call for moderation and tolerance. We are a people fragmented, persecuted, and denied our freedom, they say; Palestine is occupied and our national rights are denied. An older man with graying hair and thick glasses, declares, his voice a trifle too high "O brothers, O sisters, foreign eyes are watching us. And the criminal Begin is killing our women and children."

And so it goes on until the Chair proclaims the debate closed. The voting begins. Two hundred and forty-three votes are cast against the challenge to the credentials of the charity organizations. The total for the challenge is 114 votes.

Everybody breaks for lunch.

The corridors have a profusion of T-shirts proclaiming revolutionary legends, scarves with "Palestine" printed on them, gold necklaces made in the shape of Palestine to be worn around the necks of men and women, *hattas*, and Palestinian embroidered dresses. Everywhere I see people whose idiom, gestures, and tensions express the world experienced and inhabited by Palestinians. Though they were at each others' throats only a moment ago, tearing apart each others' concepts, they all share a common sense, a common resource, of feeling. To all these Palestinians—though at different transformational points in their intellectual development and embracing a diversity of ideological currents and social sensibilities—Palestine as a country, as a vision of liberation, has always been a dominant value in their lives. Its pain and joy, the ebb and flow of its struggle, have been an indivisible part of their identity. They have come to realize, these last three decades, that when their heads were pushed against the whetstone of persecution, the persecutor did not ask if they were radical or conservative, rich or poor, Muslim or Christian, secular or sectarian. The persecutor merely asked if they were Palestinian.

I think to myself that if I know our people and their inner resources, this congress will succeed.

I walk out of the hotel with a friend who has recently arrived in the capital to study at Georgetown University. He has only been in town for a couple of days but, though he had spent all his life in the Arab

165

world, seems very much at ease here. At ease with himself and with his identity. It does not bother him much that he does not know what the waitress means when she asks "what kind of dressing" he wants with his salad. He was as amused at the word "dressing" as he was shocked that a salad dressing came prepackaged in a little plastic container.

"May Americans be damned by both their parents for the way they cook and eat their food," he says flippantly.

We talk about Beirut, where he works at WAFA, the Palestinian news agency, and about how Palestinians living in diverse locales around the world should visit "the liberated zone" in Lebanon. Literally thousands of Palestinians, he tells me, have been converging on Lebanon in the last year or two, from Kuwait, Jordan, England, South America, the United States, Canada, and other parts of the world where there are large Palestinian émigré centers. I tell him that Palestinian groups had been arranging for Palestinian-American children to go to Lebanon to live with Palestinian families, attend Palestinian schools, meet with other Palestinian children, and pick up Palestinian Arabic as a second language.

"We have Palestinian children from South America doing that every summer," he says. "But beyond the children, we also need adults who will do the same thing. An individual life history, no matter how rich, will remain meaningless when divorced from its social, cultural, and political milieu."

I realize how right he is as I listen to him talk in his Palestinian idiom, which not only has remained intact but includes all the new modes of speech that have emerged over the last twenty years. I, in effect, am listening to words that I no longer use, a turn of phrase that is no longer part of my syntax, an idiom that I am no longer at ease with. What he is doing, just by talking to me in the authentic *argot* of my native tongue, is restoring the emotional atmosphere of my culture.

"You must go to Beirut, and you must do it at once," he says seriously, as if reading my thoughts.

"I will, I will," I respond with passion. "And how I need to be there!"

Please be seated. Please be seated. The delegates take ten minutes to do so.

The preamble in the constitution is to be discussed and voted upon. The majority, representing Fatah, wants to amend a phrase in the preamble that reads, "The Palestinian community in North America affirms its support of the Palestinian people's struggle to realize its national rights, including its right to return to its national homeland, to national self-determination, and to its national independence and sovereignty in all of Palestine."

They want to delete the words "all of."

Immediately, the gathering is charged with enormous tensions— and all hell breaks loose. Even I, a writer who has long since resigned himself to accepting the existence of diverse ideological sensibilities among my people, am shocked.

Please be seated. Please be seated.

The logic behind the majority's motion, presumably, is to ensure that, in the event that a "separate" state in the West Bank and Gaza Strip are established, the preamble will not bind Palestinian-Americans to go against it. The opposition is accusing the other delegates of treason. The women in the opposition, for a reason I cannot discern, are far more vociferous than the men. One of them, with a baby on her arm, is gesticulating wildly and claiming that no one, but no one, has the right to alter the phrase "in all of Palestine" in the proposed constitution. Her voice is reaching a crescendo. Her child begins to cry, trying to free himself. She moves him to the other arm in a distracted, impatient manner. "Palestine is sacrosanct. Palestine is sacrosanct, I tell you!" she screams.

Please be seated. Please be seated. Please be seated.

A Fatah woman—though less vociferously—is shouting back that not one can accuse "us" of not wanting the liberation of "the whole of Palestine."

Not to be outdone, another woman from the opposition is hollering: "You bunch of 242s!"

"I struggle more than you do. I was in jail. I was tortured!" This is from a Fatah woman wearing glasses. "Do you accuse *us* of not wanting the liberation of *the whole* of Palestine?"

For a while it seems that this is a battle of Palestinian women. Palestinian women, in this congress at least, are clearly more emotionally and ideologically involved than the men.

Across the hall, some people are shouting "communists" at the opposition.

"I am not a communist. I just don't want to compromise my history and my country," someone shouts back.

Brothers and sisters, be calm. Do you want to destroy your congress? Are they questioning our revolutionary integrity? Do we struggle less than they do?

Please be seated. Please be seated.

To change the preamble, there are 243 for, 127 against, and 4 abstentions.

Please be seated. Please be seated. I will not recognize anyone who is standing.

Everybody, in the end, is seated.

A delegate from the opposition comes forward and proposes an amendment to the proposed constitution calling for condemnation of Zionism, imperialism, and Arab reaction.

Another ruckus greets this.

Those in favor take to the microphone to argue, one after another, that this is already an integrated slogan, not a contested idea, in the Palestinian Revolution. Those opposed say, defensively, that it may "offend" some Arab regimes who are "currently with us."

A PLO representative in an oil-producing country who is attending the conference is challenged by a Popular Front woman "to take the microphone and tell us, once and for all, whether or not you are against Arab reaction."

The Chair calls on him to do that.

Right then, as the PLO representative leaves his seat, all the microphones break down, incredibly enough. They were probably too weak to take this flow of energy, these impassioned arguments.

The meeting is adjourned for ten minutes and resumes in another hall.

Like everybody else, I am eager to hear what the PLO representative is going to say. Will he, being put on the spot like this, admit that "Arab reaction" is a target of the Palestine liberation movement?

Instead, he stands up and chastises the audience for being "disorganized." He adds that he had no idea his people would "stoop" to such levels of chaos. He does not mention "Arab reaction." Yet he gets a standing ovation from his bloc, who are the majority by a ratio of two to one. The opposition and the independents smile bitterly.

Please be seated. Please be seated.

A vote is taken. The phrase "Arab reaction" will not to appear in the constitution.

The opposition delegates pound on their tables, calling out "traitors, traitors." A man shouts hoarsely: "The masses will judge you. History will judge you. The people will struggle till the total liberation of Palestine from the river to the sea. Down with the accommodationists."

In the back of the hall two people are on the verge of a fistfight; in the front, two groups accuse each other of treason, seemingly a hair short of actual violence. In the midst of it all, an old man wearing a red *hatta* is screaming, to no one in particular, that everybody should remember that "the success of this congress is the success of your people and its failure is their failure. Please be calm."

Please be seated. Please be seated. Pleeeeeeeese!

Yet another man says, "If you want the liberation of Palestine from the river to the sea, from the north to the south, I urge you to be calm. Our people, which has no freedom in its occupied homeland, has democracy in its exiled society. Please, everybody, be calm."

Everything is out of control.

Then an older woman in traditional Palestinian dress starts ululating from the gallery. Other women join in. The ululation drowns out the verbal confrontations.

The meeting turns to the last item in the day's debate on the constitution—one that, mercifully, generates little controversy.

Someone moves that the name of the congress, the Palestine American Congress, be changed to the Palestine Congress of North America.

For the motion, a woman argues that "we are Palestinians first and foremost." Against it, a gray-haired delegate wearing a business suit claims that "if changed, the name would sound foreign."

Laughter greets this from all around the hall.

The delegates from Canada say they have a good reason to change the name to "North" America. A man well known in the Washington area for his pamphleteering on theological questions in the Palestine problem says in heavily accented English that he is against the change "because my sons are American."

He is booed repeatedly.

The name change passes by an overwhelming majority.

The chairman, his voice virtually gone at this point, reminds the audience that the congress has called a demonstration for tonight outside the White House. Buses, chartered in advance, will be ready to take people there at five o'clock. He urges everyone to go. Around five hundred individuals respond.

They arrive outside the White House in early evening. President Carter is out on the Mississippi cruising on a riverboat called the Delta Queen.

In the United States, many Palestinians think of Carter as essentially a decent man. His secretary of state, Cyrus Vance, is also a decent man, in that middle-class, middle-brow, middle-American, middle-aged way that middle-class, middle-brow, middle-American, middle-aged WASPS have about them. And Robert Strauss, the American envoy at the "autonomy talks," is also, if one wants to stretch a point, a decent man. But they, along with other officials responsible for America's Palestine policy, do not understand Palestinians. Many Arabs do not understand Palestinians. Many Palestinians do not understand Palestinians.

What they do not understand is that over the last six decades the struggle for Palestine has created a dialectic that has governed the interaction of Palestinians and Zionists, a dialectic based on the zero-sum dichotomy of oppressor-oppressed. And that Palestinians have assimilated this oppression, internalized it, interpreted it subjectively and cognitively, become transformed by it, and acted spontaneously upon it to struggle for freedom.

The struggle for freedom, by any people, is a living dialogue between that people and history. And this struggle, whether conducted by an individual, or collectively by a nation, is what gives life—that journey between birth and death—its meaning, its coherence, its justification. Without this struggle, life is a cliché, inert, hollow. Every open system in the universe, including humanity, is in constant motion. And the struggle for freedom surely represents the poetry of motion.

The six decades that the Palestinians have struggled through in their search for freedom are six decades only in calendar time. Since time has a dynamic relationship to space, the intensity of the transactions that Palestinians have conducted with history, in the experiential domain, has transformed them at a formidably accelerated pace. Like other people before them who have internalized substantial doses of oppression and been sparked by it to revolt, the

170

Palestinians have such energy packed within them, and have so enriched themselves, that no power on earth is likely to defeat them.

At the demonstration today, outside the White House, these five hundred Palestinians are not just shouting slogans—they are echoing the deep recesses of their soul. A young woman is crying out "Long live Palestine," and the crowd is ecstatically repeating it after her. This is not just a slogan. She, and they, are singing the words, ululating them, caressing them, burning with them a hole in the fabric of the surrounding environment. And as the demonstrators shout back, with a rational and moral optimism, the words overflow with the mystery of a human struggle that has become for Palestinians, in a complex way, an instrument of self-definition.

At one point, I find myself marching next to three Iranians. I ask them if they are attending the congress. They say no; they were driving by, saw the Palestinian flag, realized it was a Palestinian affair, and so parked their car (illegally as it turned out) to join the demonstration.

An American youngster, who was part of the congress as a guest, fired either by the slogans or by the need to look for a dream to dream, decides to jump over the White House fence. He is immediately picked up by the police and taken into custody.

As the demonstration is ending two hours later the organizers ask me to "make a short speech." I stand up on the railing of the White House lawn and tell the demonstrators that "the Palestinian people shall never recognize the Irgun Gang who now head the illegal regime in Palestine." Our struggle, I add, is a struggle "for the total liberation of Palestine from Zionist *apartheid*." I have come a long way since 1972, when I called for coexistence.

The political statement (especially when combined with the poetic impulse and the dance form) organizes, explores, and synthesizes the consciousness of the Palestinian character. And Palestinians, over the years, have created a rich ensemble of political statements.

Again today, the last day of the conference, the Palestinians here are seeking to apprehend and reenact the complexity of their struggle, and its relatedness to their private lives, through statements as politically charged as their language can yield.

171

The major task before the delegates is electing an executive committee of nine members to make preparations for the first annual conference of the Palestine Congress of North America. The conference, to be held in September 1980, will develop a national program and submit its recommendations to its general assembly.

Thirteen people are nominated. This alone takes two tense hours, during which two delegates from opposing factions confront each other physically. The elections bring into the executive committee two supporters of the PFLP, five supporters of Fatah, and two independents.

The chairman, about to call the meeting closed, is mobbed by a large crowd who carry him on their shoulders shouting: "Revolution, revolution till victory."

Everywhere in the hall people shout slogans, sing and dance the *dabki*; old ladies ululate and' children sing the national anthem.

In the corridors small groups knot in discussion. I overhear angry voices complaining about the deletion of "all of Palestine" from the constitution and the defeat of the "Arab reaction" clause. Some delegates are very bitter. An older man with a peasant accent confides to me that "we should beware of those who trade in Palestine," adding, "When the axe comes to the forest, the trees say the handle is one of us."

Another man tells me that though he was head of a UHLF delegation, he "took" three delegates with him and voted consistently with the PFLP. "I did that not because I'm a communist," he said, and left it at that.

I talk to a well-dressed, middle-aged couple whom I had come to know in Cleveland, who say they were pained by the divisiveness demonstrated at the congress. "Why can't we be united? Why can't we be united and civilized? Why not?" the wife asks ponderously. And the husband chimes in, asking "And what are the media going to say about us?"

I have a formidable urge to scream: *Don't you all understand? Don't you understand? It could not have happened any other way.* Instead, I walk down the corridors to the lobby and out into the street.

The Palestine Congress of North America, with which the Palestinian community had been pregnant for a few years, was given birth to, the way it was given birth to.

In retrospect, one thing is strangely certain about the statement

172

the congress made: in the national psyche of Palestinians, no set of circumstances, outside the physical elimination of all Palestinians, could drive Palestine into oblivion. The Palestinians live because Palestine lives—in their hearts, in their minds, and in the essential repertoire of their consciousness.

7

People in national struggle—especially those among them to whom national struggle has come to shape the meaning they carry of life—operate from and within a context of existential reference located somewhere north of the future. Communities in struggle feel habitual comfort only in the future tense, finding the strength to overcome extinction in their shared perception of "potentiality," of the inevitable succession of what they have mapped ahead.

By 1979, eleven years after the battle of Karameh launched this generation's own struggle for independence, the Palestinians were still no nearer their goal. On the contrary. By that time, the whole of Palestine was under occupation and those Palestinians still living there were subjected daily to the institutionalized sadism of that occupation: collective punishment, land expropriation, deportation, imprisonment, torture, censorship, the rule of the gun by the army and the rule of the hoodlum by the settlers, slow death by economic

174

strangulation, and repeated indignities as a subjugated people. Now in 1979, even their right to statehood on 18 percent of their land was considered unacceptable. The outlook for the future seemed bleak. An underlying sense of futility should have nagged at the core of their history: where do we go from here in the aftermath of Black September, the Lebanon civil war, Tel Zaatar, and Camp David? Yet it was precisely these military, political, and diplomatic defeats that, paradoxically, seemed to trigger the transition of the Palestinian movement from a provincial to an international organization in control of itself. The legacy of these defeats was a resurgence in confidence, a national mood of defiance and its elegant articulation in poetry, literature, polemics, and style, and, above all, a reinforcement of the organic link that Palestinians inside felt with those outside Palestine, and those outside Lebanon felt with those living and fighting in the "liberated zone." Palestinians from the West Bank/Gaza were constantly visiting Palestinians in the United States, and Palestinians from the United States were constantly visiting Palestine and Lebanon. And Palestinians from Kuwait, North Africa, and South America were visiting Palestinians in the United States and Lebanon. Palestinians had never been so frequently in physical contact with each other. Beyond this, the proliferation of periodicals, newspapers, books, films, and poetry journals enabled them to speak to each other about each other. Never had so many Palestinian organizations existed around the world. Never had Palestinians been so organized in their lives, so tied together. Never had they experienced so much national unity.

It was time for me also to visit with Palestinians "in the liberated zone." I had better make the visit soon, I thought, before the Palestinian springs of life in my identity run dry. I have been away from *el Blad* for twenty years. *El Blad*. This term, so uniquely Palestinian, literally means "the countries," that is, where Palestinians live. In Palestinian idiom, however, *el Blad* connotes the covert exaltation of a homeland without boundaries, a refuge of the national sensibility as it ferments in exile before it is transplanted home during the *awda*—another one of those Palestinian words that belong to a language within another language: the Return.

Over the next few days, as I make preparations for my first visit to *el Blad*, I experience a hysterical onrush of crazy fear. And strain. What is a shrill writer like me going to Lebanon for? A writer, at that, who has merely appropriated the struggle and pain of others in the liberated zone and, through some subtle literary larceny, claimed these two decades as his own? Yet, I argue, have I not all these years felt that struggle and that pain to be an indivisible part of my own daily existence? Have they not been, all these years, a focus for my emotions more real than any reality I have created around me? Besides, Beirut is the only place in the world where I have left toys in the attic, a shadow in the streets, a mesh of words by the sea. When I get there, I may find that the mirror has long since cracked, and the image I may see there will be blurred. But I will be there, in the liberated zone, mocking death by my prodigal presence.

There is something about airports and Palestinians. An airport is a place like no other for them. It used to be that when they found themselves in one, Palestinians never failed to experience a quickening in the pulse of their private consciousness, a vehement restatement of their national mood of helplessness, a formidable sense of terror and turbulence at their very core.

Airports, after all, are where Palestinians have traditionally been turned away, held up, detained, questioned. Few Palestinians alive today have not at one time or another clutched a stateless travel document at an airport somewhere in the world. with aching resentment during questioning about their identity. At airports, the very pivot of Palestinians' being is stripped of meaning, right there before their eyes; every sheltering symbol of their national self is wrenched away from them as they stand abjectly arguing with immigration officials. And always as they do, Palestinians feel the need, that desperate need, to lunge out at their tormentors and scream how it is all an affront to their dignity as humans and as Palestinians to be thus treated.

At the beginning, when it all started, Palestinians spoke about airports to themselves. Then to each other. And then later, when it had all moved retroactively into focus in the consciousness of a new generation, they spoke about it *at* airports. It was, after all, the Palestinians, beginning in 1970, who made plane hijacking fashionable, who went from airport to airport around the globe commandeering planes and blowing them up. Were they realizing, in a manner beyond their consciousness, their right to travel? Was that kind of violence, at airports, a metaphrase taken from the *argot* of the stateless, the damned, the repudiated? Were Palestinians, by singling out airports as a theater to play the contradictions of their condition in, unconsciously saying to the world: if we're not good enough to travel through your airports, we shall make sure they're not good enough for everybody else to travel through?

At Dulles International, in Washington, I go through security and recall how these electronic gadgets were initially introduced in response to all that terror that we began to inflict at airports nine years ago. This is our damn legacy. We have succeeded in making it as difficult for other people to travel as it has always been for us. I have ambivalent feelings about that.

I arrive in Beirut on a cold day when the city's wounds from the civil war and its class engagements are still raw, still unhealed. Off the plane, I am met by a middle-aged Palestinian from the Movement who is wearing a Russian woolen hat. "I am Abu Karim," he says.

My first moment here. This is a real Palestinian, with a name like Abu Karim, speaking with an authentic Palestinian accent, standing there on the tarmac, smiling and putting his had out for me to shake. I hold back an onrush of tears. (I have to restrain myself, I think; if I cry now, how will I react to more emotionally charged encounters, to revisiting the Bourj el Barajneh refugee camp where I grew up, and other camps, the source of a great deal of the complex energy in our Palestinianness and our history?)

Abu Karim and I hug, kissing each other on both cheeks as is the custom in our culture. He smiles at me with great warmth, mumbling repeatedly, "Welcome, welcome, welcome to you, brother."

Inside the airport, behind the customs and immigration barriers, hundreds of Lebanese Arabs are awaiting the arrival of friends and relatives. They all have beautiful Arab faces, ancient Semitic faces with dark skin and dark eyes. I stare at them. To me this is different from seeing Arabs in a social situation or a lecture hall in the United States. These are Arabs in the Arab world, who have gone through various wars in Lebanon, their lives ripped apart by uncounted

177

agonies. As I look at the faces, wondering how they have been transformed by the sustained tensions of the last two decades, I realize that I am staring at the faces with a kind of apprehension, anxiety, as if a sensitive chord has been hit in me, triggering old fears. Perhaps it was the fear I had always had in the Arab world, in those days when to be a Palestinian was to be the other, the lesser in the scheme of things, fair game for abuse by those who wanted you always close to the door for easy eviction or deportation or incarceration.

I turn away. Abu Karim is asking me to give him my passport and luggage tags. I do, and soon we go through customs without a luggage check and through immigration, where my passport is swiftly stamped in my absence. How can he do that, I am wondering, when we are *Palestinians?*

Though I am intellectually, at least, aware of the changes that have taken place here, I am still afflicted with the brutalized images that I had taken with me when I left twenty years before. I keep thinking, any minute now some police official will arrest me as a Palestinian Godless Communist and implicate me in some plot to bring about transformation in society. I am like someone who goes blind and continues to perceive his reality in the context of remembered images.

Outside the airport I am caught in a breathless scene so intimate and so integral to my childhood in Beirut that all my senses flinch. Taxi drivers milling around their vehicles, peddlers, chewing gum boys, porters, money changers, and a diversity of other people who have chosen the airport area to conduct their business, all shouting at each other, and the world around them, or singing the virtues of whatever it is they are selling. I feel faint with the exquisiteness and pain of it. This is where and how I grew up, peddling, stealing, starving, brawling, and hustling a living. This is where I acquired my original education before I began to acquire the semblance of an academic one. In these very streets. A child who was barely ten years old, with an oversized man's jacket hanging over him, extends a box of chewing gum in my direction. "Chewing gum, please!"

This is not true. This is not real. Has nothing changed in Lebanon? A civil war that took the lives of thousands, both fighters and civilians, and nothing has changed. How could anything be said to have changed in Lebanon if children still sell chewing gum in the streets?

"I am an Arab," I say to all the children crowding around with their boxes of Chiclets extended toward me as if they were badges of misery and defeat. "I am not foreign. I am Palestinian." I say that to them as they speak to me in their version of English.

"I am an Arab. I am a Palestinian," I keep saying. Suddenly I want to shed all the intellectual grime that I have acquired in my Western *ghourba* off my body and soul. I want to stand, just stand, in their midst. To scream "I am a Palestinian. An Arab like you. Not so long ago, your pain was mine. I don't feel it today, but it is still my pain. It is still part of my convention of statement and my contours of vision. Everything I have learnt in the West, every idea I have espoused, is merely cosmetic, added on to that first leap to maturity I took right here. With you. I understand it all. I understand. I understand why men and women and children stood abjectly in line outside an UNRWA food depot each month, to receive their food rations, at the Bourj el Barajneh refugee camp, and why they threw furtive glances at each other, with their voices, like their faces, full of calm despair. I understand why men in tens of thousands went to the Arabian Peninsula to work in the oil fields for a pittance, sleeping in prefabricated tin boxes, ten to a box, leaving children, wives, and parents behind. I understand why the kids shivered under their clothing in classrooms in the dead of winter. I understand why Palestinians were shunted back and forth, for months on end, at the Aliens Department of the Ministry of Interior when they wanted only to get a permit to travel outside the country (and sometimes inside the country) to visit a relative or seek employment.

Tomorrow is the fourteenth anniversary of the emergence of the Palestinian Revolution. Commemorative banners are flying in the Basta district where I grew up, now controlled by elements from the Palestinian "Armed Struggle Command" and the Lebanese National Movement. Tomorrow ten thousand Palestinian guerrillas will parade in the sports stadium, before an expected one hundred thousand spectators. Soon, tonight, I may see my family, at least those fragments of it that have not been driven out of the country or killed. But my mother has left Beirut to join her sister in Aleppo. My sister Jasmine, long since married to a Palestinian engineer, live in Kuwait.

My aunts and uncles and other relatives, who still live here, I will not recognize if I meet them. My nieces and nephews and their husbands and wives I have never met. And my friends from Awlad Falasteen, with whom I grew up in these very streets, I have no idea where they could be—who is here, who is overseas, who is dead, who is alive, who is in the Movement, who is not.

A car carries me toward the city. The driver, Mahmoud, one of Abu Karim's men, is a youngster in his late teens. I learned later that he belonged to a reserve unit in Fatah and was a veteran of the war against the Syrian forces that invaded Lebanon in June 1976 and of what Palestinians call the Eight Day War, the Israeli invasion of the south of Lebanon in March 1978.

He wants to know what "they" have done to me in the United States. "Brother, you look like one of them, with your beard and hair," he says with much facetious gesturing.

I ask him how Abu Karim was able to get me through immigration and customs with such ease. He says there is an understanding between the Lebanese National Movement, the Syrian army, and the local police on the one hand, and the Palestine Liberation Organization (PLO) on the other, for the Palestinian Movement to have a free hand in letting "guests of the Revolution" into the country. They had no such agreement with the "Lebanese government" because that entity had long since ceased to exist. Lebanon has been divided, since 1976, into separate "zones." Some of them, such as the south, were totally controlled by the Palestinian-Lebanese coalition. Others, such as the Jounieh area, were under the control of the fascist forces. Still other zones, such as those in the Bekaa Valley, were patrolled exclusively by the Syrian army. And others such as sensitive areas in West Beirut were jointly controlled by the Syrians and the Palestinian-Lebanese forces.

"Some airport officials," Mahmoud tells me as he drives along the airport road leading us to West Beirut, "respond to other things too."

"What's that?"

"Bribery," he tells me off-handedly.

"Bribery?"

"Just bribery. These officials would do anything for a bribe," he says and adds after a short silence, with a hint of contempt in his voice: "These people don't deserve to have a homeland of their own. I swear a state is wasted on these people. They don't appreciate what they have. They abuse their country. We bribe them simply to let our people in, but they deserve nothing from us but contempt."

We stop at the entrance of a three-story building. "Well, brother," Mahmoud says, "this is where we have breakfast, at the cafeteria of the General Union of Palestinian Women, up on the third floor."

When we get there, Mahmoud banters with everybody—he seems to know all the people there too. The walls of the cafeteria are covered with posters about the revolutionary role women should play in Palestinian society. Most tables are occupied by groups of men and women in earnest conversation. Many of the faces look European, Oriental, African, Latin.

"These are visiting delegations, here to express solidarity with us," Mahmoud tells me. "Some of them are here to work with us. Some are doctors, nurses, engineers, and some are students, workers, unionists, and the like. You find them operating in hospitals or building shelters or digging trenches for sewage in the camps. Some of these people, mind you, are also romantics, or alienated souls, or rejects from their own society, or what have you. But they are all here and they are our guests."

We eat a typical Palestinian breakfast of goat cheese, black olives, and *foule,* mashed fava beans with olive oil and lemon.

"Mahmoud, I want to ask you a question," I begin, sipping my tea. "I'm trying to locate a friend. I'm almost certain he is in the Movement."

What's his Movement name?"

"I don't know," I say with frustration. "His real name is Samir Salfiti."

"Doesn't ring a bell."

"I grew up with him. We called him Brazil-Japan or Bee-Jay for short. He's with Fatah. At least I think he's still with Fatah."

Mahmoud asks me a few questions about his background, his age, and what he looked like. I say I can't possibly describe what he looks like now.

"I mean, I haven't seen the brother for twenty years. We also used to call him Abu Saksuki (Father of the Beard) because he had a beard even then."

181

Suddenly Mahmoud sits up straight. "Of course, you mean Abu Hinchel, the brother with a wooden leg. He lost the real one at the battle of Karameh in 1968. We call him Abu Saksuki from time to time too. Good heavens above, man, who *doesn't* know Abu Hinchel? I'll take you to him later on today. But now we have to hurry on to meet with brother Labadi."

"Bee-Jay lost a leg at Karameh?"

"Yes. Hasn't stopped him from fighting though. He led the battles against the fascists at the Hotel District in June 1976."

"With a wooden leg?"

"Brother, in our Revolution, when a fighter loses a limb, that's no excuse to stop fighting. We have a whole bunch of *fedayeen* running around with the best of them, though minus an arm or a leg here and there. If you have the will to fight and you can use a weapon, why not do it? Ours is not an army. Nobody is drafted to fight. A Palestinian becomes a *fedayi* by free choice. He drops out, when and if he wants to, by free choice. All the brothers and sisters here are in the Movement, fighting in their own way, the best way they know how, not because someone told them to, or because some siren went off somewhere, like a Muezzin's call to prayer, telling people to come and be involved. They just came here. The Revolution stems from a place in every one of us."

I am too excited by the news that Bee-Jay is in town to pay much attention to what Mahmoud is saying. I ask him how he can be sure we are talking about the same man, and he says it has to be, since Bee-Jay is also known as Abu Saksuki, has been with Fatah from the outset, grew up in Lebanon, and the rest of it.

Mahmoud drives me to the Samed school for orphans of Tel Zaatar in his Land Rover. From the outside, the Samed school, an innocuous, unimposing three-story building with a school-size yard on a quiet street in West Beirut. I ask him why the lunacy on our part, in 1976, of insisting on the defense of the camp to begin with. If we had avoided the confrontation, all that death and suffering would have been avoided.

"Tel Zaatar was our camp," he says evenly, "it was our home. We lived there. The cowardly Syrians and their fascist allies attacked. We defended ourselves. As simple as that."

"But why the heroic display, why the sacrifice, the stubbornness throughout the whole siege?" I ask.

"At first the military command of the Revolution sent orders by radio to the *fedayeen* there not to surrender, not to evacuate. I guess the command was convinced that the Syrians would not persist in their attack for too long, since the political pressure on Assad from the left-wing faction inside his party, or his masses, would bring about the collapse of his regime; or perhaps they assumed that Tel Zaatar, with its complex of shelters and well-armed and trained militias and *fedayeen* would withstand the siege. But the assault was too ferocious; dozens of people were being killed or dying in the rubble every day, right up to August 17, when the camp fell. Obviously, the Syrian regime didn't fall, though its troops were dealt one humiliating defeat after another elsewhere in Lebanon in the kind of engagements with our *fedayeen* that Syrian soldiers weren't trained to fight. By the first week of August the command in West Beirut was sending radio messages telling the defenders of Tel Zaatar to lay down their arms and trust in a truce that was being arranged with the Red Cross for safe conduct for all women and children.

"The response came back from Tel Zaatar: 'No. We don't trust the word of the fascists or their Syrian allies.' And as we know, when the population had been virtually decimated and they did accept the safe conduct, their fears turned out to be justified—the survivors trekking to West Beirut were waylaid by fascist forces, robbed, killed, choked, stabbed, and cut down; virtually every Palestinian over the age of ten. Red Cross officials watched helplessly—and sent reports to Geneva. The commandos, who had not been offered "safe conduct," were the luckiest: they went up through the mountains and many of them arrived safely in Bhamdoun, which was controlled by our leftist allies." He fell silent.

The surviving children of Tel Zaatar who arrived in West Beirut will never be the same again. These were children who walked all the way from their camp and on the way found themselves walking alone. Children who saw their parents bayoneted to death in front of their eyes. Children who were shellshocked. Children who, before the siege, had been physically and mentally healthy and were now deaf-mute. Children who went into convulsions when they heard the word "water." Children who woke up in the middle of the night screaming. Children who lost every member of their families. Children who did not play, or run around, but sat staring, responding

183

neither to questions nor the offer of food. Children whose experiences had already entered our history books.

The Samed school is home to some of these kids. It is run by the General Union of Palestinian Women, itself one of the diverse political, social, economic, and civic associations, committees, councils, organizations, and institutions belonging to—and making up—the Palestine Liberation Organization.

Wearing khaki pants and a white blouse, Dr. Hanan Taha, the school director, a middle-aged woman in her early forties, looks more like someone who has just finished a game of tennis than someone with the awesome responsibility of rehabilitating 115 children from Tel Zaatar. The first thing she says to me: "Brother, I want to tell you that we don't call this place a school, simply because it is not a school. It is a home."

She explains that the children are divided into "families" of five, with a surrogate mother for each, in most cases a woman who is herself a survivor of Tel Zaatar. In the building, where each family has an "apartment," the groups live, eat, play, and interact with one another as if they are normal families. In the morning, the children go to school and their mothers are there when they arrive "home."

"They do their homework, play in the yard you see outside," I am told, "and try to live normal lives, to the extent that it's possible at this time."

Dr. Taha sounds very businesslike, betraying no emotion as she tells me how the Samed home opened on August 17, 1977, the first anniversary of the fall of Tel Zaatar; how the General Union of Palestinian Women has opened six similar homes; and how, though she already has 115 kids, she hopes to absorb another 35 over the next year—hundreds of children have been placed in foster homes in the refugee camps and with middle-class Palestinian families living outside, she says. Her voice breaks when she starts telling me about the first few months, when the kids were "Masakeen" (packages of tragedy).

"At the beginning," she says, "the kids seemed beyond help, beyond therapy or affection. We would ask them to do drawings of anything they wanted and they would draw planes dropping bombs on houses, figures lying on the ground in pools of blood, buildings in rubble with bodies half sticking out. When they projected these fears, or aggressions, outward, they just went around hitting each other,

184

pulling each others' hair or sulking for hours in their bedrooms, refusing to eat or talk. These were the norm. We had extreme cases as well. One kid arrived safely in West Beirut in his uncle's arms. But somewhere en route, the shock of what he had seen had turned him into a mute. For months he would not say a word. Another kid refused to use his legs and had to be carried everywhere. Until recently, many of the children were waking up in the middle of the night whenever they heard any shooting outside and going into their mothers' bedrooms to beg them not to go out 'to get water.' "

As she talks, a young woman walks in with a teapot and two tiny glasses. She is introduced as one of the surrogate mothers. We pour tea.

As if the ordeal of talking about all of this is too much for her, Dr. Taha asks me where I lived in the United States. I say in Washington. To my amazement, her response is, "Where in Washington?" When I tell her, she smiles and says she knows the neighborhood very well. After getting her Ph.D. in psychology at Georgetown University, she says, she remained in the District for five years working at the Federal Forensic Medicine Department, treating parolees, convicted rapists, and youth offenders from the inner city. The experience transformed her, she tells me; before that she had wanted to escape her Palestinianness, refused to be political or have anything to do with Palestinians.

"I practiced a wishy-washy kind of therapy," she reminisces, "till one day I realized that the psychotic impulse in ghetto people is derived totally from and is molded by the political, social, and economic conditions they've labored under since the day they were born. Of course radical psychologists had been telling us that for years, but I had not been affected by them. I had lived what I was convincing myself was a happy life in the United States till I began interacting with the world of black Americans in the inner city— going to cocktail parties and embassy functions, attending conferences and annual conventions of hopelessly pathetic Arab-American organizations like the National Association of Arab-Americans (NAAA) that wanted to lobby on the Hill for Palestinian rights."

I ask her whether the children interact with surrogate fathers. She says there are none, but the children have many father figures as models. A lot of men drop by almost daily just to be there and play with the children—*fedayeen,* militia, students, instructors and artists from the Institute of Palestinian Folk Art, officials from the "office crowd," and so on.

Our tea drinking continues. Soon, however, the kids start arriving. I hear their laughter in the yard, in the hallways outside, in their homes close by. I stand up to steal a glance through the window and see a dozen or so running around the yard. *The children of Tel Zaatar.* My God, I'm looking at the children of Tel Zaatar! I want to run outside and hug them and kiss them and love them. I want to ask them to forgive me. I want to tell them that ever since they came into my life on August 17, 1976, as the trekked to West Beirut carrying a past innocent of guilt, I have addressed myself endlessly. Ever since that day I have inhabited a gulf of emptiness. It was as if the walled city of our dreams has burned down, and our sea was wounded by its own waves. Why weren't we there to save our children from such a wanton fate? My parents' generation had known Deir Yassein, where, on the night of April 8, 1948, 248 innocent men, women, and children were butchered and some of their bodies thrown into the village well, by the Irgun and the Stern Gang. That should have been the last massacre. Now my own generation has already lived through two more, Black September and Tel Zaatar, in the short span of six years. Will they never, ever want to look into the forlorn bleeding eyes of our nation and stop killing us? Will our nation never, ever know the joyful chorus of a people living free?

I go out to the yard with Dr. Taha, who suggests I walk around by myself and speak with the children. I stand there, unsure of myself, of what to do. Why had I thought this was going to be a poignant moment, my first encounter with the children of Tel Zaatar? These kids look no different from other kids elsewhere. They are running around, playing with each other, going in or coming our of their homes like normal kids. Some of them, pointed out to me as the school's folk troupe, are emerging from the building into the yard dressed for rehearsal in the Palestinian national costume. Others are beginning to crowd around me to ask questions. Still others want me to take their picture as they stand in a group with their arms around each other or holding the victory sign over their heads. They are loud, noisy, mischievous. They betray no tragic looks of pain. I know how my generation dealt with its own pain and became transformed by it. How will this generation do it?

Beautiful Palestinian children. With beautiful faces. Beautiful, brown Semitic faces. Happy faces of Palestinian children who have had no respite, this whole century, from pain and violence and destitution. Boys and girls crowding around me. Some of them holding my hand. "Are you Palestinian? Hey, are you Palestinian?"

I say yes, and they want to know where in Palestine I come from. I say Haifa, and they call out, "I'm from Safad." "I'm from Genin." "I'm from Lydda." "I'm from Acre." "I'm from Ramaleh."

"And what's your name?" I ask a little girl of eight or nine who is holding on to my hand.

"My name is Jamila Abdel Rahman. I was named after Jamila, the Algerian *fedaya* who fell in 1958."

The practice of naming Palestinian children after Palestinian patriots or Palestinian notions such as *thaaer* (revolutionary), *nidal* (struggle), or *awda* (return) is as old as the Palestinian struggle itself, but by the 1960s it had reached a point where virtually every child born to a family of patriots had a *watani* name like that given it at birth.

Many children born in the 1950s and after were given names of non-Palestinian revolutionaries such as Castro, Lenin, Gamal (Nasser), and Guevara (a very popular name indeed among Palestinian children today).

Jamila asks me if I could take her picture. When I try to do that, she won't let go of my hand. I say that she will have to stand a few feet away from me if she wants me to take her picture. She just looks up at me and says nothing, still holding on to my hand. Then she drags me to her home to visit her "mother," "sisters," and two "brothers." Only her mother and one brother are there. He is named after Omar ben Khatab, the legendary Arab general who led his forces out of the Arabian Peninsula to defeat the Persian and Byzantine empires in the seventh century. Omar does not know how old he is. He immediately shows me his drawing book. Only a Palestinian child, a survivor of Tel Zaatar, could have done those drawings. Page after page holds images of *fedayeen* with kalashnikovs, tanks and jet fighters, and *ashbal*, plural of *shibil*, a young fighter training to become a *fedayi*.

"This is a *fedayi*," he says.

"What does a *fedayi* do?" I ask.

"He fights."

"And a *shibil*?"

"He trains."

187

"What does a plane do?"

"It drops bombs."

The children's mother does not ask me if I want tea. She just brings a pot over and we start drinking it out of the tiny glasses.

"Where do you come from, brother?" she asks. She is wearing her *hatta* loosely around her neck.

"I'm from Haifa."

"Bless you, you must be of the crowd of 1948."

"That's right."

"So was my husband. He fell on the Hill," she says, referring to Tel Zaatar, the Hill of Thyme. "I'm from Jaffa, but I was born on the Hill two years after the *nakbi* [the start of our exile in 1948]. Have you been away from the countries a long time?"

When I tell her that I've been away for twenty years, she says "Well, that's our lot. Surely I don't know of any Palestinian family, anywhere in the world, that has stayed together. I surely don't know of any Palestinian family that has not suffered. But God willing, we shall soon return."

I ask her what it was like at Tel Zaatar.

"What happened on the Hill, brother, happened. They attacked us. We defended ourselves," she says quietly. "But what happened on the trek was something else. What they did to the nurses, for example—and may the Lord's rage lodge in their souls—demonstrated their savagery. I saw it all. With my own eyes," she says. And what I see in *her* eyes is not grief but anger. "Those beautiful nurses. All so young and so beautiful. Still in their beautiful white uniforms. Their only crime was to be Palestinian and work for the Palestine Red Crescent. The fascists just lined them up against the wall and shot them dead. All of them. I remember one of those nurses, like a beautiful rose she was, the last to get killed, she just stood there. And just when the fascists cocked their machine guns she put her arms out, palms up, as if to ward off the bullets. They killed them all. I saw it all."

She breaks down, sobbing quietly. But not for long. Suddenly she looks up, her voice firm, and stares at me for an instant before saying, "We shall avenge what those sons of whores did, not only on the Hill but on the trek. They shall pay. And their punishment shall be truly terrible."

Just another young Palestinian. Skilled in the art of survival and

188

averting madness. Does she know I'm here with her to look for new suffering to suffer? Can she know what I truly am and still accept me?

"Come," she says, removing the teapot and cups to the kitchen. "Let's go visit Um Ismael next door. You have much in common with her. She has seen much more than I have. She is an educated woman."

Um Ismael is much younger and very attractive, with a look of assured determination, almost of impatience. She has none of the traditional mannerisms or patterns of speech of a woman of peasant background like Um Omar.

"I never grew up in a refugee camp," she tells me immediately. "I come from a bourgeois Palestinian family. When I graduated from the American University in Cairo in 1975 I came back to Beirut. The Revolution wanted teachers for Palestinian schools in the camps. I volunteered and was sent to the Hill, where I was till the evacuation.

"I thought I had learned something at college that I could teach the kids at the Hill. It was the other way around. At least I learned that for some people a cup of water can be more valuable than a cup of gold. During the siege, after we ran out of water, we would go out to the pumps at night, five or six at a time. Every time someone would get killed by fascist sniper fire. The Syrians had given them the weapons. When we tried to bury the dead the next day, some of the mourners would get killed too. It just went on. The mother of some of the kids I had taught went out one night to get water in a bucket. She crawled all the way to the pump safely. On the way back she was hit. But she still clutched her bucket, now half full with water. Some of the fighters rushed from behind their sandbags to help her as did some of us. She still would not let go of her bucket and mumbled about how her kids were dying of thirst. When we got her home, she was bleeding profusely and we discovered the water in the bucket was totally red. Her blood had been falling into it the whole time. Two days later, she died."

Um Omar is nodding her head repeatedly, angrily, looking for a gap in Um Ismael's narrative, her peasant face contorted with pain. Palestinian pain. That no one knows exists. Um Omar says: "After Marwan, my husband, fell, I moved into my brother's house. One night I went out with one of his sons—my brother was a fighter and we hardly saw him—to fetch water. While we were filling our jerrycans, the boy was hit in the shoulder. He refused to leave the jerry-can, even with me, and be taken to the clinic. He insisted on being taken home. He wanted to bring the water to his mother and two sisters himself. He wanted to see them smile. He died before we got home. The Hill had become a cemetery."

On the way back to the guest house Mahmoud tells me he has a surprise for me. Bee-Jay, whom he had tracked down while I was at the Samed school, will be waiting for me at the guest house. He is taking me and the guerrillas on leave I had met that morning at the guest house for dinner at his home near Bourj el Barajneh, the biggest and most populous Palestinians refugee camp anywhere.

When I get there I don't recognize Bee-Jay, nor he me. Mahmoud brings me to him.

"*Ya hala, Ya hala, Ya hala,*" Bee-Jay intones as he approaches, both arms extended, to hug me warmly for the longest time. "My God, it is a blessing from the Lord to have you with us."

"Brother, how are you?" I ask breathlessly, a bit irrelevantly.

"I'm here, brother, I'm here," he says in that typical Palestinian way of responding to the question *how* you are by identifying *where* you are.

We all sit down in the living room and Abu Medienne, the guerrilla commander, chides me for not giving him Bee-Jay's *nom de guerre* when I asked for his whereabouts in the morning, since "there is no one in Beirut who doesn't know your friend here."

Bee-Jay looks so old, though I know he is only two years older than I am. He is married, he tells me, and has six daughters. His wife is pregnant again and he hopes for a son. That's his paramount aspiration in life.

"Don't raise your hopes, Abu Hinchel," one of Abu Medienne's fellow guerrillas says teasingly. "Some men like you are married to women good enough to give birth only to daughters." Everybody laughs, including Bee-Jay.

"Hey, what's wrong with daughters anyway," he answers; "what about Dalal Moughrabi?"

"Just kidding, Abu Hinchel."

Inevitably, we start talking politics. We just drift into it, with the casualness and ease of men to whom it is an aspect of their daily existence.

Sadat's name is mentioned, in the context of the Camp David Accords. Everybody snickers. The Egyptian president's name always evokes contempt among Palestinians nowadays. Not anger, or frustration, just contempt.

"That offspring of sixty whores," one of the men says, "does he really think he'll get away with it? Are Americans really *that* dumb to think they can mutilate our destiny like that?"

"Well, whether we like it or not," another responds, "they have mutilated it."

Bee-Jay says, "Brothers, Americans have affected our destiny, true, and affected it dramatically since 1948, but we have also affected theirs. Granted, our national life would have been different if America had not chosen to support Israel the way it has, but the national life of Americans would have been different too if Sirhan Sirhan, a Palestinian, had not chosen to kill Bobby Kennedy."

Bee-Jay, Brazil-Japan, has not changed.

"Everything we do as a national liberation movement in this part of the world, changing the balance of power among radical and moderate regimes, as American calls them, contributing to a change in the political order in Iran, turning Lebanon into a liberated zone for Arab and other third world revolutionaries to cement their links in, all of this will change, or at least affect, the imperialist designs of Washington. And we have a great advantage, an important weapon at our disposal, in addition to our commitments, and that is the fact that American policymakers and strategists are fools. They are new at the game of Big Power and you can't go wrong underestimating their intelligence in that field. They see history, and human struggle, mechanistically, as a forward motion of events dependent on the law of causality—A leads to B and B leads to C—with everything else constant. But one event in the life of a people's struggle—an invasion by a foreign army, a defeat in battle, the imposition of an unpopular regime, economic destitution, colonial occupation, civil war, name it—could, in the dialectic of things, unlock forces antithetical to the goals intended by a policy move, forces that may otherwise have remained dormant but now, once emergent, will overcome the policy and its initiators."

On the way to his house for dinner, Bee-Jay asks me "to guess" who was in Beirut recently, visiting from the United States. I imagine he is referring to some Palestinian-American activist or some official from the PLO mission to the UN whom I know.

"Who?"

"Our old buddy Ibrahim," he says.

"Which Ibrahim are you talking about?" I ask, not daring to guess that he is speaking of Ibrahim Adel, our childhood friend who shined shoes while I peddled chewing gum.

"Not . . . not him?"

"Yes, no other."

Suddenly, I'm recollecting the day he was willing to kiss the *zaim*'s foot because he was hungry; the day he talked down Lebanon's prime minister; the day he graduated at the top of his class; the day, twenty years ago, he said goodbye to us all to go to Berkeley.

"He wasn't here as a guest of the Revolution. He just came to visit his parents," Bee-Jay says wearily.

"From where?"

"From California, man; he still lives in Berkeley."

"But he can't. I would have met him."

"He's not active. He's dead. Like a zombie. Something happened to the kid. He is not anywhere near his old self. There is no semblance of Palestinian life about him, no carryover from our generation's political spirit. There is nothing there, man."

"What could have happened?"

"Beats me, brother."

And every time I had thought of Ibrahim, all those years, I had imagined him at least involved, if not prominent in, the Free Speech Movement and going on to join the Revolution—or something, for God's sake. But there he was, I complain to Bee-Jay, in Berkeley all the time when I came to speak on campus, to address the Palestinian community so many times and to participate in seminars sponsored by Arab and other third world student bodies—and he didn't know, didn't come up and introduce himself. I mean, what the fuck is the man doing?

Bee-Jay gives me not only Ibrahim's address but his phone number. I promise to look him up, to visit him, to see for myself what's happened to him, the moment I return to the United States.

8

I call Ibrahim up in Berkeley and tell him who I am. A long silence
fills the phone before he answers, "You mean—it can't be!"

I say it is and tell him that I'm going to be in San Francisco three
days hence to give a lecture but I want to come a day earlier to be with
him. We have so much to say, so much to talk about, that we end up
saying nothing. He is almost tongue-tied and responds to my
questions in monosyllables. So I just say that I will call him when I
arrive in town.

Is it possible that Ibrahim has been in Berkeley *all* these years?
And if he has, for fuck's sake, how come he wasn't *involved*? If he
had been involved in any way at all, surely our paths would have
crossed. What is he *doing*, my old shoeshine friend, the boy who
marched with us in demonstrations and saw his first prison cell at
age thirteen?

When I arrive in Berkeley I give him a call from just outside the campus, where the airport limo drops me, and tell him that I'll be taking a cab over to his place.

The door opens. I see a short, older-looking man with a moustache. I recognize him immediately. All this time, thinking of this moment, I had imagined that when we met I would feel our pulses ticking in unison as we looked at each other; and when we shook hands, I would feel the weight of our common life swiftly passing between us. When we shake hands, however, and then hug with infinite lavishness, as we are expected to, I feel nothing. Absolutely nothing. No energy. Not in the touch. Not in the face. Not in the way his body moves. Not in the voice. Not in the eyes. I sense a deadness of spirit about the man. In the man. When he speaks, his words yield so little. Even his living room looks gray and lifeless as he sits in it, across from me, hunched over like a scarecrow, describing his life over the previous two decades. He got his Ph.D. a year ago, he tells me, "in anthropology, you know," and he now works for some local Arab-American organization agitating against anti-Arab discrimination in the media, adding, "but I'm looking for a better job." The shock comes when he tells me that he has "converted to Islam." He met a religious figure, or a figure who represented an Islamic institution in the Gulf, who won him over from his Greek Orthodox faith to Islam by offering a not insubstantial financial reward. I want to applaud his survivalist instinct—or his gift for the Palestinian hucksterism that we have all become adept at over the years—but he persists in trying to convince me that he is serious in his religious beliefs. When his wife walks in later in the day, she turns out to be a woman of few words who smiles swiftly and endearingly at every word he utters. Over dinner, he complains constantly of a toothache, that he is losing most of his teeth, and that he couldn't possibly hack it without codeine.

"Thank God for codeine," he says.

"Oh yes," his wife adds eagerly, "thank God for codeine."

As I lie in bed that night my memories tangle with the shadow of my old friend. And a kind of shadow spills out to tangle with the shadow. Time uses insidious weapons against some of us, a chilling knife to our spirit. I can't figure out what happened to my friend Ibrahim. I do know that certain things cannot be lost. Certain things cannot be thrown away. Like the memories I have of him in the streets of Beirut, that brutal directness of political feeling that characterized our Palestinian childhood, by the Corniche, before we went our separate ways.

Those memories I will keep.

The winter of 1982. The Palestinian Movement was at the peak of its power. And, as some would later say in the cold light of hindsight, also at the nadir of its strength. Something had gone wrong. Haywire. Maybe lots of things. The bureaucratization of its functionaries. The regimentation of its guerrillas. The corruption of some of its leading cadres in the field. The alienation of the Lebanese from it. The massive amounts of money that poured into it. And, perhaps above all, the lack of insight the Movement had shown in assessing, reconsidering, and transforming its tactical and strategic objectives in response to the ebb and flow of daily struggle against its many enemies in the region.

To be sure, the élan of the 1960s and the middle 1970s was still there, but it had acquired a blustering edge. The heroism in combat that had characterized the performance of the *fedayeen* was still there, but it had become directionless. And the organic relationship that had always bound the Palestinian people and their Movement into a cohesive whole, though also still there, was becoming uneasy. Something sinister had lodged in the soul of our nation. And people sensed it in the winter of 1982 as they talked about the coming war.

We have been at war with Zionism for eighty years. With no let up. No respite. And yet another war was coming. Though a truce had been negotiated between the PLO and Israel through Philip Habib, U.S. envoy to the Middle East, in July 1981, Palestinians knew— even the media knows—that Israel was preparing an invasion of Lebanon with the declared intention of "wiping out" the physical presence and institutional structure of Palestinian nationalism.

In the United States, those Palestinians who had been trained as guerrillas, or were part of the reserves, were picking up their bags and traveling to Lebanon to join their units. The rest were marching in demonstrations, organizing rallies, putting on *haflis* (community functions), collecting donations, and sponsoring lectures. A frenzy of activity, a defiance of mood, gripped Palestinian communities in exile everywhere. I found myself on a "lecture" tour around the country, living out of the proverbial suitcase for two or three months on end. Indeed, even before, long before, the imminence of war gripped our attention and preoccupied us all, I was already living a lifestyle that at times gave me the impression of living not in the United States but somewhere else, in some other country inhabited only by Palestinians. I sensed American society around me only marginally.

I wake up in the morning and find myself in a room in a sponsor's home, in a city at the back of beyond of a Western state. Yes, I'm still on the road, I say to myself, and get ready for yet another lecture, followed by a gathering at somebody's house for a long political discussion, interspersed with dancing and singing, going on till dawn. Then I go to bed and wake up in the morning to discuss the news on television that day with my hosts and get ready to fly to Los Angeles to join a picket line somewhere in town. In the late afternoon, I'm in San Diego to address a gathering of the General Union of Palestinian Students (GUPS) on the PLO's strategy for the coming war in Lebanon. I give a poetry recital in Berkeley, then attend a GUPS local election in San Francisco, where I speak on the occasion of the forty-sixth anniversary of the death of Izz el Deen el Kassam, the Palestinian peasant revolutionary. I join a community picnic in Sacramento. In Detroit, I get drunk with three professors from Bir Zeit University on a short fund-raising visit to the United States and discuss home, politics, and history. In Boston, I cross paths with two Palestinian activists similarly engaged, Fouad Moughrabi and Naseer Aruri, and spend the whole night at the Hyatt Regency Hotel, where the three of us are staying, talking about the concept of "the Arab nation." I get to Chicago in time for the last day of the Association of Arab-American University Graduates (AAUG) conference and for an opportunity to watch the Palestine Folk Troupe from Beirut perform its exquisite *dabki* numbers. I attend the annual *hafli* of supporters of the PFLP in New York. Back in Detroit, which has the highest concentration of Palestinians, I join more than two thousand other people at the wedding of a Palestinian friend where all the songs, dances, expressions of joy, and telegrams of congratulations express commitment to the struggle. I spend a morning drafting a booklet commissioned by the Palestine Congress of North America about the strange case of Ziad Abu Ain, the Palestinian kid Israel accused of "terrorism" and extradited from the United States. I spend an afternoon writing, typing, and mailing my monthly editorial to *Palestine Perspectives,* the PLO publication in the United States, and my monthly column to *Arab Perspectives,* the Arab League journal. I sit in a hotel room in Austin, Texas, waiting for someone to pick me up and take me to a lecture hall, and write down more notes for a long paper, already way beyond its deadline, that I promised the *Journal of Palestine Studies.* And in yet another city, in yet another hotel, I stay on the phone for an hour talking to my lawyer in Washington about a court case pending against me in connection with the time I punched a fellow Palestinian writer on the nose at a party thrown for both of us.

All this went on smoothly, happily, normally, with little concern on my part about everyday life in the United States. I was in the country but not of it. Its passions, raging around me like a storm, seemed mockingly remote from my reality. To be sure, I would speak to the waiter in my neighborhood restaurant, be mildly bemused by Walter Cronkite on CBS News, exchange a few pleasantries with my neighbor, read an odd commentary or two in the *Washington Post,* listen to some of the engagingly naive babble that passed for political debate on the Martin Agronsky show, and, after many years of interacting with him on a drinking basis, earn my bartender's respect—but for all intents and purposes, I was removed from the natives. And it feels good to be turning the tables on them: I was a third world person in a Western country who disdained the natives, formed no lasting friendships with any of them, made no effort to learn about their culture, and did not eat their food.

Meanwhile, winter was coming to a close, and the war was inexorably approaching. The Palestinians had not marshaled the kind of support they needed from their allies—few as they were in the Arab world—to stand up to the military might of their Israeli enemy. It seemed they were going to have to fight with their bare hands. To be sure, they reinforced some of their positions in the south and augmented their numbers in Beirut. But they obviously were not going to withstand massive attacks by land, sea, and air forces with their limited arsenal of small weapons. No amount of heroism in battle was going to save the day without direct logistical support from Arab allies with credible armaments, prepared to fight alongside them. The only such allies were the Syrians. And the Syrians, as their history of confrontation with the Palestinian movement attested, wished nothing more than to see the PLO destroyed so they could become the undisputed arbiters of a Palestinian settlement with Israel.

Though everyone expected "the war of destiny," as many Palestinians were already calling it, we didn't know it would come on the fifteenth anniversary of the June War of 1967. When the assault began, I was in Paris for a short vacation.

The siege of Beirut brought with it all the ancient terrors of sieges—city gates broken, libraries burned down, fire dropped on defenders. A truly medieval event recalling the sieges of Jerusalem in 1099 and Acre in 1189. This siege also was a metaphor of confrontation between East and West and a fascinating symbol of the clash of self-definitions between settler-colonialism and native resistance. It was a mirage from the medieval age that bespoke, as sieges then often did, the most dreadful catastrophe that could befall people: the destruction of their city and their subsequent wanderings in search of shelter to house their passions and the outward expression of their culture. To Palestinians everywhere, the siege of Beirut became the most monumental event in their modern history—even more monumental than the dismemberment of, and exodus from, Palestine in 1948.

The Israelis tried everything during the siege. To starve the city. To bomb it to rubble. To terrorize its inhabitants with psychological warfare. To cut its water, medical, and food supplies.

Still, the city held.

And still, relieving Arab armies did not arrive.

And still, the bombs fell.

A man driving to West Beirut from the east was stopped at an Israeli army checkpoint. His sandwich was confiscated.

In the West Bank, an older Palestinian woman attacked an Israeli soldier with a kitchen knife. She did not let go until she had stabbed him, and herself been shot, to death.

One evening, eager to find out how the Arab world was reacting to the war, my friends and I turned on our shortwave radio. Without much difficulty, we got the broadcast from Algeria—the land of the long, bloody war of independence against the French, the land for which I had gone to jail when as a teenager I demonstrated in support of its revolution. The land for which I, selling ice-cream bars fourteen hours a day, kept aside at least 15 percent of my earnings.

Algerian radio was singing. The music blared "*El akel el saleem, fee el jisim al salim*" (Healthy minds are in healthy bodies).

Egyptian radio was also playing a song, "I am hooked on my darling love, though he deserted me."

Libyan radio was beaming an impassioned narration of the "lofty" philosophy of the Green Book by "the brother struggler."

And Damascus—yes, Damascus—was giving cooking lessons. "Take the banana in the right hand, and cut sideways, before you sprinkle it with brown sugar."

While Beirut crumbled, the Arab world was gripped with World Cup fever. The day after the Kuwaiti team lost, on the very Sunday when Beirut was subjected to its heaviest raid yet and hospital corridors were full of patients dying of unattended wounds, the Kuwaiti Embassy in London bought a full-page ad in the *London Times* to explain "to the British people at large" why its national team had lost. It was terribly unfair, the ad complained, for the Kuwaiti team to be robbed of victory by a "biased" referee.

As Beirut bled, besieged by a foreign army that killed and ravaged at will, Arab rulers and their peoples neither said nor did anything meaningful. They stayed well behind the frontiers of history, living, wallowing, and pimping in their whorehouse of moderation. Meanwhile Israel dragged her war wagon from one Arab capital to another, marching on like a vulture hobbling after a dead carcass, leaving after her a charred landscape and a dossier of national humiliations. And always Arab rulers are ruled by the intoning "*Ma bidna niza'el el America'an*" [We don't want to alienate Americans]— while *americani* warplanes dropped *americani* bombs from air-conditioned *americani* cockpits by soldiers backed by *americani* vetoes at the United Nations who were sent to wage war financed by *americani* aid.

Beirut was and remains a special place for me. It contained the tensions of my last day in Palestine and my first day in exile. And the siege continued. Bombs flew from the air, the sea, and the ground.

Still, miraculously, the center held.

Beyond the brute chaos of siege was that Palestinian habit of spirit whose very origins are rooted in some mysterious essence of *el ard*. It affirms that, in struggle, there is a thing of beauty, a spontaneity freed from the constraints of rational reason. Its intensities outweigh the passing terrors of death, of thirst, of hunger, of siege. In struggle, this spirit holds that no catastrophe, from the death of one *shahid* to the dismemberment of home and homeland, is final. For every end is a beginning. *Elli bi khallef ma bimout* goes the Palestinian proverb, "He who begets, never dies." And here lies the mystery of reciprocity as perceived by Palestinians—if only allegorically—between life and death. The energy of those who die never disperses, it is assimilated by the whole to animate new apprehensions in the reservoir of national consciousness.

That is why, in Palestinian society, when a *shahid* falls, people go to his home to congratulate his family. By his death he has enriched life for those who stay behind.

What happened in Lebanon in the summer of 1982, and the haunting way it was dealt with, is hard to translate to an outsider; it is all irreducibly Palestinian.

Then the evacuation began, a scene the likes of which the world has rarely witnessed. It had a curious, haughty magic to it, as if it were a parable dealing with death and resurrection. In its final moments, amid the ululation and the din of the *takhikha*, it was a scene of grief and joy, of lament over the fall of our city and joy in our assured sense of imminent rebirth.

The evacuation of Palestinians from Beirut in the summer of 1982, unlike their exodus from Palestine in 1948, embodied the mystery inherent in the rules of relations between Israel and Palestine. Israelis can win a war, but in doing so they submit to us. They can occupy Palestine, yet they remain captive to the dialectic of its existence. They can banish the native presence, but cannot ostracize its reality.

Behind the fearful nobility of Palestinian resistance to the siege is a

200

richer, more eloquent statement: national struggle has now become the mainspring of Palestinian existence, a daily currency of rational exchange, a layer of reality in the process of human renewal, more intimately enfolding than their own skin.

Palestinians *always* go on, leaving failed history behind. They *always* pick up, reassembling themselves as they do so, and proceed afresh.

Do they? And how long would it take? How long would it take us, this time, to reassemble ourselves, to proceed afresh? And what goes on in the interim, between the reassembly and the procession?

Hysteria! And grief and bitterness. That's what goes on. Not satisfied that our fighters evacuated the city, the enemy went after their women and children whom they left behind in the refugee camps of Sabra and Shatila, slaughtered them, and left their bodies stacked in grotesque piles in the muddy lanes, fly-covered, rotting in the sun. They went after our Palestine Research Center, the repository of our culture and history in exile, whose treasures we had been collecting since the day we left Palestine, looted it and then burned it to the ground. Fifteen thousand of our people, including boys under the age of twelve and men over the age of eighty, were picked up and put in a concentration camp called Ansar. Our community in Lebanon, half a million men, women, and children, found itself suddenly severed from the institutions (educational, medical, cultural, economic, and social) they had depended on for their everyday living, which the enemy destroyed. Our fighters, the mainspring of our national struggle, were shipped to the deserts of Algeria, the outback of Sudan, and the scorching plain of Yemen. Our leadership sought refuge in Tunisia. And when the choked psyche of our nation gasped for air, some months later, we lunged at each other in civil war, because we had failed our people and ourselves. Our promises had proved illusory.

The horrors that my generation wrought upon our nation were unspeakable. And the pain that generation suffered as a consequence was beyond comprehension.

201

Less than two years after the siege of Beirut, our history stood as if empty. Later we were to harvest whatever faint echoes it emitted in the cries of our crushed people left to the mercy of murderous street gangs in Lebanon and the institutionalized sadism of the military occupation in Palestine.

What goes on in the interim between reassembly and procession is hysteria. And grief and bitterness.

Nothing works between silence and tomorrow, between words and redemption. I supported the rebels in their drive against the mainstream leadership; that didn't work. I went to Mecca to do the Hajj; that didn't work. I called for a struggle of blood and fire against the enemy; that didn't work. I passed the poisoned chalice around to my fellow Palestinian activists whenever I met them; that didn't work. I avoided my son, lest he look at me with mockery in his eyes; that didn't work. I even took to getting into fistfights at the Childe Harold, my neighborhood bar, and that didn't work either. Finally I withdrew to write—as my aunt had done in Aleppo a quarter century before when I visited her as a teenager—about the mythology of hope of my generation, its nostalgia for the absolutes of the battle of Karameh in 1968 and for the metaphoric necessity of the future tense in our life of struggle.

There is nothing else to do. I am forty-five years old and I find no emotional logic in my introspections, no relevance in my dogmatic certitudes. A new generation, bringing with it a new order of reality, an alternative order of meaning, is emerging to supplant ours. No individuals who hold themselves responsible, as I do, and no generation that holds itself responsible, as mine must, for the monstrous evil of Sabra and Shatila can make their reality durable by any means other than final release from that evil.

I sit at the bar and Archie assures me that "Larry Holmes was robbed of the title" in his fight against Leon Spinks. "Robbed. Robbed, I tell you."

"I am sure he was," I say, "definitely robbed."

Two women in their early twenties, both dressed in black, walk in and sit at the bar next to me.

"Do us, Jimmy," one says to the bartender.

"Thanks a bunch," she says before downing her drink. The other simply says "Yummy!" They hug each other and giggle.

Scarlet and Dennis are sitting at a table sipping beer, strung out on coke, as is their wont at this early hour. They overhear Jimmy and me talk about the meeting of the nonaligned nations in Zimbabwe.

"All it would take is one bomb," Scarlet says. "Just drop one bomb on the bastards, right?"

In this bar, which when I first arrived in town was a hangout for a generation of young Americans that talked of "American imperialism" and the onslaught on the environment by "the military-industrial complex," there is now a poster in support of Vietnam veterans. The "anti-imperialist" generation itself is captive to the national hysteria about "hostages" and "terrorism" and "commies."

"Do me, Jimmy," I tell the bartender over and over again before I finally leave the bar and stagger home. I want to lose time forever, to leave a door open in the dream about the way we dream our dreams, about the way we write the history of our cloudless summer and coarse wounds of morning. Surely our meaning, the meaning of what we did with our history, must reside not in the events, but inside them. Inside the tension of their own dialectic.

It seems only yesterday that I was twenty-five and the battle of Karameh thrust me and my generation into a life of struggle. Now another Palestinian revolutionary and his generation are twenty-five, and all that we have lived for—every conviction, every feeling, every whisper, every outcry—is a part, only a part, of their own repertoire of consciousness, their own motivations. Though we have failed in struggle, our failure is not a bastard mode of existence. Though we have died in life, this death is not a negation of our nexus of being. Nothing dies without leaving its seed behind. Nothing ends without creating a beginning. Nothing goes to forgotten dust except nothingness. Nothing, absolutely nothing, will ever make human beings who have struggled for freedom return to a life that is hollow and meaningless without it.

It matters not that we, the native people of Palestine, keep carrying bricks to Babel, year after year, generation after generation, in a desperate, monotonous reach for the heavens, although we know the tower may never be completed. What does matter is to proceed. And if on the way, thunder is God's answer to every question we ask, then so be it. The dream is too magnetic, too entrenched in our social consciousness.

I look out my window, right here in this whatnotland, right here on Connecticut Avenue, and I hear nothing but voices from Black

203

September and Tel Zaatar and Sabra/Shatila tumbling over my head, tangling with spring and the way I hug my son. Their tones are woven into my walls and sheets and the divine language of the god who created my God. And when I do not look out the window, I just sit here, my silence silhouetted against the night, armed only with the memory of these past twenty years, trying to ape, with a clash of sounds from my typewriter, the pungency of my generation's pain. Something is metaphysically absurd about a man, sitting alone in a room on Connecticut Avenue, defining his solitude at the keys of his typewriter in a fraternity of silent screams. And every day, I lie waiting for the coming of cruel and bitter morning, when I will write more about the enormity of our darkness. And every morning the darkness closes in on me like a clenched fist. If only the children of my generation had had a childhood to speak of, we would not have become so abused by time. We were all born around the *nakbi* of 1948, yet we have seen ages pass by, time behind time, yielding an echo of so many tragedies and so much anguish. And I am confused by all the stillness, all the aloneness that I see out of my window overlooking Connecticut Avenue. I am confused by all the legends I bring with me from a place where the Mediterranean disgorges its waves on a shore gray with time and full of our memories. This is why we shall continue celebrating the fury of who we are. Everyone needs the security of a liberated zone to live in. And if we die seeking passage to it, still carrying bricks to a Babel that never seems to get completed, the generation that follows ours will understand. They alone will understand. People who die for the freedom of others are, like women who die in childbirth, difficult to explain except to those for whom they died. Our children have drunk all our suffering as they sat on our laps hugging three thousand years of history. They will understand.

Fawaz Turki, Palestinian writer, poet, and activist, is author of the widely acclaimed book *The Disinherited* (Monthly Review Press, 1972), as well as a book of poems *Tel Zaatar Was the Hill of Thyme* (Palestine Review Press, 1979). Former president of the General Union of Palestinian Writers in North America, he represented the Palestinian people at the UNESCO Conference on World Culture in 1982.